SUPER HOROSCOPE
SAGITTARIUS

2007

NOVEMBER 23 – DECEMBER 20

BERKLEY BOOKS, NEW YORK

THE BERKLEY PUBLISHING GROUP
Published by the Penguin Group
Penguin Group (USA) Inc.
375 Hudson Street, New York, New York 10014, USA
Penguin Group (Canada), 90 Eglinton Avenue East, Suite 700, Toronto, Ontario M4P 2Y3, Canada
(a division of Pearson Penguin Canada Inc.)
Penguin Books Ltd., 80 Strand, London WC2R 0RL, England
Penguin Group Ireland, 25 St. Stephen's Green, Dublin 2, Ireland (a division of Penguin Books Ltd.)
Penguin Group (Australia), 250 Camberwell Road, Camberwell, Victoria 3124, Australia
(a division of Pearson Australia Group Pty. Ltd.)
Penguin Books India Pvt. Ltd., 11 Community Centre, Panchsheel Park, New Delhi—110 017, India
Penguin Group (NZ), Cnr. Airborne and Rosedale Roads, Albany, Auckland 1310, New Zealand
(a division of Pearson New Zealand Ltd.)
Penguin Books (South Africa) (Pty.) Ltd., 24 Sturdee Avenue, Rosebank, Johannesburg 2196,
South Africa

Penguin Books Ltd., Registered Offices: 80 Strand, London WC2R 0RL, England

2007 SUPER HOROSCOPE SAGITTARIUS

The publishers regret that they cannot answer individual letters requesting personal horoscope information.

PRINTING HISTORY
Berkley trade paperback edition / July 2006

Berkley trade paperback ISBN: 0-425-20935-0

Library of Congress Cataloging-in-Publication Data

ISSN: 1535-8992

PRINTED IN THE UNITED STATES OF AMERICA

10   9   8   7   6   5   4   3   2   1

CONTENTS

THE CUSP-BORN SAGITTARIUS

Are you *really* a Sagittarius? If your birthday falls around the fourth week in November, at the very beginning of Sagittarius, will you still retain the traits of Scorpio, the sign of the Zodiac before Sagittarius? And what if you were born near Christmas—are you more Capricorn than Sagittarius? Many people born at the edge, or cusp, of a sign have great difficulty determining exactly what sign they are. If you are one of these people, here's how you can figure it out once and for all.

Consult the cusp table on the facing page, then locate the year of your birth. The table will tell you the precise days on which the Sun entered and left your sign for the year of your birth. In that way you can determine if you are a true Sagittarius—or whether you are a Scorpio or Capricorn—according to the variations in cusp dates from year to year (see also page 17).

If you were born at the beginning or end of Sagittarius, yours is a lifetime reflecting a process of subtle transformation. Your life on Earth will symbolize a significant change in consciousness, for you are about to enter a whole new way of living or are leaving one behind.

If you were born at the beginning of Sagittarius, you may want to read the horoscope for Scorpio as well as Sagittarius, for Scorpio holds the key to many of your hidden weaknesses, sexual uncertainties, wishes, fantasies, and spiritual potentials. You are the symbol of the human mind awakening to its higher capabilities. You are preparing the way for the liberation of your soul into the realms of wisdom and truth. You leave behind greed, blind desire, and shallow lust, as you learn to create and understand yourself. You travel, see new places, see how people live, figure yourself out, acquire knowledge.

You may hide a stubborn and dangerous extremism and you may rely too much on luck, but at some crisis point in your life a change of consciousness will occur to shift your behavior patterns. New worlds open up, as you become aware of immortality and the infinite possibilities of your own mind.

If you were born at the end of Sagittarius, you may want to read the horoscope book for Capricorn as well as Sagittarius, for Capricorn is a deep part of your materialistic values. You were born with the need to bring your dreams into reality and put your talents and ambitions to practical use.

You need to conquer worry and depression and inhibition. You will learn to take life seriously, but without losing your sense of humor and hope. You must find a balance between believing nothing and believing too much. You need to find the firm middle ground between cynicism and idealism.

THE CUSPS OF SAGITTARIUS

DATES SUN ENTERS SAGITTARIUS (LEAVES SCORPIO)

November 22 every year from 1900 to 2010,
except for the following:

November 21		November 23		
1976	1993	1902	1915	1931
80	1996	03	19	35
84	2000	07	23	39
88	2004	10	27	43
92	2008	11		

DATES SUN LEAVES SAGITTARIUS (ENTERS CAPRICORN)

December 22 every year from 1900 to 2010,
except for the following:

December 21						
1912	1944	1964	1977	1989	2000	2010
16	48	65	80	92	2001	
20	52	68	81	93	2002	
23	53	69	84	94	2004	
28	56	72	85	96	2005	
32	57	73	86	97	2008	
36	60	76	88	98	2009	
40	61					

THE ASCENDANT: SAGITTARIUS RISING

Could you be a "double" Sagittarius? That is, could you have Sagittarius as your Rising sign as well as your Sun sign? The tables on pages 8–9 will tell you Sagittarius what your Rising sign happens to be. Just find the hour of your birth, then find the day of your birth, and you will see which sign of the Zodiac is your Ascendant, as the Rising sign is called. The Ascendant is called that because it is the sign rising on the eastern horizon at the time of your birth. For a more detailed discussion of the Rising sign and the twelve houses of the Zodiac, see pages 17–20.

The Ascendant, or Rising sign, is placed on the 1st house in a horoscope, of which there are twelve houses. The 1st house represents your response to the environment—your unique response. Call it identity, personality, ego, self-image, facade, come-on, body-mind-spirit—whatever term best conveys to you the meaning of the you that acts and reacts in the world. It is a you that is always changing, discovering a new you. Your identity started with birth and early environment, over which you had little conscious control, and continues to experience, to adjust, to express itself. The 1st house also represents how others see you. Has anyone ever guessed your sign to be your Rising sign? People may respond to that personality, that facade, that body type governed by your Rising sign.

Your Ascendant, or Rising sign, modifies your basic Sun sign personality, and it affects the way you act out the daily predictions for your Sun sign. If your Rising sign indeed is Sagittarius, what follows is a description of its effects on your horoscope. If your Rising sign is not Sagittarius, but some other sign of the Zodiac, you may wish to read the horoscope book for that sign.

With Sagittarius on the Ascendant, the planet rising in the 1st house is Jupiter, ruler of Sagittarius. In this position Jupiter confers good health, a pleasing personality, a generous disposition, and an increased vitality. It also confers honors or wealth at some point in your lifetime. You may reap unexpected good fortune in times of hardship. At some point, too, you may exile yourself from everyday life to serve a larger dedication. You will sacrifice for your ideals. Because you are zealous in your beliefs, you could make enemies behind your back. Again, the influence of Jupiter works to overcome the opposition.

You are the student, the idealist. Your need for wisdom is boundless. And you think big! You are not satisfied gathering concrete facts or analyzing practical information. You want to infer the grand patterns, to abstract, to generalize, and finally to generate new ideas. You are a visionary, a dreamer, a futurist. Philosophy, law, and religion attract you, for their truths go beyond the limits of everyday experience. Though you firmly hold your beliefs, you are not dogmatic. Rather, you romanticize them, and your method of persuasion is more seductive than shrill. You restless types are very adaptable, changing your ideas with each new discovery. Your mind is completely open.

With Sagittarius Rising you can be attracted to great causes. Your ideas are not generated merely to erect an impressive intellectual framework. Enlightened by your deep compassion, they become ideals in the service of humanity. There may be an inspirational quality to the causes you join or to the ideals you generate for a cause. Justice and mercy are concepts to be translated into action. You work hard to do that, but you are not rebellious or bossy or demanding. You are brave and forthright, without being reckless or combative. Cooperation and communication are important goals. You like working in groups; your friendly good humor is a model for all social relationships.

There is another you, a private you, that people do not necessarily know very well but may glimpse when you have gone out of their lives. That you is restless, opportunistic, seemingly rootless. You live so much in your mind that you don't want to be tied down by mundane obligations. In fact, you will escape from situations that limit your freedom of choice or action, even if you must dishonor a commitment to do so. You could shirk responsibility by flying off to some greener pasture, yet be no richer for the new experience. Carried to extremes, your quest for adventure could be self-indulgent, yet wasteful of yourself and selfish to the people around you.

Like the Archer, the zodiacal symbol of Sagittarius, you like to roam and hunt, though ideas and people may be your terrain and game. But some of you really prefer the outdoor life and sports. You certainly like to travel. Change recharges your happy-go-lucky nature. You like to get around but not get stuck in a rut, so just as swiftly as you appear on a scene, you disappear. Many jobs and places of residence are outcomes of your journeys.

The key words for Sagittarius Rising are buoyancy and expansiveness. Channel these forces into modes of industriousness so you do not waste your noble visions.

RISING SIGNS FOR SAGITTARIUS

Hour of Birth*	Day of Birth		
	November 21–25	November 26–30	December 1–5
Midnight	Virgo	Virgo	Virgo
1 AM	Virgo	Virgo	Virgo
2 AM	Libra	Libra	Libra
3 AM	Libra	Libra	Libra
4 AM	Libra	Libra; Scorpio 11/29	Libra
5 AM	Scorpio	Scorpio	Scorpio
6 AM	Scorpio	Scorpio	Scorpio
7 AM	Sagittarius	Sagittarius	Sagittarius
8 AM	Sagittarius	Sagittarius	Sagittarius
9 AM	Sagittarius	Capricorn	Capricorn
10 AM	Capricorn	Capricorn	Capricorn
11 AM	Capricorn; Aquarius 11/25	Aquarius	Aquarius
Noon	Aquarius	Aquarius; Pisces 12/3	Aquarius;
1 PM	Pisces	Pisces	Pisces
2 PM	Aries	Aries	Aries
3 PM	Aries	Taurus	Taurus
4 PM	Taurus	Taurus; Gemini 12/2	Taurus;
5 PM	Gemini	Gemini	Gemini
6 PM	Gemini	Gemini; Cancer 12/2	Gemini;
7 PM	Cancer	Cancer	Cancer
8 PM	Cancer	Cancer	Cancer
9 PM	Leo	Leo	Leo
10 PM	Leo	Leo	Leo
11 PM	Leo	Leo; Virgo 11/30	Virgo

*Hour of birth given here is for Standard Time in any time zone. If your hour of birth was recorded in Daylight Saving Time, subtract one hour from it and consult that hour in the table above. For example, if you were born at 7 AM D.S.T., see 6 AM above.

Hour of Birth*	Day of Birth		
	December 6–10	December 11–16	December 17–22
Midnight	Virgo	Virgo	Virgo; Libra 12/22
1 AM	Libra	Libra	Libra
2 AM	Libra	Libra	Libra
3 AM	Libra	Libra; Scorpio 12/14	Scorpio
4 AM	Scorpio	Scorpio	Scorpio
5 AM	Scorpio	Scorpio	Scorpio; Sagittarius 12/21
6 AM	Sagittarius	Sagittarius	Sagittarius
7 AM	Sagittarius	Sagittarius	Sagittarius
8 AM	Sagittarius	Capricorn	Capricorn
9 AM	Capricorn	Capricorn	Capricorn
10 AM	Capricorn; Aquarius 12/10	Aquarius	Aquarius
11 AM	Aquarius	Aquarius	Aquarius; Pisces 12/18
Noon	Pisces	Pisces	Pisces; Aries 12/22
1 PM	Aries	Aries	Aries
2 PM	Aries	Taurus	Taurus
3 PM	Taurus	Taurus	Taurus; Gemini 12/19
4 PM	Gemini	Gemini	Gemini
5 PM	Gemini	Gemini	Cancer
6 PM	Cancer	Cancer	Cancer
7 PM	Cancer	Cancer	Cancer; Leo 12/22
8 PM	Leo	Leo	Leo
9 PM	Leo	Leo	Leo
10 PM	Leo	Leo; Virgo 12/15	Virgo
11 PM	Virgo	Virgo	Virgo

*See note on facing page.

THE PLACE OF ASTROLOGY IN TODAY'S WORLD

Does astrology have a place in the fast-moving, ultra-scientific world we live in today? Can it be justified in a sophisticated society whose outriders are already preparing to step off the moon into the deep space of the planets themselves? Or is it just a hangover of ancient superstition, a psychological dummy for neurotics and dreamers of every historical age?

These are the kind of questions that any inquiring person can be expected to ask when they approach a subject like astrology which goes beyond, but never excludes, the materialistic side of life.

The simple, single answer is that astrology works. It works for many millions of people in the western world alone. In the United States there are 10 million followers and in Europe, an estimated 25 million. America has more than 4000 practicing astrologers, Europe nearly three times as many. Even down-under Australia has its hundreds of thousands of adherents. In the eastern countries, astrology has enormous followings, again, because it has been proved to work. In India, for example, brides and grooms for centuries have been chosen on the basis of their astrological compatibility.

Astrology today is more vital than ever before, more practicable because all over the world the media devotes much space and time to it, more valid because science itself is confirming the precepts of astrological knowledge with every new exciting step. The ordinary person who daily applies astrology intelligently does not have to wonder whether it is true nor believe in it blindly. He can see it working for himself. And, if he can use it—and this book is designed to help the reader to do just that—he can make living a far richer experience, and become a more developed personality and a better person.

Astrology and Relationships

Astrology is the science of relationships. It is not just a study of planetary influences on man and his environment. It is the study of man himself.

We are at the center of our personal universe, of all our relationships. And our happiness or sadness depends on how we act, how we relate to the people and things that surround us. The emotions that we generate have a distinct effect—for better or worse—on the world around us. Our friends and our enemies will confirm this. Just look in the mirror the next time you are angry. In other words, each of us is a kind of sun or planet or star radiating our feelings on the environment around us. Our influence on our personal universe, whether loving, helpful, or destructive, varies with our changing moods, expressed through our individual character.

Our personal "radiations" are potent in the way they affect our moods and our ability to control them. But we usually are able to throw off our emotion in some sort of action—we have a good cry, walk it off, or tell someone our troubles—before it can build up too far and make us physically ill. Astrology helps us to understand the universal forces working on us, and through this understanding, we can become more properly adjusted to our surroundings so that we find ourselves coping where others may flounder.

The Challenge of Love

The challenge of love lies in recognizing the difference between infatuation, emotion, sex, and, sometimes, the intentional deceit of the other person. Mankind, with its record of broken marriages, despair, and disillusionment, is obviously not very good at making these distinctions.

Can astrology help?

Yes. In the same way that advance knowledge can usually help in any human situation. And there is probably no situation as human, as poignant, as pathetic and universal, as the failure of man's love.

Love, of course, is not just between man and woman. It involves love of children, parents, home, and friends. But the big problems usually involve the choice of partner.

Astrology has established degrees of compatibility that exist between people born under the various signs of the Zodiac. Because people are individuals, there are numerous variations and modifications. So the astrologer, when approached on mate and marriage matters, makes allowances for them. But the fact remains that some groups of people are suited for each other and some are not, and astrology has expressed this in terms of characteristics we all can study and use as a personal guide.

No matter how much enjoyment and pleasure we find in the different aspects of each other's character, if it is not an overall compatibility, the chances of our finding fulfillment or enduring happiness in each other are pretty hopeless. And astrology can help us to find someone compatible.

Astrology and Science

Closely related to our emotions is the "other side" of our personal universe, our physical welfare. Our body, of course, is largely influenced by things around us over which we have very little control. The phone rings, we hear it. The train runs late. We snag our stocking or cut our face shaving. Our body is under a constant bombardment of events that influence our daily lives to varying degrees.

The question that arises from all this is, what makes each of us act so that we have to involve other people and keep the ball of activity and evolution rolling? This is the question that both science and astrology are involved with. The scientists have attacked it from different angles: anthropology, the study of human evolution as body, mind and response to environment; anatomy, the study of bodily structure; psychology, the science of the human mind; and so on. These studies have produced very impressive classifications and valuable information, but because the approach to the problem is fragmented, so is the result. They remain "branches" of science. Science generally studies effects. It keeps turning up wonderful answers but no lasting solutions. Astrology, on the other hand, approaches the question from the broader viewpoint. Astrology began its inquiry with the totality of human experience and saw it as an effect. It then looked to find the cause, or at least the prime movers, and during thousands of years of observation of man and his *universal* environment came up with the extraordinary principle of planetary influence—or astrology, which, from the Greek, means the science of the stars.

Modern science, as we shall see, has confirmed much of astrology's foundations—most of it unintentionally, some of it reluctantly, but still, indisputably.

It is not difficult to imagine that there must be a connection between outer space and Earth. Even today, scientists are not too sure how our Earth was created, but it is generally agreed that it is only a tiny part of the universe. And as a part of the universe, people on Earth see and feel the influence of heavenly bodies in almost every aspect of our existence. There is no doubt that the Sun has the greatest influence on life on this planet. Without it there would be no life, for without it there would be no warmth, no division into day and night, no cycles of time or season at all. This is clear and easy to see. The influence of the Moon, on the other hand, is more subtle, though no less definite.

There are many ways in which the influence of the Moon manifests itself here on Earth, both on human and animal life. It is a well-known fact, for instance, that the large movements of water on our planet—that is the ebb and flow of the tides—are caused by the Moon's gravitational pull. Since this is so, it follows that these water movements do not occur only in the oceans, but that all bodies of water are affected, even down to the tiniest puddle.

The human body, too, which consists of about 70 percent water, falls within the scope of this lunar influence. For example the menstrual cycle of most women corresponds to the 28-day lunar month; the period of pregnancy in humans is 273 days, or equal to nine lunar months. Similarly, many illnesses reach a crisis at the change of the Moon, and statistics in many countries have shown that the crime rate is highest at the time of the Full Moon. Even human sexual desire has been associated with the phases of the Moon. But it is in the movement of the tides that we get the clearest demonstration of planetary influence, which leads to the irresistible correspondence between the so-called metaphysical and the physical.

Tide tables are prepared years in advance by calculating the future positions of the Moon. Science has known for a long time that the Moon is the main cause of tidal action. But only in the last few years has it begun to realize the possible extent of this influence on mankind. To begin with, the ocean tides do not rise and fall as we might imagine from our personal observations of them. The Moon as it orbits around Earth sets up a circular wave of attraction which pulls the oceans of the world after it, broadly in an east to west direction. This influence is like a phantom wave crest, a loop of power stretching from pole to pole which passes over and around the Earth like an invisible shadow. It travels with equal effect across the land masses and, as scientists were recently amazed to observe, caused oysters placed in the dark in the middle of the United States where there is no sea to open their shells to receive the nonexistent tide. If the land-locked oysters react to this invisible signal, what effect does it have on us who not so long ago in evolutionary time came out of the sea and still have its salt in our blood and sweat?

Less well known is the fact that the Moon is also the primary force behind the circulation of blood in human beings and animals, and the movement of sap in trees and plants. Agriculturists have established that the Moon has a distinct influence on crops, which explains why for centuries people have planted according to Moon cycles. The habits of many animals, too, are directed by the movement of the Moon. Migratory birds, for instance, depart only at or near the time of the Full Moon. And certain sea creatures, eels in particular, move only in accordance with certain phases of the Moon.

Know Thyself—Why?

In today's fast-changing world, everyone still longs to know what the future holds. It is the one thing that everyone has in common: rich and poor, famous and infamous, all are deeply concerned about tomorrow.

But the key to the future, as every historian knows, lies in the past. This is as true of individual people as it is of nations. You cannot understand your future without first understanding your past, which is simply another way of saying that you must first of all know yourself.

The motto "know thyself" seems obvious enough nowadays, but it was originally put forward as the foundation of wisdom by the ancient Greek philosophers. It was then adopted by the "mystery religions" of the ancient Middle East, Greece, Rome, and is still used in all genuine schools of mind training or mystical discipline, both in those of the East, based on yoga, and those of the West. So it is universally accepted now, and has been through the ages.

But how do you go about discovering what sort of person you are? The first step is usually classification into some sort of system of types. Astrology did this long before the birth of Christ. Psychology has also done it. So has modern medicine, in its way.

One system classifies people according to the source of the impulses they respond to most readily: the muscles, leading to direct bodily action; the digestive organs, resulting in emotion; or the brain and nerves, giving rise to thinking. Another such system says that character is determined by the endocrine glands, and gives us such labels as "pituitary," "thyroid," and "hyperthyroid" types. These different systems are neither contradictory nor mutually exclusive. In fact, they are very often different ways of saying the same thing.

Very popular, useful classifications were devised by Carl Jung, the eminent disciple of Freud. Jung observed among the different faculties of the mind, four which have a predominant influence on character. These four faculties exist in all of us without exception, but not in perfect balance. So when we say, for instance, that someone is a "thinking type," it means that in any situation he or she tries to be rational. Emotion, which may be the opposite of thinking, will be his or her weakest function. This thinking type can be sensible and reasonable, or calculating and unsympathetic. The emotional type, on the other hand, can often be recognized by exaggerated language—everything is either marvelous or terrible—and in extreme cases they even invent dramas and quarrels out of nothing just to make life more interesting.

The other two faculties are intuition and physical sensation. The sensation type does not only care for food and drink, nice clothes and furniture; he or she is also interested in all forms of physical experience. Many scientists are sensation types as are athletes and nature-lovers. Like sensation, intuition is a form of perception and we all possess it. But it works through that part of the mind which is not under conscious control—consequently it sees meanings and connections which are not obvious to thought or emotion. Inventors and original thinkers are always intuitive, but so, too, are superstitious people who see meanings where none exist.

Thus, sensation tells us what is going on in the world, feeling (that is, emotion) tells us how important it is to ourselves, thinking enables us to interpret it and work out what we should do about it, and intuition tells us what it means to ourselves and others. All four faculties are essential, and all are present in every one of us. But some people are guided chiefly by one, others by another. In addition, Jung also observed a division of the human personality into the extrovert and the introvert, which cuts across these four types.

A disadvantage of all these systems of classification is that one cannot tell very easily where to place oneself. Some people are reluctant to admit that they act to please their emotions. So they deceive themselves for years by trying to belong to whichever type they think is the "best." Of course, there is no best; each has its faults and each has its good points.

The advantage of the signs of the Zodiac is that they simplify classification. Not only that, but your date of birth is personal—

it is unarguably yours. What better way to know yourself than by going back as far as possible to the very moment of your birth? And this is precisely what your horoscope is all about, as we shall see in the next section.

WHAT IS A HOROSCOPE?

If you had been able to take a picture of the skies at the moment of your birth, that photograph would be your horoscope. Lacking such a snapshot, it is still possible to recreate the picture—and this is at the basis of the astrologer's art. In other words, your horoscope is a representation of the skies with the planets in the exact positions they occupied at the time you were born.

The year of birth tells an astrologer the positions of the distant, slow-moving planets Jupiter, Saturn, Uranus, Neptune, and Pluto. The month of birth indicates the Sun sign, or birth sign as it is commonly called, as well as indicating the positions of the rapidly moving planets Venus, Mercury, and Mars. The day and time of birth will locate the position of our Moon. And the moment—the exact hour and minute—of birth determines the houses through what is called the Ascendant, or Rising sign.

With this information the astrologer consults various tables to calculate the specific positions of the Sun, Moon, and other planets relative to your birthplace at the moment you were born. Then he or she locates them by means of the Zodiac.

The Zodiac

The Zodiac is a band of stars (constellations) in the skies, centered on the Sun's apparent path around the Earth, and is divided into twelve equal segments, or signs. What we are actually dividing up is the Earth's path around the Sun. But from our point of view here on Earth, it seems as if the Sun is making a great circle around our planet in the sky, so we say it is the Sun's apparent path. This twelvefold division, the Zodiac, is a reference system for the astrologer. At any given moment the planets—and in astrology both the Sun and Moon are considered to be planets—can all be located at a specific point along this path.

Now where in all this are you, the subject of the horoscope? Your character is largely determined by the sign the Sun is in. So that is where the astrologer looks first in your horoscope, at your Sun sign.

16

The Sun Sign and the Cusp

There are twelve signs in the Zodiac, and the Sun spends approximately one month in each sign. But because of the motion of the Earth around the Sun—the Sun's apparent motion—the dates when the Sun enters and leaves each sign may change from year to year. Some people born near the cusp, or edge, of a sign have difficulty determining which is their Sun sign. But in this book a Table of Cusps is provided for the years 1900 to 2010 (page 5) so you can find out what your true Sun sign is.

Here are the twelve signs of the Zodiac, their ancient zodiacal symbol, and the dates when the Sun enters and leaves each sign for the year 2007. Remember, these dates may change from year to year.

ARIES	Ram	March 20–April 20
TAURUS	Bull	April 20–May 21
GEMINI	Twins	May 21–June 21
CANCER	Crab	June 21–July 23
LEO	Lion	July 23–August 23
VIRGO	Virgin	August 23–September 23
LIBRA	Scales	September 23–October 23
SCORPIO	Scorpion	October 23–November 22
SAGITTARIUS	Archer	November 22–December 22
CAPRICORN	Sea Goat	December 22–January 20
AQUARIUS	Water Bearer	January 20–February 18
PISCES	Fish	February 18–March 20

It is possible to draw significant conclusions and make meaningful predictions based simply on the Sun sign of a person. There are many people who have been amazed at the accuracy of the description of their own character based only on the Sun sign. But an astrologer needs more information than just your Sun sign to interpret the photograph that is your horoscope.

The Rising Sign and the Zodiacal Houses

An astrologer needs the exact time and place of your birth in order to construct and interpret your horoscope. The illustration on the next page shows the flat chart, or natural wheel, an astrologer uses. Note the inner circle of the wheel labeled 1 through 12. These 12 divisions are known as the houses of the Zodiac.

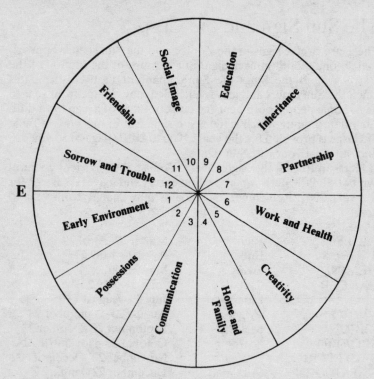

The 1st house always starts from the position marked E, which corresponds to the eastern horizon. The rest of the houses 2 through 12 follow around in a "counterclockwise" direction. The point where each house starts is known as a cusp, or edge.

The cusp, or edge, of the 1st house (point E) is where an astrologer would place your Rising sign, the Ascendant. And, as already noted, the exact time of your birth determines your Rising sign. Let's see how this works.

As the Earth rotates on its axis once every 24 hours, each one of the twelve signs of the Zodiac appears to be "rising" on the horizon, with a new one appearing about every 2 hours. Actually it is the turning of the Earth that exposes each sign to view, but in our astrological work we are discussing apparent motion. This Rising sign marks the Ascendant, and it colors the whole orientation of a horoscope. It indicates the sign governing the 1st house of the chart, and will thus determine which signs will govern all the other houses.

To visualize this idea, imagine two color wheels with twelve divisions superimposed upon each other. For just as the Zodiac is divided into twelve constellations that we identify as the signs, another twelvefold division is used to denote the houses. Now imagine one wheel (the signs) moving slowly while the other wheel (the houses) remains still. This analogy may help you see how the signs keep shifting the "color" of the houses as the Rising sign continues to change every two hours. To simplify things, a Table of Rising Signs has been provided (pages 8–9) for your specific Sun sign.

Once your Rising sign has been placed on the cusp of the 1st house, the signs that govern the rest of the 11 houses can be placed on the chart. In any individual's horoscope the signs do not necessarily correspond with the houses. For example, it could be that a sign covers part of two adjacent houses. It is the interpretation of such variations in an individual's horoscope that marks the professional astrologer.

But to gain a workable understanding of astrology, it is not necessary to go into great detail. In fact, we just need a description of the houses and their meanings, as is shown in the illustration above and in the table below.

THE 12 HOUSES OF THE ZODIAC

1st	Individuality, body appearance, general outlook on life	Personality house
2nd	Finance, possessions, ethical principles, gain or loss	Money house
3rd	Relatives, communication, short journeys, writing, education	Relatives house
4th	Family and home, parental ties, land and property, security	Home house
5th	Pleasure, children, creativity, entertainment, risk	Pleasure house
6th	Health, harvest, hygiene, work and service, employees	Health house
7th	Marriage and divorce, the law, partnerships and alliances	Marriage house
8th	Inheritance, secret deals, sex, death, regeneration	Inheritance house
9th	Travel, sports, study, philosophy Ω house	Travel house
10th	Career, social standing, success and honor	Business house
11th	Friendship, social life, hopes and wishes	Friends house
12th	Troubles, illness, secret enemies, hidden agendas	Trouble house

The Planets in the Houses

An astrologer, knowing the exact time and place of your birth, will use tables of planetary motion in order to locate the planets in your horoscope chart. He or she will determine which planet or planets are in which sign and in which house. It is not uncommon, in an individual's horoscope, for there to be two or more planets in the same sign and in the same house.

The characteristics of the planets modify the influence of the Sun according to their natures and strengths.

Sun: Source of life. Basic temperament according to the Sun sign. The conscious will. Human potential.

Moon: Emotions. Moods. Customs. Habits. Changeable. Adaptive. Nurturing.

Mercury: Communication. Intellect. Reasoning power. Curiosity. Short travels.

Venus: Love. Delight. Charm. Harmony. Balance. Art. Beautiful possessions.

Mars: Energy. Initiative. War. Anger. Adventure. Courage. Daring. Impulse.

Jupiter: Luck. Optimism. Generous. Expansive. Opportunities. Protection.

Saturn: Pessimism. Privation. Obstacles. Delay. Hard work. Research. Lasting rewards after long struggle.

Uranus: Fashion. Electricity. Revolution. Independence. Freedom. Sudden changes. Modern science.

Neptune: Sensationalism. Theater. Dreams. Inspiration. Illusion. Deception.

Pluto: Creation and destruction. Total transformation. Lust for power. Strong obsessions.

Superimpose the characteristics of the planets on the functions of the house in which they appear. Express the result through the character of the Sun sign, and you will get the basic idea.

Of course, many other considerations have been taken into account in producing the carefully worked out predictions in this book: the aspects of the planets to each other; their strength according to position and sign; whether they are in a house of exaltation or decline; whether they are natural enemies or not; whether a planet occupies its own sign; the position of a planet in relation to its own house or sign; whether the sign is male or female; whether the sign is a fire, earth, water, or air sign. These are only a few of the colors on the astrologer's pallet which he or she must mix with the inspiration of the artist and the accuracy of the mathematician.

How To Use These Predictions

A person reading the predictions in this book should understand that they are produced from the daily position of the planets for a group of people and are not, of course, individually specialized. To get the full benefit of them our readers should relate the predictions to their own character and circumstances, coordinate them, and draw their own conclusions from them.

If you are a serious observer of your own life, you should find a definite pattern emerging that will be a helpful and reliable guide.

The point is that we always retain our free will. The stars indicate certain directional tendencies but we are not compelled to follow. We can do or not do, and wisdom must make the choice.

We all have our good and bad days. Sometimes they extend into cycles of weeks. It is therefore advisable to study daily predictions in a span ranging from the day before to several days ahead.

Daily predictions should be taken very generally. The word "difficult" does not necessarily indicate a whole day of obstruction or inconvenience. It is a warning to you to be cautious. Your caution will often see you around the difficulty before you are involved. This is the correct use of astrology.

In another section (pages 78–84), detailed information is given about the influence of the Moon as it passes through each of the twelve signs of the Zodiac. There are instructions on how to use the Moon Tables (pages 85–92), which provide Moon Sign Dates throughout the year as well as the Moon's role in health and daily affairs. This information should be used in conjunction with the daily forecasts to give a fuller picture of the astrological trends.

HISTORY OF ASTROLOGY

The origins of astrology have been lost far back in history, but we do know that reference is made to it as far back as the first written records of the human race. It is not hard to see why. Even in primitive times, people must have looked for an explanation for the various happenings in their lives. They must have wanted to know why people were different from one another. And in their search they turned to the regular movements of the Sun, Moon, and stars to see if they could provide an answer.

It is interesting to note that as soon as man learned to use his tools in any type of design, or his mind in any kind of calculation, he turned his attention to the heavens. Ancient cave dwellings reveal dim crescents and circles representative of the Sun and Moon, rulers of day and night. Mesopotamia and the civilization of Chaldea, in itself the foundation of those of Babylonia and Assyria, show a complete picture of astronomical observation and well-developed astrological interpretation.

Humanity has a natural instinct for order. The study of anthropology reveals that primitive people—even as far back as prehistoric times—were striving to achieve a certain order in their lives. They tried to organize the apparent chaos of the universe. They had the desire to attach meaning to things. This demand for order has persisted throughout the history of man. So that observing the regularity of the heavenly bodies made it logical that primitive peoples should turn heavenward in their search for an understanding of the world in which they found themselves so random and alone.

And they did find a significance in the movements of the stars. Shepherds tending their flocks, for instance, observed that when the cluster of stars now known as the constellation Aries was in sight, it was the time of fertility and they associated it with the Ram. And they noticed that the growth of plants and plant life corresponded with different phases of the Moon, so that certain times were favorable for the planting of crops, and other times were not. In this way, there grew up a tradition of seasons and causes connected with the passage of the Sun through the twelve signs of the Zodiac.

Astrology was valued so highly that the king was kept informed of the daily and monthly changes in the heavenly bodies, and the results of astrological studies regarding events of the future. Head astrologers were clearly men of great rank and position, and the office was said to be a hereditary one.

Omens were taken, not only from eclipses and conjunctions of the Moon or Sun with one of the planets, but also from storms and earthquakes. In the eastern civilizations, particularly, the reverence inspired by astrology appears to have remained unbroken since the very earliest days. In ancient China, astrology, astronomy, and religion went hand in hand. The astrologer, who was also an astronomer, was part of the official government service and had his own corner in the Imperial Palace. The duties of the Imperial astrologer, whose office was one of the most important in the land, were clearly defined, as this extract from early records shows:

> This exalted gentleman must concern himself with the stars in the heavens, keeping a record of the changes and movements of the Planets, the Sun and the Moon, in order to examine the movements of the terrestrial world with the object of prognosticating good and bad fortune. He divides the territories of the nine regions of the empire in accordance with their dependence on particular celestial bodies. All the fiefs and principalities are connected with the stars and from this their prosperity or misfortune should be ascertained. He makes prognostications according to the twelve years of the Jupiter cycle of good and evil of the terrestrial world. From the colors of the five kinds of clouds, he determines the coming of floods or droughts, abundance or famine. From the twelve winds, he draws conclusions about the state of harmony of heaven and earth, and takes note of good and bad signs that result from their accord or disaccord. In general, he concerns himself with five kinds of phenomena so as to warn the Emperor to come to the aid of the government and to allow for variations in the ceremonies according to their circumstances.

The Chinese were also keen observers of the fixed stars, giving them such unusual names as Ghost Vehicle, Sun of Imperial Concubine, Imperial Prince, Pivot of Heaven, Twinkling Brilliance, Weaving Girl. But, great astrologers though they may have been, the Chinese lacked one aspect of mathematics that the Greeks applied to astrology—deductive geometry. Deductive geometry was the basis of much classical astrology in and after the time of the Greeks, and this explains the different methods of prognostication used in the East and West.

Down through the ages the astrologer's art has depended, not so much on the uncovering of new facts, though this is important, as on the interpretation of the facts already known. This is the essence of the astrologer's skill.

But why should the signs of the Zodiac have any effect at all on the formation of human character? It is easy to see why people thought they did, and even now we constantly use astrological expressions in our everyday speech. The thoughts of "lucky star," "ill-fated," "star-crossed," "mooning around," are interwoven into the very structure of our language.

Wherever the concept of the Zodiac is understood and used, it could well appear to have an influence on the human character. Does this mean, then, that the human race, in whose civilization the idea of the twelve signs of the Zodiac has long been embedded, is divided into only twelve types? Can we honestly believe that it is really as simple as that? If so, there must be pretty wide ranges of variation within each type. And if, to explain the variation, we call in heredity and environment, experiences in early childhood, the thyroid and other glands, and also the four functions of the mind together with extroversion and introversion, then one begins to wonder if the original classification was worth making at all. No sensible person believes that his favorite system explains everything. But even so, he will not find the system much use at all if it does not even save him the trouble of bothering with the others.

In the same way, if we were to put every person under only one sign of the Zodiac, the system becomes too rigid and unlike life. Besides, it was never intended to be used like that. It may be convenient to have only twelve types, but we know that in practice there is every possible gradation between aggressiveness and timidity, or between conscientiousness and laziness. How, then, do we account for this?

A person born under any given Sun sign can be mainly influenced by one or two of the other signs that appear in their individual horoscope. For instance, famous persons born under the sign of Gemini include Henry VIII, whom nothing and no one could have induced to abdicate, and Edward VIII, who did just that. Obviously, then, the sign Gemini does not fully explain the complete character of either of them.

Again, under the opposite sign, Sagittarius, were both Stalin, who was totally consumed with the notion of power, and Charles V, who freely gave up an empire because he preferred to go into a monastery. And we find under Scorpio many uncompromising characters such as Luther, de Gaulle, Indira Gandhi, and Montgomery, but also Petain, a successful commander whose name later became synonymous with collaboration.

A single sign is therefore obviously inadequate to explain the differences between people; it can only explain resemblances, such as the combativeness of the Scorpio group, or the far-reaching devotion of Charles V and Stalin to their respective ideals—the Christian heaven and the Communist utopia.

But very few people have only one sign in their horoscope chart.

In addition to the month of birth, the day and, even more, the hour to the nearest minute if possible, ought to be considered. Without this, it is impossible to have an actual horoscope, for the word horoscope literally means "a consideration of the hour."

The month of birth tells you only which sign of the Zodiac was occupied by the Sun. The day and hour tell you what sign was occupied by the Moon. And the minute tells you which sign was rising on the eastern horizon. This is called the Ascendant, and, as some astrologers believe, it is supposed to be the most important thing in the whole horoscope.

The Sun is said to signify one's heart, that is to say, one's deepest desires and inmost nature. This is quite different from the Moon, which signifies one's superficial way of behaving. When the ancient Romans referred to the Emperor Augustus as a Capricorn, they meant that he had the Moon in Capricorn. Or, to take another example, a modern astrologer would call Disraeli a Scorpion because he had Scorpio Rising, but most people would call him Sagittarius because he had the Sun there. The Romans would have called him Leo because his Moon was in Leo.

So if one does not seem to fit one's birth month, it is always worthwhile reading the other signs, for one may have been born at a time when any of them were rising or occupied by the Moon. It also seems to be the case that the influence of the Sun develops as life goes on, so that the month of birth is easier to guess in people over the age of forty. The young are supposed to be influenced mainly by their Ascendant, the Rising sign, which characterizes the body and physical personality as a whole.

It is nonsense to assume that all people born at a certain time will exhibit the same characteristics, or that they will even behave in the same manner. It is quite obvious that, from the very moment of its birth, a child is subject to the effects of its environment, and that this in turn will influence its character and heritage to a decisive extent. Also to be taken into account are education and economic conditions, which play a very important part in the formation of one's character as well.

People have, in general, certain character traits and qualities which, according to their environment, develop in either a positive or a negative manner. Therefore, selfishness (inherent selfishness, that is) might emerge as unselfishness; kindness and consideration as cruelty and lack of consideration toward others. In the same way, a naturally constructive person may, through frustration, become destructive, and so on. The latent characteristics with which people are born can, therefore, through environment and good or bad training, become something that would appear to be its opposite, and so give the lie to the astrologer's description of their character.

But this is not the case. The true character is still there, but it is buried deep beneath these external superficialities.

Careful study of the character traits of various signs of the Zodiac are of immeasurable help, and can render beneficial service to the intelligent person. Undoubtedly, the reader will already have discovered that, while he is able to get on very well with some people, he just "cannot stand" others. The causes sometimes seem inexplicable. At times there is intense dislike, at other times immediate sympathy. And there is, too, the phenomenon of love at first sight, which is also apparently inexplicable. People appear to be either sympathetic or unsympathetic toward each other for no apparent reason.

Now if we look at this in the light of the Zodiac, we find that people born under different signs are either compatible or incompatible with each other. In other words, there are good and bad interrelating factors among the various signs. This does not, of course, mean that humanity can be divided into groups of hostile camps. It would be quite wrong to be hostile or indifferent toward people who happen to be born under an incompatible sign. There is no reason why everybody should not, or cannot, learn to control and adjust their feelings and actions, especially after they are aware of the positive qualities of other people by studying their character analyses, among other things.

Every person born under a certain sign has both positive and negative qualities, which are developed more or less according to our free will. Nobody is entirely good or entirely bad, and it is up to each of us to learn to control ourselves on the one hand and at the same time to endeavor to learn about ourselves and others.

It cannot be emphasized often enough that it is free will that determines whether we will make really good use of our talents and abilities. Using our free will, we can either overcome our failings or allow them to rule us. Our free will enables us to exert sufficient willpower to control our failings so that they do not harm ourselves or others.

Astrology can reveal our inclinations and tendencies. Astrology can tell us about ourselves so that we are able to use our free will to overcome our shortcomings. In this way astrology helps us do our best to become needed and valuable members of society as well as helpmates to our family and our friends. Astrology also can save us a great deal of unhappiness and remorse.

Yet it may seem absurd that an ancient philosophy could be a prop to modern men and women. But below the materialistic surface of modern life, there are hidden streams of feeling and thought. Symbology is reappearing as a study worthy of the scholar; the psychosomatic factor in illness has passed from the writings of the crank to those of the specialist; spiritual healing in all its forms is no longer a pious hope but an accepted phenomenon. And it is into this context that we consider astrology, in the sense that it is an analysis of human types.

Astrology and medicine had a long journey together, and only parted company a couple of centuries ago. There still remain in medical language such astrological terms as "saturnine," "choleric," and "mercurial," used in the diagnosis of physical tendencies. The herbalist, for long the handyman of the medical profession, has been dominated by astrology since the days of the Greeks. Certain herbs traditionally respond to certain planetary influences, and diseases must therefore be treated to ensure harmony between the medicine and the disease.

But the stars are expected to foretell and not only to diagnose.

Astrological forecasting has been remarkably accurate, but often it is wide of the mark. The brave person who cares to predict world events takes dangerous chances. Individual forecasting is less clear cut; it can be a help or a disillusionment. Then we come to the nagging question: if it is possible to foreknow, is it right to foretell? This is a point of ethics on which it is hard to pronounce judgment. The doctor faces the same dilemma if he finds that symptoms of a mortal disease are present in his patient and that he can only prognosticate a steady decline. How much to tell an individual in a crisis is a problem that has perplexed many distinguished scholars. Honest and conscientious astrologers in this modern world, where so many people are seeking guidance, face the same problem.

Five hundred years ago it was customary to call in a learned man who was an astrologer who was probably also a doctor and a philosopher. By his knowledge of astrology, his study of planetary influences, he felt himself qualified to guide those in distress. The world has moved forward at a fantastic rate since then, and yet people are still uncertain of themselves. At first sight it seems fantastic in the light of modern thinking that they turn to the most ancient of all studies, and get someone to calculate a horoscope for them. But is it really so fantastic if you take a second look? For astrology is concerned with tomorrow, with survival. And in a world such as ours, tomorrow and survival are the keywords for the twenty-first century.

ASTROLOGICAL BRIDGE TO THE 21st CENTURY

Themes connecting past, present, and future are in play as the first decade reveals hidden paths and personal hints for achieving your potential. Make the most of the messages from the planets.

With the dawning of the twenty-first century look first to Jupiter, the planet of good fortune. Each new yearly Jupiter cycle follows the natural progression of the Zodiac. First is Jupiter in Aries and in Taurus through spring 2000, next Jupiter is in Gemini to summer 2001, then in Cancer to midsummer 2002, in Leo to late summer 2003, in Virgo to early autumn 2004, in Libra to midautumn 2005, and so on through Jupiter in Pisces through June 2010. The beneficent planet Jupiter promotes your professional and educational goals while urging informed choice and deliberation, providing a rich medium for creativity. Planet Jupiter's influence is protective, the generous helper that comes to the rescue just in the nick of time. And while safeguarding good luck, Jupiter can turn unusual risks into achievable aims.

In order to take advantage of luck and opportunity, to gain wisdom from experience, to persevere against adversity, look to beautiful planet Saturn. Saturn, planet of reason and responsibility, began a new cycle in earthy Taurus at the turn of the century. Saturn in Taurus until spring 2001 inspires industry and affection, blends practicality and imagination, all the while inviting caution and care. Saturn in Taurus lends beauty, order, and structure to your life. Then Saturn is in Gemini, the sign of mind and communication, until June 2003. Saturn in Gemini gives a lively intellectual capacity, so the limits of creativity can be stretched and boundaries broken. Saturn in Gemini holds the promise of fruitful endeavor through sustained study, learning, and application. Saturn in Cancer from early June 2003 to mid-July 2005 poses issues of long-term security versus immediate gratification. Rely on deliberation and choice to make sense out of diversity and change. Saturn in Cancer can be a revealing cycle, leading to the desired outcomes of growth and maturity. Saturn in Leo from mid-July 2005 to early September 2007 can be a test of boldness versus caution. Here every challenge must be met with benevolent authority, matched by a caring and generous outlook. Saturn in Virgo early September 2007 into October 2009 sharpens and deepens the mind, conferring precise writing and teaching skills. Saturn in Virgo presents chances to excel, to accomplish a great deal, and to gain prominence through good words and good works.

Uranus, planet of innovation and surprise, started an important new cycle in January of 1996. At that time Uranus entered its natural home in airy Aquarius. Uranus in Aquarius into the year 2003 has a profound effect on your personality and the lens through which you see the world. A basic change in the way you project yourself is just one impact of Uranus in Aquarius. More significantly, a whole new consciousness is evolving. Winds of change blowing your way emphasize movement and freedom. Uranus in Aquarius poses involvement in the larger community beyond self, family, friends, lovers, associates. Radical ideas and progressive thought signal a journey of liberation. As the new century begins, follow Uranus on the path of humanitarianism. A new Uranus cycle begins March 2003 when Uranus visits Pisces, briefly revisits Aquarius, then returns late in 2003 to Pisces where it will stay into May 2010. Uranus in Pisces, a strongly intuitive force, urges work and service for the good of humankind to make the world a better place for all people.

Neptune, planet of vision and mystery, is enjoying a long cycle that excites creativity and imaginative thinking. Neptune is in airy Aquarius from November 1998 to February of 2012. Neptune in Aquarius, the sign of the Water Bearer, represents two sides of the coin of wisdom: inspiration and reason. Here Neptune stirs powerful currents bearing a rich and varied harvest, the fertile breeding ground for idealistic aims and practical considerations. Neptune's fine intuition tunes in to your dreams, your imagination, your spirituality. You can never turn your back on the mysteries of life. Uranus and Neptune, the planets of enlightenment and idealism, give you glimpses into the future, letting you peek through secret doorways into the twenty-first century.

Pluto, planet of beginnings and endings, began a new cycle of growth and learning late in 1995. Pluto entered fiery Sagittarius and remains there into the year 2008. Pluto in Sagittarius during its long stay over twelve years can create significant change. The great power of Pluto in Sagittarius is already starting its transformation of your character and lifestyle. Pluto in Sagittarius takes you on a new journey of exploration and learning. The awakening you experience on intellectual and artistic levels heralds a new cycle of growth. Uncompromising Pluto, seeker of truth, challenges your identity, persona, and self-expression. Uncovering the real you, Pluto holds the key to understanding and meaningful communication. Pluto in Sagittarius can be the guiding light illuminating the first decade of the twenty-first century. Good luck is riding on the waves of change.

THE SIGNS OF THE ZODIAC

Dominant Characteristics

Aries: March 21–April 20

The Positive Side of Aries

The Aries has many positive points to his character. People born under this first sign of the Zodiac are often quite strong and enthusiastic. On the whole, they are forward-looking people who are not easily discouraged by temporary setbacks. They know what they want out of life and they go out after it. Their personalities are strong. Others are usually quite impressed by the Ram's way of doing things. Quite often they are sources of inspiration for others traveling the same route. Aries men and women have a special zest for life that can be contagious; for others, they are a fine example of how life should be lived.

The Aries person usually has a quick and active mind. He is imaginative and inventive. He enjoys keeping busy and active. He generally gets along well with all kinds of people. He is interested in mankind, as a whole. He likes to be challenged. Some would say he thrives on opposition, for it is when he is set against that he often does his best. Getting over or around obstacles is a challenge he generally enjoys. All in all, Aries is quite positive and young-thinking. He likes to keep abreast of new things that are happening in the world. Aries are often fond of speed. They like things to be done quickly, and this sometimes aggravates their slower colleagues and associates.

The Aries man or woman always seems to remain young. Their whole approach to life is youthful and optimistic. They never say die, no matter what the odds. They may have an occasional setback, but it is not long before they are back on their feet again.

The Negative Side of Aries

Everybody has his less positive qualities—and Aries is no exception. Sometimes the Aries man or woman is not very tactful in communicating with others; in his hurry to get things done he is apt to be a little callous or inconsiderate. Sensitive people are likely to find him somewhat sharp-tongued in some situations. Often in his eagerness to get the show on the road, he misses the mark altogether and cannot achieve his aims.

At times Aries can be too impulsive. He can occasionally be stubborn and refuse to listen to reason. If things do not move quickly enough to suit the Aries man or woman, he or she is apt to become rather nervous or irritable. The uncultivated Aries is not unfamiliar with moments of doubt and fear. He is capable of being destructive if he does not get his way. He can overcome some of his emotional problems by steadily trying to express himself as he really is, but this requires effort.

Taurus: April 21–May 20

The Positive Side of Taurus

The Taurus person is known for his ability to concentrate and for his tenacity. These are perhaps his strongest qualities. The Taurus man or woman generally has very little trouble in getting along with others; it's his nature to be helpful toward people in need. He can always be depended on by his friends, especially those in trouble.

Taurus generally achieves what he wants through his ability to persevere. He never leaves anything unfinished but works on something until it has been completed. People can usually take him at his word; he is honest and forthright in most of his dealings. The Taurus person has a good chance to make a success of his life because of his many positive qualities. The Taurus who aims high seldom falls short of his mark. He learns well by experience. He is thorough and does not believe in shortcuts of any kind. The Bull's thoroughness pays off in the end, for through his deliberateness he learns how to rely on himself and what he has learned. The Taurus person tries to get along with others, as a rule. He is not overly critical and likes people to be themselves. He is a tolerant person and enjoys peace and harmony—especially in his home life.

Taurus is usually cautious in all that he does. He is not a person

who believes in taking unnecessary risks. Before adopting any one line of action, he will weigh all of the pros and cons. The Taurus person is steadfast. Once his mind is made up it seldom changes. The person born under this sign usually is a good family person—reliable and loving.

The Negative Side of Taurus

Sometimes the Taurus man or woman is a bit too stubborn. He won't listen to other points of view if his mind is set on something. To others, this can be quite annoying. Taurus also does not like to be told what to do. He becomes rather angry if others think him not too bright. He does not like to be told he is wrong, even when he is. He dislikes being contradicted.

Some people who are born under this sign are very suspicious of others—even of those persons close to them. They find it difficult to trust people fully. They are often afraid of being deceived or taken advantage of. The Bull often finds it difficult to forget or forgive. His love of material things sometimes makes him rather avaricious and petty.

Gemini: May 21–June 20

The Positive Side of Gemini

The person born under this sign of the Heavenly Twins is usually quite bright and quick-witted. Some of them are capable of doing many different things. The Gemini person very often has many different interests. He keeps an open mind and is always anxious to learn new things.

Gemini is often an analytical person. He is a person who enjoys making use of his intellect. He is governed more by his mind than by his emotions. He is a person who is not confined to one view; he can often understand both sides to a problem or question. He knows how to reason, how to make rapid decisions if need be.

He is an adaptable person and can make himself at home almost anywhere. There are all kinds of situations he can adapt to. He is a person who seldom doubts himself; he is sure of his talents and his ability to think and reason. Gemini is generally most satisfied when he is in a situation where he can make use of his intellect. Never

short of imagination, he often has strong talents for invention. He is rather a modern person when it comes to life; Gemini almost always moves along with the times—perhaps that is why he remains so youthful throughout most of his life.

Literature and art appeal to the person born under this sign. Creativity in almost any form will interest and intrigue the Gemini man or woman.

The Gemini is often quite charming. A good talker, he often is the center of attraction at any gathering. People find it easy to like a person born under this sign because he can appear easygoing and usually has a good sense of humor.

The Negative Side of Gemini

Sometimes the Gemini person tries to do too many things at one time—and as a result, winds up finishing nothing. Some Twins are easily distracted and find it rather difficult to concentrate on one thing for too long a time. Sometimes they give in to trifling fancies and find it rather boring to become too serious about any one thing. Some of them are never dependable, no matter what they promise.

Although the Gemini man or woman often appears to be well-versed on many subjects, this is sometimes just a veneer. His knowledge may be only superficial, but because he speaks so well he gives people the impression of erudition. Some Geminis are sharp-tongued and inconsiderate; they think only of themselves and their own pleasure.

Cancer: June 21–July 20

The Positive Side of Cancer

The Moon Child's most positive point is his understanding nature. On the whole, he is a loving and sympathetic person. He would never go out of his way to hurt anyone. The Cancer man or woman is often very kind and tender; they give what they can to others. They hate to see others suffering and will do what they can to help someone in less fortunate circumstances than themselves. They are often very concerned about the world. Their interest in people generally goes beyond that of just their own families and close friends; they have a deep sense of community and respect humanitarian values. The Moon Child means what he says, as a rule; he is honest about his feelings.

The Cancer man or woman is a person who knows the art of patience. When something seems difficult, he is willing to wait until the situation becomes manageable again. He is a person who knows how to bide his time. Cancer knows how to concentrate on one thing at a time. When he has made his mind up he generally sticks with what he does, seeing it through to the end.

Cancer is a person who loves his home. He enjoys being surrounded by familiar things and the people he loves. Of all the signs, Cancer is the most maternal. Even the men born under this sign often have a motherly or protective quality about them. They like to take care of people in their family—to see that they are well loved and well provided for. They are usually loyal and faithful. Family ties mean a lot to the Cancer man or woman. Parents and in-laws are respected and loved. Young Cancer responds very well to adults who show faith in him. The Moon Child has a strong sense of tradition. He is very sensitive to the moods of others.

The Negative Side of Cancer

Sometimes Cancer finds it rather hard to face life. It becomes too much for him. He can be a little timid and retiring, when things don't go too well. When unfortunate things happen, he is apt to just shrug and say, "Whatever will be will be." He can be fatalistic to a fault. The uncultivated Cancer is a bit lazy. He doesn't have very much ambition. Anything that seems a bit difficult he'll gladly leave to others. He may be lacking in initiative. Too sensitive, when he feels he's been injured, he'll crawl back into his shell and nurse his imaginary wounds. The immature Moon Child often is given to crying when the smallest thing goes wrong.

Some Cancers find it difficult to enjoy themselves in environments outside their homes. They make heavy demands on others, and need to be constantly reassured that they are loved. Lacking such reassurance, they may resort to sulking in silence.

Leo: July 21–August 21

The Positive Side of Leo

Often Leos make good leaders. They seem to be good organizers and administrators. Usually they are quite popular with others. Whatever group it is that they belong to, the Leo man or woman is almost sure to be or become the leader. Loyalty, one of the Lion's noblest traits, enables him or her to maintain this leadership position.

Leo is generous most of the time. It is his best characteristic. He or she likes to give gifts and presents. In making others happy, the Leo person becomes happy himself. He likes to splurge when spending money on others. In some instances it may seem that the Lion's generosity knows no boundaries. A hospitable person, the Leo man or woman is very fond of welcoming people to his house and entertaining them. He is never short of company.

Leo has plenty of energy and drive. He enjoys working toward some specific goal. When he applies himself correctly, he gets what he wants most often. The Leo person is almost never unsure of himself. He has plenty of confidence and aplomb. He is a person who is direct in almost everything he does. He has a quick mind and can make a decision in a very short time.

He usually sets a good example for others because of his ambitious manner and positive ways. He knows how to stick to something once he's started. Although Leo may be good at making a joke, he is not superficial or glib. He is a loving person, kind and thoughtful.

There is generally nothing small or petty about the Leo man or woman. He does what he can for those who are deserving. He is a person others can rely upon at all times. He means what he says. An honest person, generally speaking, he is a friend who is valued and sought out.

The Negative Side of Leo

Leo, however, does have his faults. At times, he can be just a bit too arrogant. He thinks that no one deserves a leadership position except him. Only he is capable of doing things well. His opinion of himself is often much too high. Because of his conceit, he is

sometimes rather unpopular with a good many people. Some Leos are too materialistic; they can only think in terms of money and profit.

Some Leos enjoy lording it over others—at home or at their place of business. What is more, they feel they have the right to. Egocentric to an impossible degree, this sort of Leo cares little about how others think or feel. He can be rude and cutting.

Virgo: August 22–September 22

The Positive Side of Virgo

The person born under the sign of Virgo is generally a busy person. He knows how to arrange and organize things. He is a good planner. Above all, he is practical and is not afraid of hard work.

Often called the sign of the Harvester, Virgo knows how to attain what he desires. He sticks with something until it is finished. He never shirks his duties, and can always be depended upon. The Virgo person can be thoroughly trusted at all times.

The man or woman born under this sign tries to do everything to perfection. He doesn't believe in doing anything halfway. He always aims for the top. He is the sort of a person who is always learning and constantly striving to better himself—not because he wants more money or glory, but because it gives him a feeling of accomplishment.

The Virgo man or woman is a very observant person. He is sensitive to how others feel, and can see things below the surface of a situation. He usually puts this talent to constructive use.

It is not difficult for the Virgo to be open and earnest. He believes in putting his cards on the table. He is never secretive or underhanded. He's as good as his word. The Virgo person is generally plainspoken and down to earth. He has no trouble in expressing himself.

The Virgo person likes to keep up to date on new developments in his particular field. Well-informed, generally, he sometimes has a keen interest in the arts or literature. What he knows, he knows well. His ability to use his critical faculties is well-developed and sometimes startles others because of its accuracy.

Virgos adhere to a moderate way of life; they avoid excesses. Virgo is a responsible person and enjoys being of service.

The Negative Side of Virgo

Sometimes a Virgo person is too critical. He thinks that only he can do something the way it should be done. Whatever anyone else does is inferior. He can be rather annoying in the way he quibbles over insignificant details. In telling others how things should be done, he can be rather tactless and mean.

Some Virgos seem rather emotionless and cool. They feel emotional involvement is beneath them. They are sometimes too tidy, too neat. With money they can be rather miserly. Some Virgos try to force their opinions and ideas on others.

Libra: September 23–October 22

The Positive Side of Libra

Libras love harmony. It is one of their most outstanding character traits. They are interested in achieving balance; they admire beauty and grace in things as well as in people. Generally speaking, they are kind and considerate people. Libras are usually very sympathetic. They go out of their way not to hurt another person's feelings. They are outgoing and do what they can to help those in need.

People born under the sign of Libra almost always make good friends. They are loyal and amiable. They enjoy the company of others. Many of them are rather moderate in their views; they believe in keeping an open mind, however, and weighing both sides of an issue fairly before making a decision.

Alert and intelligent, Libra, often known as the Lawgiver, is always fair-minded and tries to put himself in the position of the other person. They are against injustice; quite often they take up for the underdog. In most of their social dealings, they try to be tactful and kind. They dislike discord and bickering, and most Libras strive for peace and harmony in all their relationships.

The Libra man or woman has a keen sense of beauty. They appreciate handsome furnishings and clothes. Many of them are artistically inclined. Their taste is usually impeccable. They know how to use color. Their homes are almost always attractively arranged and inviting. They enjoy entertaining people and see to it that their guests always feel at home and welcome.

Libra gets along with almost everyone. He is well-liked and socially much in demand.

The Negative Side of Libra

Some people born under this sign tend to be rather insincere. So eager are they to achieve harmony in all relationships that they will even go so far as to lie. Many of them are escapists. They find facing the truth an ordeal and prefer living in a world of make-believe.

In a serious argument, some Libras give in rather easily even when they know they are right. Arguing, even about something they believe in, is too unsettling for some of them.

Libras sometimes care too much for material things. They enjoy possessions and luxuries. Some are vain and tend to be jealous.

Scorpio: October 23–November 22

The Positive Side of Scorpio

The Scorpio man or woman generally knows what he or she wants out of life. He is a determined person. He sees something through to the end. Scorpio is quite sincere, and seldom says anything he doesn't mean. When he sets a goal for himself he tries to go about achieving it in a very direct way.

The Scorpion is brave and courageous. They are not afraid of hard work. Obstacles do not frighten them. They forge ahead until they achieve what they set out for. The Scorpio man or woman has a strong will.

Although Scorpio may seem rather fixed and determined, inside he is often quite tender and loving. He can care very much for others. He believes in sincerity in all relationships. His feelings about someone tend to last; they are profound and not superficial.

The Scorpio person is someone who adheres to his principles no matter what happens. He will not be deterred from a path he believes to be right.

Because of his many positive strengths, the Scorpion can often achieve happiness for himself and for those that he loves.

He is a constructive person by nature. He often has a deep understanding of people and of life, in general. He is perceptive and unafraid. Obstacles often seem to spur him on. He is a positive person who enjoys winning. He has many strengths and resources; challenge of any sort often brings out the best in him.

The Negative Side of Scorpio

The Scorpio person is sometimes hypersensitive. Often he imagines injury when there is none. He feels that others do not bother to recognize him for his true worth. Sometimes he is given to excessive boasting in order to compensate for what he feels is neglect.

Scorpio can be proud, arrogant, and competitive. They can be sly when they put their minds to it and they enjoy outwitting persons or institutions noted for their cleverness.

Their tactics for getting what they want are sometimes devious and ruthless. They don't care too much about what others may think. If they feel others have done them an injustice, they will do their best to seek revenge. The Scorpion often has a sudden, violent temper; and this person's interest in sex is sometimes quite unbalanced or excessive.

Sagittarius: November 23–December 20

The Positive Side of Sagittarius

People born under this sign are honest and forthright. Their approach to life is earnest and open. Sagittarius is often quite adult in his way of seeing things. They are broad-minded and tolerant people. When dealing with others the person born under the sign of the Archer is almost always open and forthright. He doesn't believe in deceit or pretension. His standards are high. People who associate with Sagittarius generally admire and respect his tolerant viewpoint.

The Archer trusts others easily and expects them to trust him. He is never suspicious or envious and almost always thinks well of others. People always enjoy his company because he is so friendly and easygoing. The Sagittarius man or woman is often good-humored. He can always be depended upon by his friends, family, and co-workers.

The person born under this sign of the Zodiac likes a good joke every now and then. Sagittarius is eager for fun and laughs, which makes him very popular with others.

A lively person, he enjoys sports and outdoor life. The Archer is fond of animals. Intelligent and interesting, he can begin an ani-

mated conversation with ease. He likes exchanging ideas and discussing various views.

He is not selfish or proud. If someone proposes an idea or plan that is better than his, he will immediately adopt it. Imaginative yet practical, he knows how to put ideas into practice.

The Archer enjoys sport and games, and it doesn't matter if he wins or loses. He is a forgiving person, and never sulks over something that has not worked out in his favor.

He is seldom critical, and is almost always generous.

The Negative Side of Sagittarius

Some Sagittarius are restless. They take foolish risks and seldom learn from the mistakes they make. They don't have heads for money and are often mismanaging their finances. Some of them devote much of their time to gambling.

Some are too outspoken and tactless, always putting their feet in their mouths. They hurt others carelessly by being honest at the wrong time. Sometimes they make promises which they don't keep. They don't stick close enough to their plans and go from one failure to another. They are undisciplined and waste a lot of energy.

Capricorn: December 21–January 19

The Positive Side of Capricorn

The person born under the sign of Capricorn, known variously as the Mountain Goat or Sea Goat, is usually very stable and patient. He sticks to whatever tasks he has and sees them through. He can always be relied upon and he is not averse to work.

An honest person, Capricorn is generally serious about whatever he does. He does not take his duties lightly. He is a practical person and believes in keeping his feet on the ground.

Quite often the person born under this sign is ambitious and knows how to get what he wants out of life. The Goat forges ahead and never gives up his goal. When he is determined about something, he almost always wins. He is a good worker—a hard worker. Although things may not come easy to him, he will not complain, but continue working until his chores are finished.

He is usually good at business matters and knows the value of money. He is not a spendthrift and knows how to put something away for a rainy day; he dislikes waste and unnecessary loss.

Capricorn knows how to make use of his self-control. He can apply himself to almost anything once he puts his mind to it. His ability to concentrate sometimes astounds others. He is diligent and does well when involved in detail work.

The Capricorn man or woman is charitable, generally speaking, and will do what is possible to help others less fortunate. As a friend, he is loyal and trustworthy. He never shirks his duties or responsibilities. He is self-reliant and never expects too much of the other fellow. He does what he can on his own. If someone does him a good turn, then he will do his best to return the favor.

The Negative Side of Capricorn

Like everyone, Capricorn, too, has faults. At times, the Goat can be overcritical of others. He expects others to live up to his own high standards. He thinks highly of himself and tends to look down on others.

His interest in material things may be exaggerated. The Capricorn man or woman thinks too much about getting on in the world and having something to show for it. He may even be a little greedy.

He sometimes thinks he knows what's best for everyone. He is too bossy. He is always trying to organize and correct others. He may be a little narrow in his thinking.

Aquarius: January 20–February 18

The Positive Side of Aquarius

The Aquarius man or woman is usually very honest and forthright. These are his two greatest qualities. His standards for himself are generally very high. He can always be relied upon by others. His word is his bond.

Aquarius is perhaps the most tolerant of all the Zodiac personalities. He respects other people's beliefs and feels that everyone is entitled to his own approach to life.

He would never do anything to injure another's feelings. He is never unkind or cruel. Always considerate of others, the Water

Bearer is always willing to help a person in need. He feels a very strong tie between himself and all the other members of mankind.

The person born under this sign, called the Water Bearer, is almost always an individualist. He does not believe in teaming up with the masses, but prefers going his own way. His ideas about life and mankind are often quite advanced. There is a saying to the effect that the average Aquarius is fifty years ahead of his time.

Aquarius is community-minded. The problems of the world concern him greatly. He is interested in helping others no matter what part of the globe they live in. He is truly a humanitarian sort. He likes to be of service to others.

Giving, considerate, and without prejudice, Aquarius have no trouble getting along with others.

The Negative Side of Aquarius

Aquarius may be too much of a dreamer. He makes plans but seldom carries them out. He is rather unrealistic. His imagination has a tendency to run away with him. Because many of his plans are impractical, he is always in some sort of a dither.

Others may not approve of him at all times because of his unconventional behavior. He may be a bit eccentric. Sometimes he is so busy with his own thoughts that he loses touch with the realities of existence.

Some Aquarius feel they are more clever and intelligent than others. They seldom admit to their own faults, even when they are quite apparent. Some become rather fanatic in their views. Their criticism of others is sometimes destructive and negative.

Pisces: February 19–March 20

The Positive Side of Pisces

Known as the sign of the Fishes, Pisces has a sympathetic nature. Kindly, he is often dedicated in the way he goes about helping others. The sick and the troubled often turn to him for advice and assistance. Possessing keen intuition, Pisces can easily understand people's deepest problems.

He is very broad-minded and does not criticize others for their faults. He knows how to accept people for what they are. On the whole, he is a trustworthy and earnest person. He is loyal to his friends and will do what he can to help them in time of need. Generous and good-natured, he is a lover of peace; he is often willing to help others solve their differences. People who have taken a wrong turn in life often interest him and he will do what he can to persuade them to rehabilitate themselves.

He has a strong intuitive sense and most of the time he knows how to make it work for him. Pisces is unusually perceptive and often knows what is bothering someone before that person, himself, is aware of it. The Pisces man or woman is an idealistic person, basically, and is interested in making the world a better place in which to live. Pisces believes that everyone should help each other. He is willing to do more than his share in order to achieve cooperation with others.

The person born under this sign often is talented in music or art. He is a receptive person; he is able to take the ups and downs of life with philosophic calm.

The Negative Side of Pisces

Some Pisces are often depressed; their outlook on life is rather glum. They may feel that they have been given a bad deal in life and that others are always taking unfair advantage of them. Pisces sometimes feel that the world is a cold and cruel place. The Fishes can be easily discouraged. The Pisces man or woman may even withdraw from the harshness of reality into a secret shell of his own where he dreams and idles away a good deal of his time.

Pisces can be lazy. He lets things happen without giving the least bit of resistance. He drifts along, whether on the high road or on the low. He can be lacking in willpower.

Some Pisces people seek escape through drugs or alcohol. When temptation comes along they find it hard to resist. In matters of sex, they can be rather permissive.

Sun Sign Personalities

ARIES: Hans Christian Andersen, Pearl Bailey, Marlon Brando, Wernher Von Braun, Charlie Chaplin, Joan Crawford, Da Vinci, Bette Davis, Doris Day, W.C. Fields, Alec Guinness, Adolf Hitler, William Holden, Thomas Jefferson, Nikita Khrushchev, Elton John, Arturo Toscanini, J.P. Morgan, Paul Robeson, Gloria Steinem, Sarah Vaughn, Vincent van Gogh, Tennessee Williams

TAURUS: Fred Astaire, Charlotte Brontë, Carol Burnett, Irving Berlin, Bing Crosby, Salvador Dali, Tchaikovsky, Queen Elizabeth II, Duke Ellington, Ella Fitzgerald, Henry Fonda, Sigmund Freud, Orson Welles, Joe Louis, Lenin, Karl Marx, Golda Meir, Eva Peron, Bertrand Russell, Shakespeare, Kate Smith, Benjamin Spock, Barbra Streisand, Shirley Temple, Harry Truman

GEMINI: Ruth Benedict, Josephine Baker, Rachel Carson, Carlos Chavez, Walt Whitman, Bob Dylan, Ralph Waldo Emerson, Judy Garland, Paul Gauguin, Allen Ginsberg, Benny Goodman, Bob Hope, Burl Ives, John F. Kennedy, Peggy Lee, Marilyn Monroe, Joe Namath, Cole Porter, Laurence Olivier, Harriet Beecher Stowe, Queen Victoria, John Wayne, Frank Lloyd Wright

CANCER: "Dear Abby," Lizzie Borden, David Brinkley, Yul Brynner, Pearl Buck, Marc Chagall, Princess Diana, Babe Didrikson, Mary Baker Eddy, Henry VIII, John Glenn, Ernest Hemingway, Lena Horne, Oscar Hammerstein, Helen Keller, Ann Landers, George Orwell, Nancy Reagan, Rembrandt, Richard Rodgers, Ginger Rogers, Rubens, Jean-Paul Sartre, O.J. Simpson

LEO: Neil Armstrong, James Baldwin, Lucille Ball, Emily Brontë, Wilt Chamberlain, Julia Child, William J. Clinton, Cecil B. De Mille, Ogden Nash, Amelia Earhart, Edna Ferber, Arthur Goldberg, Alfred Hitchcock, Mick Jagger, George Meany, Annie Oakley, George Bernard Shaw, Napoleon, Jacqueline Onassis, Henry Ford, Francis Scott Key, Andy Warhol, Mae West, Orville Wright

VIRGO: Ingrid Bergman, Warren Burger, Maurice Chevalier, Agatha Christie, Sean Connery, Lafayette, Peter Falk, Greta Garbo, Althea Gibson, Arthur Godfrey, Goethe, Buddy Hackett, Michael Jackson, Lyndon Johnson, D.H. Lawrence, Sophia Loren, Grandma Moses, Arnold Palmer, Queen Elizabeth I, Walter Reuther, Peter Sellers, Lily Tomlin, George Wallace

LIBRA: Brigitte Bardot, Art Buchwald, Truman Capote, Dwight D. Eisenhower, William Faulkner, F. Scott Fitzgerald, Gandhi, George Gershwin, Micky Mantle, Helen Hayes, Vladimir Horowitz, Doris Lessing, Martina Navratalova, Eugene O'Neill, Luciano Pavarotti, Emily Post, Eleanor Roosevelt, Bruce Springsteen, Margaret Thatcher, Gore Vidal, Barbara Walters, Oscar Wilde

SCORPIO: Vivien Leigh, Richard Burton, Art Carney, Johnny Carson, Billy Graham, Grace Kelly, Walter Cronkite, Marie Curie, Charles de Gaulle, Linda Evans, Indira Gandhi, Theodore Roosevelt, Rock Hudson, Katherine Hepburn, Robert F. Kennedy, Billie Jean King, Martin Luther, Georgia O'Keeffe, Pablo Picasso, Jonas Salk, Alan Shepard, Robert Louis Stevenson

SAGITTARIUS: Jane Austen, Louisa May Alcott, Woody Allen, Beethoven, Willy Brandt, Mary Martin, William F. Buckley, Maria Callas, Winston Churchill, Noel Coward, Emily Dickinson, Walt Disney, Benjamin Disraeli, James Doolittle, Kirk Douglas, Chet Huntley, Jane Fonda, Chris Evert Lloyd, Margaret Mead, Charles Schulz, John Milton, Frank Sinatra, Steven Spielberg

CAPRICORN: Muhammad Ali, Isaac Asimov, Pablo Casals, Dizzy Dean, Marlene Dietrich, James Farmer, Ava Gardner, Barry Goldwater, Cary Grant, J. Edgar Hoover, Howard Hughes, Joan of Arc, Gypsy Rose Lee, Martin Luther King, Jr., Rudyard Kipling, Mao Tse-tung, Richard Nixon, Gamal Nasser, Louis Pasteur, Albert Schweitzer, Stalin, Benjamin Franklin, Elvis Presley

AQUARIUS: Marian Anderson, Susan B. Anthony, Jack Benny, John Barrymore, Mikhail Baryshnikov, Charles Darwin, Charles Dickens, Thomas Edison, Clark Gable, Jascha Heifetz, Abraham Lincoln, Yehudi Menuhin, Mozart, Jack Nicklaus, Ronald Reagan, Jackie Robinson, Norman Rockwell, Franklin D. Roosevelt, Gertrude Stein, Charles Lindbergh, Margaret Truman

PISCES: Edward Albee, Harry Belafonte, Alexander Graham Bell, Chopin, Adelle Davis, Albert Einstein, Golda Meir, Jackie Gleason, Winslow Homer, Edward M. Kennedy, Victor Hugo, Mike Mansfield, Michelangelo, Edna St. Vincent Millay, Liza Minelli, John Steinbeck, Linus Pauling, Ravel, Renoir, Diana Ross, William Shirer, Elizabeth Taylor, George Washington

The Signs and Their Key Words

		POSITIVE	NEGATIVE
ARIES	self	courage, initiative, pioneer instinct	brash rudeness, selfish impetuosity
TAURUS	money	endurance, loyalty, wealth	obstinacy, gluttony
GEMINI	mind	versatility	capriciousness, unreliability
CANCER	family	sympathy, homing instinct	clannishness, childishness
LEO	children	love, authority, integrity	egotism, force
VIRGO	work	purity, industry, analysis	faultfinding, cynicism
LIBRA	marriage	harmony, justice	vacillation, superficiality
SCORPIO	sex	survival, regeneration	vengeance, discord
SAGITTARIUS	travel	optimism, higher learning	lawlessness
CAPRICORN	career	depth	narrowness, gloom
AQUARIUS	friends	human fellowship, genius	perverse unpredictability
PISCES	confine-ment	spiritual love, universality	diffusion, escapism

The Elements and Qualities of The Signs

Every sign has both an *element* and a *quality* associated with it. The element indicates the basic makeup of the sign, and the quality describes the kind of activity associated with each.

Element	Sign	Quality	Sign
FIRE	ARIES LEO SAGITTARIUS	CARDINAL ...	ARIES LIBRA CANCER CAPRICORN
EARTH ...	TAURUS VIRGO CAPRICORN	FIXED	TAURUS LEO SCORPIO AQUARIUS
AIR	GEMINI LIBRA AQUARIUS		
WATER ...	CANCER SCORPIO PISCES	MUTABLE	GEMINI VIRGO SAGITTARIUS PISCES

Signs can be grouped together according to their element and quality. Signs of the same element share many basic traits in common. They tend to form stable configurations and ultimately harmonious relationships. Signs of the same quality are often less harmonious, but they share many dynamic potentials for growth as well as profound fulfillment.

Further discussion of each of these sign groupings is provided on the following pages.

The Fire Signs

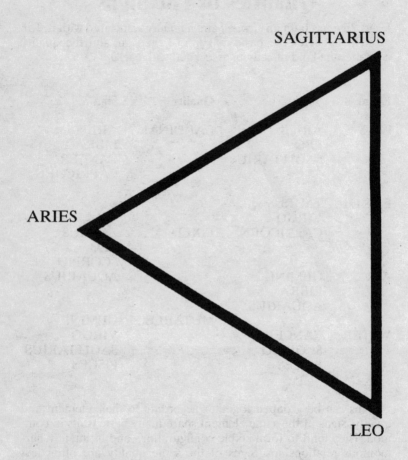

This is the fire group. On the whole these are emotional, volatile types, quick to anger, quick to forgive. They are adventurous, powerful people and act as a source of inspiration for everyone. They spark into action with immediate exuberant impulses. They are intelligent, self-involved, creative, and idealistic. They all share a certain vibrancy and glow that outwardly reflects an inner flame and passion for living.

The Earth Signs

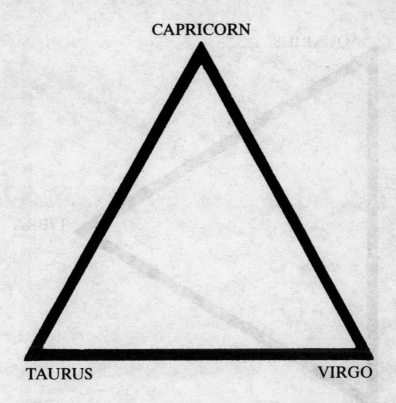

CAPRICORN

TAURUS

VIRGO

This is the earth group. They are in constant touch with the material world and tend to be conservative. Although they are all capable of spartan self-discipline, they are earthy, sensual people who are stimulated by the tangible, elegant, and luxurious. The thread of their lives is always practical, but they do fantasize and are often attracted to dark, mysterious, emotional people. They are like great cliffs overhanging the sea, forever married to the ocean but always resisting erosion from the dark, emotional forces that thunder at their feet.

The Air Signs

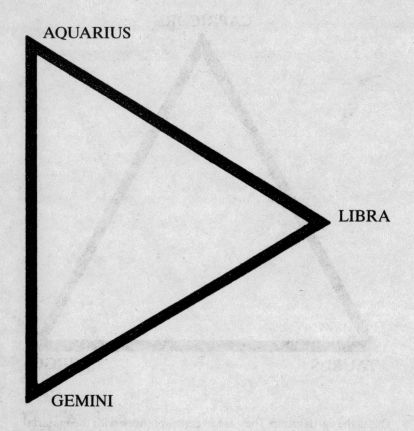

This is the air group. They are light, mental creatures desirous of contact, communication, and relationship. They are involved with people and the forming of ties on many levels. Original thinkers, they are the bearers of human news. Their language is their sense of word, color, style, and beauty. They provide an atmosphere suitable and pleasant for living. They add change and versatility to the scene, and it is through them that we can explore new territory of human intelligence and experience.

The Water Signs

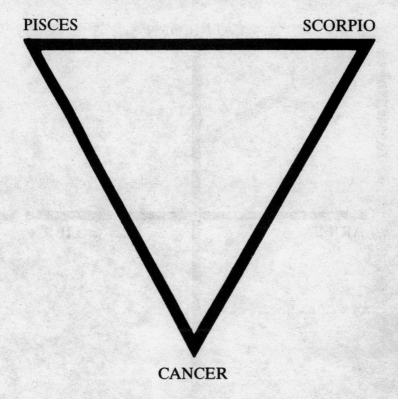

PISCES

SCORPIO

CANCER

This is the water group. Through the water people, we are all joined together on emotional, nonverbal levels. They are silent, mysterious types whose magic hypnotizes even the most determined realist. They have uncanny perceptions about people and are as rich as the oceans when it comes to feeling, emotion, or imagination. They are sensitive, mystical creatures with memories that go back beyond time. Through water, life is sustained. These people have the potential for the depths of darkness or the heights of mysticism and art.

The Cardinal Signs

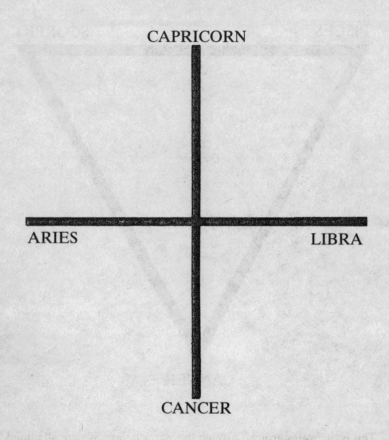

CAPRICORN

ARIES   LIBRA

CANCER

Put together, this is a clear-cut picture of dynamism, activity, tremendous stress, and remarkable achievement. These people know the meaning of great change since their lives are often characterized by significant crises and major successes. This combination is like a simultaneous storm of summer, fall, winter, and spring. The danger is chaotic diffusion of energy; the potential is irrepressible growth and victory.

The Fixed Signs

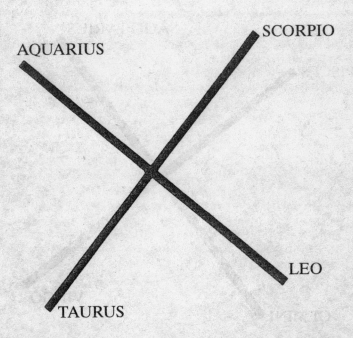

Fixed signs are always establishing themselves in a given place or area of experience. Like explorers who arrive and plant a flag, these people claim a position from which they do not enjoy being deposed. They are staunch, stalwart, upright, trusty, honorable people, although their obstinacy is well-known. Their contribution is fixity, and they are the angels who support our visible world.

The Mutable Signs

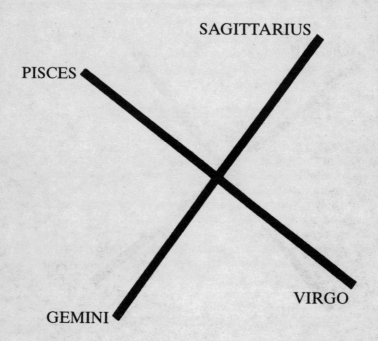

Mutable people are versatile, sensitive, intelligent, nervous, and deeply curious about life. They are the translators of all energy. They often carry out or complete tasks initiated by others. Combinations of these signs have highly developed minds; they are imaginative and jumpy and think and talk a lot. At worst their lives are a Tower of Babel. At best they are adaptable and ready creatures who can assimilate one kind of experience and enjoy it while anticipating coming changes.

THE PLANETS
OF THE SOLAR SYSTEM

This section describes the planets of the solar system. In astrology, both the Sun and the Moon are considered to be planets. Because of the Moon's influence in our day-to-day lives, the Moon is described in a separate section following this one.

The Planets and the Signs They Rule

The signs of the Zodiac are linked to the planets in the following way. Each sign is governed or ruled by one or more planets. No matter where the planets are located in the sky at any given moment, they still rule their respective signs, and when they travel through the signs they rule, they have special dignity and their effects are stronger.

Following is a list of the planets and the signs they rule. After looking at the list, read the definitions of the planets and see if you can determine how the planet ruling *your* Sun sign has affected your life.

SIGNS	RULING PLANETS
Aries	Mars, Pluto
Taurus	Venus
Gemini	Mercury
Cancer	Moon
Leo	Sun
Virgo	Mercury
Libra	Venus
Scorpio	Mars, Pluto
Sagittarius	Jupiter
Capricorn	Saturn
Aquarius	Saturn, Uranus
Pisces	Jupiter, Neptune

Characteristics of the Planets

The following pages give the meaning and characteristics of the planets of the solar system. They all travel around the Sun at different speeds and different distances. Taken with the Sun, they all distribute individual intelligence and ability throughout the entire chart.

The planets modify the influence of the Sun in a chart according to their own particular natures, strengths, and positions. Their positions must be calculated for each year and day, and their function and expression in a horoscope will change as they move from one area of the Zodiac to another.

We start with a description of the sun.

THE SUN

SUN

This is the center of existence. Around this flaming sphere all the planets revolve in endless orbits. Our star is constantly sending out its beams of light and energy without which no life on Earth would be possible. In astrology it symbolizes everything we are trying to become, the center around which all of our activity in life will always revolve. It is the symbol of our basic nature and describes the natural and constant thread that runs through everything that we do from birth to death on this planet.

To early astrologers, the Sun seemed to be another planet because it crossed the heavens every day, just like the rest of the bodies in the sky.

It is the only star near enough to be seen well—it is, in fact, a dwarf star. Approximately 860,000 miles in diameter, it is about ten times as wide as the giant planet Jupiter. The next nearest star is nearly 300,000 times as far away, and if the Sun were located as far away as most of the bright stars, it would be too faint to be seen without a telescope.

Everything in the horoscope ultimately revolves around this singular body. Although other forces may be prominent in the charts of some individuals, still the Sun is the total nucleus of being and symbolizes the complete potential of every human being alive. It is vitality and the life force. Your whole essence comes from the position of the Sun.

You are always trying to express the Sun according to its position by house and sign. Possibility for all development is found in the Sun, and it marks the fundamental character of your personal radiations all around you.

It is the symbol of strength, vigor, wisdom, dignity, ardor, and generosity, and the ability for a person to function as a mature individual. It is also a creative force in society. It is consciousness of the gift of life.

The underdeveloped solar nature is arrogant, pushy, undependable, and proud, and is constantly using force.

MERCURY

Mercury is the planet closest to the Sun. It races around our star, gathering information and translating it to the rest of the system. Mercury represents your capacity to understand the desires of your own will and to translate those desires into action.

In other words it is the planet of mind and the power of communication. Through Mercury we develop an ability to think, write, speak, and observe—to become aware of the world around us. It colors our attitudes and vision of the world, as well as our capacity to communicate our inner responses to the outside world. Some people who have serious disabilities in their power of verbal communication have often wrongly been described as people lacking intelligence.

Although this planet (and its position in the horoscope) indicates your power to communicate your thoughts and perceptions to the world, intelligence is something deeper. Intelligence is distributed throughout all the planets. It is the relationship of the planets to each other that truly describes what we call intelligence. Mercury rules speaking, language, mathematics, draft and design, students, messengers, young people, offices, teachers, and any pursuits where the mind of man has wings.

VENUS

Venus is beauty. It symbolizes the harmony and radiance of a rare and elusive quality: beauty itself. It is refinement and delicacy, softness and charm. In astrology it indicates grace, balance, and the aesthetic sense. Where Venus is we see beauty, a gentle drawing in of energy and the need for satisfaction and completion. It is a special touch that finishes off rough edges. It is sensitivity, and affection, and it is always the place for that other elusive phenomenon: love. Venus describes our sense of what is beautiful and loving. Poorly developed, it is vulgar, tasteless, and self-indulgent. But its ideal is the flame of spiritual love—Aphrodite, goddess of love, and the sweetness and power of personal beauty.

MARS

Mars is raw, crude energy. The planet next to Earth but outward from the Sun is a fiery red sphere that charges through the horoscope with force and fury. It represents the way you reach out for new adventure and new experience. It is energy and drive, initiative, courage, and daring. It is the power to start something and see it through. It can be thoughtless, cruel and wild, angry and hostile, causing cuts, burns, scalds, and wounds. It can stab its way through a chart, or it can be the symbol of healthy spirited adventure, well-channeled constructive power to begin and keep up the drive. If you have trouble starting things, if you lack the get-up-and-go to start the ball rolling, if you lack aggressiveness and self-confidence, chances are there's another planet influencing your Mars. Mars rules soldiers, butchers, surgeons, salesmen—any field that requires daring, bold skill, operational technique, or self-promotion.

JUPITER

This is the largest planet of the solar system. Scientists have recently learned that Jupiter reflects more light than it receives from the Sun. In a sense it is like a star itself. In astrology it rules good luck and good cheer, health, wealth, optimism, happiness, success, and joy. It is the symbol of opportunity and always opens the way for new possibilities in your life. It rules exuberance, enthusiasm, wisdom, knowledge, generosity, and all forms of expansion in general. It rules actors, statesmen, clerics, professional people, religion, publishing, and the distribution of many people over large areas.

Sometimes Jupiter makes you think you deserve everything, and you become sloppy, wasteful, careless and rude, prodigal and lawless, in the illusion that nothing can ever go wrong. Then there is the danger of overconfidence, exaggeration, undependability, and overindulgence.

Jupiter is the minimization of limitation and the emphasis on spirituality and potential. It is the thirst for knowledge and higher learning.

SATURN

Saturn circles our system in dark splendor with its mysterious rings, forcing us to be awakened to whatever we have neglected in the past. It will present real puzzles and problems to be solved, causing delays, obstacles, and hindrances. By doing so, Saturn stirs our own sensitivity to those areas where we are laziest.

Here we must patiently develop *method*, and only through painstaking effort can our ends be achieved. It brings order to a horoscope and imposes reason just where we are feeling least reasonable. By creating limitations and boundary, Saturn shows the consequences of being human and demands that we accept the changing cycles inevitable in human life. Saturn rules time, old age, and sobriety. It can bring depression, gloom, jealousy, and greed, or serious acceptance of responsibilities out of which success will develop. With Saturn there is nothing to do but face facts. It rules laborers, stones, granite, rocks, and crystals of all kinds.

THE OUTER PLANETS:
URANUS, NEPTUNE, PLUTO

Uranus, Neptune, Pluto are the outer planets. They liberate human beings from cultural conditioning, and in that sense are the law-breakers. In early times it was thought that Saturn was the last planet of the system—the outer limit beyond which we could never go. The discovery of the next three planets ushered in new phases of human history, revolution, and technology.

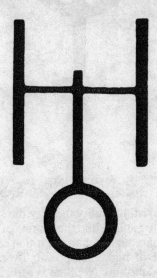

URANUS

Uranus rules unexpected change, upheaval, revolution. It is the symbol of total independence and asserts the freedom of an individual from all restriction and restraint. It is a breakthrough planet and indicates talent, originality, and genius in a horoscope. It usually causes last-minute reversals and changes of plan, unwanted separations, accidents, catastrophes, and eccentric behavior. It can add irrational rebelliousness and perverse bohemianism to a personality or a streak of unaffected brilliance in science and art. It rules technology, aviation, and all forms of electrical and electronic advancement. It governs great leaps forward and topsy-turvy situations, and *always* turns things around at the last minute. Its effects are difficult to predict, since it rules sudden last-minute decisions and events that come like lightning out of the blue.

NEPTUNE

Neptune dissolves existing reality the way the sea erodes the cliffs beside it. Its effects are subtle like the ringing of a buoy's bell in the fog. It suggests a reality higher than definition can usually describe. It awakens a sense of higher responsibility often causing guilt, worry, anxieties, or delusions. Neptune is associated with all forms of escape and can make things seem a certain way so convincingly that you are absolutely sure of something that eventually turns out to be quite different.

It is the planet of illusion and therefore governs the invisible realms that lie beyond our ordinary minds, beyond our simple factual ability to prove what is "real." Treachery, deceit, disillusionment, and disappointment are linked to Neptune. It describes a vague reality that promises eternity and the divine, yet in a manner so complex that we cannot really fathom it at all. At its worst Neptune is a cheap intoxicant; at its best it is the poetry, music, and inspiration of the higher planes of spiritual love. It has dominion over movies, photographs, and much of the arts.

PLUTO

Pluto lies at the outpost of our system and therefore rules finality in a horoscope—the final closing of chapters in your life, the passing of major milestones and points of development from which there is no return. It is a final wipeout, a closeout, an evacuation. It is a distant, subtle but powerful catalyst in all transformations that occur. It creates, destroys, then recreates. Sometimes Pluto starts its influence with a minor event or insignificant incident that might even go unnoticed. Slowly but surely, little by little, everything changes, until at last there has been a total transformation in the area of your life where Pluto has been operating. It rules mass thinking and the trends that society first rejects, then adopts, and finally outgrows.

Pluto rules the dead and the underworld—all the powerful forces of creation and destruction that go on all the time beneath, around, and above us. It can bring a lust for power with strong obsessions.

It is the planet that rules the metamorphosis of the caterpillar into a butterfly, for it symbolizes the capacity to change totally and forever a person's lifestyle, way of thought, and behavior.

THE MOON IN EACH SIGN

The Moon is the nearest planet to the Earth. It exerts more observable influence on us from day to day than any other planet. The effect is very personal, very intimate, and if we are not aware of how it works it can make us quite unstable in our ideas. And the annoying thing is that at these times we often see our own instability but can do nothing about it. A knowledge of what can be expected may help considerably. We can then be prepared to stand strong against the Moon's negative influences and use its positive ones to help us to get ahead. Who has not heard of going with the tide?

The Moon reflects, has no light of its own. It reflects the Sun—the life giver—in the form of vital movement. The Moon controls the tides, the blood rhythm, the movement of sap in trees and plants. Its nature is inconstancy and change so it signifies our moods, our superficial behavior—walking, talking, and especially thinking. Being a true reflector of other forces, the Moon is cold, watery like the surface of a still lake, brilliant and scintillating at times, but easily ruffled and disturbed by the winds of change.

The Moon takes about 27⅓ days to make a complete transit of the Zodiac. It spends just over 2¼ days in each sign. During that time it reflects the qualities, energies, and characteristics of the sign and, to a degree, the planet which rules the sign. When the Moon in its transit occupies a sign incompatible with our own birth sign, we can expect to feel a vague uneasiness, perhaps a touch of irritableness. We should not be discouraged nor let the feeling get us down, or, worse still, allow ourselves to take the discomfort out on others. Try to remember that the Moon has to change signs within 55 hours and, provided you are not physically ill, your mood will probably change with it. It is amazing how frequently depression lifts with the shift in the Moon's position. And, of course, when the Moon is transiting a sign compatible or sympathetic to yours, you will probably feel some sort of stimulation or just be plain happy to be alive.

In the horoscope, the Moon is such a powerful indicator that competent astrologers often use the sign it occupied at birth as the birth sign of the person. This is done particularly when the Sun is on the cusp, or edge, of two signs. Most experienced astrologers, however, coordinate both Sun and Moon signs by reading and confirming from one to the other and secure a far more accurate and personalized analysis.

For these reasons, the Moon tables which follow this section (see pages 86–92) are of great importance to the individual. They show the days and the exact times the Moon will enter each sign of the Zodiac for the year. Remember, you have to adjust the indicated times to local time. The corrections, already calculated for most of the main cities, are at the beginning of the tables. What follows now is a guide to the influences that will be reflected to the Earth by the Moon while it transits each of the twelve signs. The influence is at its peak about 26 hours after the Moon enters a sign. As you read the daily forecast, check the Moon sign for any given day and glance back at this guide.

MOON IN ARIES
This is a time for action, for reaching out beyond the usual self-imposed limitations and faint-hearted cautions. If you have plans in your head or on your desk, put them into practice. New ventures, applications, new jobs, new starts of any kind—all have a good chance of success. This is the period when original and dynamic impulses are being reflected onto Earth. Such energies are extremely vital and favor the pursuit of pleasure and adventure in practically every form. Sick people should feel an improvement. Those who are well will probably find themselves exuding confidence and optimism. People fond of physical exercise should find their bodies growing with tone and well-being. Boldness, strength, determination should characterize most of your activities with a readiness to face up to old challenges. Yesterday's problems may seem petty and exaggerated—so deal with them. Strike out alone. Self-reliance will attract others to you. This is a good time for making friends. Business and marriage partners are more likely to be impressed with the man and woman of action. Opposition will be overcome or thrown aside with much less effort than usual. CAUTION: Be dominant but not domineering.

MOON IN TAURUS
The spontaneous, action-packed person of yesterday gives way to the cautious, diligent, hardworking "thinker." In this period ideas will probably be concentrated on ways of improving finances. A great deal of time may be spent figuring out and going over

schemes and plans. It is the right time to be careful with detail. People will find themselves working longer than usual at their desks. Or devoting more time to serious thought about the future. A strong desire to put order into business and financial arrangements may cause extra work. Loved ones may complain of being neglected and may fail to appreciate that your efforts are for their ultimate benefit. Your desire for system may extend to criticism of arrangements in the home and lead to minor upsets. Health may be affected through overwork. Try to secure a reasonable amount of rest and relaxation, although the tendency will be to "keep going" despite good advice. Work done conscientiously in this period should result in a solid contribution to your future security. CAUTION: Try not to be as serious with people as the work you are engaged in.

MOON IN GEMINI
The humdrum of routine and too much work should suddenly end. You are likely to find yourself in an expansive, quicksilver world of change and self-expression. Urges to write, to paint, to experience the freedom of some sort of artistic outpouring, may be very strong. Take full advantage of them. You may find yourself finishing something you began and put aside long ago. Or embarking on something new which could easily be prompted by a chance meeting, a new acquaintance, or even an advertisement. There may be a yearning for a change of scenery, the feeling to visit another country (not too far away), or at least to get away for a few days. This may result in short, quick journeys. Or, if you are planning a single visit, there may be some unexpected changes or detours on the way. Familiar activities will seem to give little satisfaction unless they contain a fresh element of excitement or expectation. The inclination will be toward untried pursuits, particularly those that allow you to express your inner nature. The accent is on new faces, new places. CAUTION: Do not be too quick to commit yourself emotionally.

MOON IN CANCER
Feelings of uncertainty and vague insecurity are likely to cause problems while the Moon is in Cancer. Thoughts may turn frequently to the warmth of the home and the comfort of loved ones. Nostalgic impulses could cause you to bring out old photographs and letters and reflect on the days when your life seemed to be much more rewarding and less demanding. The love and understanding of parents and family may be important, and, if it is not forthcoming, you may have to fight against bouts of self-pity. The cordiality of friends and the thought of good times with them that are sure to be repeated will help to restore you to a happier frame

of mind. The desire to be alone may follow minor setbacks or rebuffs at this time, but solitude is unlikely to help. Better to get on the telephone or visit someone. This period often causes peculiar dreams and upsurges of imaginative thinking which can be helpful to authors of occult and mystical works. Preoccupation with the personal world of simple human needs can overshadow any material strivings. CAUTION: Do not spend too much time thinking—seek the company of loved ones or close friends.

MOON IN LEO

New horizons of exciting and rather extravagant activity open up. This is the time for exhilarating entertainment, glamorous and lavish parties, and expensive shopping sprees. Any merrymaking that relies upon your generosity as a host has every chance of being a spectacular success. You should find yourself right in the center of the fun, either as the life of the party or simply as a person whom happy people like to be with. Romance thrives in this heady atmosphere and friendships are likely to explode unexpectedly into serious attachments. Children and younger people should be attracted to you and you may find yourself organizing a picnic or a visit to a fun-fair, the movies, or the beach. The sunny company and vitality of youthful companions should help you to find some unsuspected energy. In career, you could find an opening for promotion or advancement. This should be the time to make a direct approach. The period favors those engaged in original research. CAUTION: Bask in popularity, not in flattery.

MOON IN VIRGO

Off comes the party cap and out steps the busy, practical worker. He wants to get his personal affairs straight, to rearrange them, if necessary, for more efficiency, so he will have more time for more work. He clears up his correspondence, pays outstanding bills, makes numerous phone calls. He is likely to make inquiries, or sign up for some new insurance and put money into gilt-edged investment. Thoughts probably revolve around the need for future security—to tie up loose ends and clear the decks. There may be a tendency to be "finicky," to interfere in the routine of others, particularly friends and family members. The motive may be a genuine desire to help with suggestions for updating or streamlining their affairs, but these will probably not be welcomed. Sympathy may be felt for less fortunate sections of the community and a flurry of some sort of voluntary service is likely. This may be accompanied by strong feelings of responsibility on several fronts and health may suffer from extra efforts made. CAUTION: Everyone may not want your help or advice.

MOON IN LIBRA

These are days of harmony and agreement and you should find yourself at peace with most others. Relationships tend to be smooth and sweet-flowing. Friends may become closer and bonds deepen in mutual understanding. Hopes will be shared. Progress by cooperation could be the secret of success in every sphere. In business, established partnerships may flourish and new ones get off to a good start. Acquaintances could discover similar interests that lead to congenial discussions and rewarding exchanges of some sort. Love, as a unifying force, reaches its optimum. Marriage partners should find accord. Those who wed at this time face the prospect of a happy union. Cooperation and tolerance are felt to be stronger than dissension and impatience. The argumentative are not quite so loud in their bellowings, nor as inflexible in their attitudes. In the home, there should be a greater recognition of the other point of view and a readiness to put the wishes of the group before selfish insistence. This is a favorable time to join an art group. CAUTION: Do not be too independent—let others help you if they want to.

MOON IN SCORPIO

Driving impulses to make money and to economize are likely to cause upsets all around. No area of expenditure is likely to be spared the ax, including the household budget. This is a time when the desire to cut down on extravagance can become near fanatical. Care must be exercised to try to keep the aim in reasonable perspective. Others may not feel the same urgent need to save and may retaliate. There is a danger that possessions of sentimental value will be sold to realize cash for investment. Buying and selling of stock for quick profit is also likely. The attention turns to organizing, reorganizing, tidying up at home and at work. Neglected jobs could suddenly be done with great bursts of energy. The desire for solitude may intervene. Self-searching thoughts could disturb. The sense of invisible and mysterious energies in play could cause some excitability. The reassurance of loves ones may help. CAUTION: Be kind to the people you love.

MOON IN SAGITTARIUS

These are days when you are likely to be stirred and elevated by discussions and reflections of a religious and philosophical nature. Ideas of faraway places may cause unusual response and excitement. A decision may be made to visit someone overseas, perhaps a person whose influence was important to your earlier character development. There could be a strong resolution to get away from present intellectual patterns, to learn new subjects, and to meet more interesting people. The superficial may be rejected in all its forms. An impatience with old ideas and unimaginative contacts could lead to a change of companions and interests. There may be an upsurge of religious feeling and metaphysical inquiry. Even a new insight into the significance of astrology and other occult studies is likely under the curious stimulus of the Moon in Sagittarius. Physically, you may express this need for fundamental change by spending more time outdoors: sports, gardening, long walks appeal. CAUTION: Try to channel any restlessness into worthwhile study.

MOON IN CAPRICORN

Life in these hours may seem to pivot around the importance of gaining prestige and honor in the career, as well as maintaining a spotless reputation. Ambitious urges may be excessive and could be accompanied by quite acquisitive drives for money. Effort should be directed along strictly ethical lines where there is no possibility of reproach or scandal. All endeavors are likely to be characterized by great earnestness, and an air of authority and purpose which should impress those who are looking for leadership or reliability. The desire to conform to accepted standards may extend to sharp criticism of family members. Frivolity and unconventional actions are unlikely to amuse while the Moon is in Capricorn. Moderation and seriousness are the orders of the day. Achievement and recognition in this period could come through community work or organizing for the benefit of some amateur group. CAUTION: Dignity and esteem are not always self-awarded.

MOON IN AQUARIUS

Moon in Aquarius is in the second last sign of the Zodiac where ideas can become disturbingly fine and subtle. The result is often a mental "no-man's land" where imagination cannot be trusted with the same certitude as other times. The dangers for the individual are the extremes of optimism and pessimism. Unless the imagination is held in check, situations are likely to be misread, and rosy conclusions drawn where they do not exist. Consequences for the unwary can be costly in career and business. Best to think twice and not speak or act until you think again. Pessimism can be a cruel self-inflicted penalty for delusion at this time. Between the two extremes are strange areas of self-deception which, for example, can make the selfish person think he is actually being generous. Eerie dreams which resemble the reality and even seem to continue into the waking state are also possible. CAUTION: Look for the fact and not just for the image in your mind.

MOON IN PISCES

Everything seems to come to the surface now. Memory may be crystal clear, throwing up long-forgotten information which could be valuable in the career or business. Flashes of clairvoyance and intuition are possible along with sudden realizations of one's own nature, which may be used for self-improvement. A talent, never before suspected, may be discovered. Qualities not evident before in friends and marriage partners are likely to be noticed. As this is a period in which the truth seems to emerge, the discovery of false characteristics is likely to lead to disenchantment or a shift in attachments. However, when qualities are accepted, it should lead to happiness and deeper feeling. Surprise solutions could bob up for old problems. There may be a public announcement of the solving of a crime or mystery. People with secrets may find someone has "guessed" correctly. The secrets of the soul or the inner self also tend to reveal themselves. Religious and philosophical groups may make some interesting discoveries. CAUTION: Not a time for activities that depend on secrecy.

NOTE: When you read your daily forecasts, use the Moon Sign Dates that are provided in the following section of Moon Tables. Then you may want to glance back here for the Moon's influence in a given sign.

MOON TABLES

CORRECTION FOR NEW YORK TIME, FIVE HOURS WEST OF GREENWICH

Atlanta, Boston, Detroit, Miami, Washington, Montreal,
Ottawa, Quebec, Bogota, Havana, Lima, Santiago ... Same time
Chicago, New Orleans, Houston, Winnipeg, Churchill,
Mexico City .... Deduct 1 hour
Albuquerque, Denver, Phoenix, El Paso, Edmonton,
Helena .... Deduct 2 hours
Los Angeles, San Francisco, Reno, Portland,
Seattle, Vancouver .... Deduct 3 hours
Honolulu, Anchorage, Fairbanks, Kodiak .... Deduct 5 hours
Nome, Samoa, Tonga, Midway .... Deduct 6 hours
Halifax, Bermuda, San Juan, Caracas, La Paz,
Barbados .... Add 1 hour
St. John's, Brasilia, Rio de Janeiro, Sao Paulo,
Buenos Aires, Montevideo .... Add 2 hours
Azores, Cape Verde Islands .... Add 3 hours
Canary Islands, Madeira, Reykjavik .... Add 4 hours
London, Paris, Amsterdam, Madrid, Lisbon,
Gibraltar, Belfast, Raba .... Add 5 hours
Frankfurt, Rome, Oslo, Stockholm, Prague,
Belgrade .... Add 6 hours
Bucharest, Beirut, Tel Aviv, Athens, Istanbul, Cairo,
Alexandria, Cape Town, Johannesburg .... Add 7 hours
Moscow, Leningrad, Baghdad, Dhahran,
Addis Ababa, Nairobi, Teheran, Zanzibar .... Add 8 hours
Bombay, Calcutta, Sri Lanka .... Add 10½
Hong Kong, Shanghai, Manila, Peking, Perth ...... Add 13 hours
Tokyo, Okinawa, Darwin, Pusan .... Add 14 hours
Sydney, Melbourne, Port Moresby, Guam .... Add 15 hours
Auckland, Wellington, Suva, Wake .... Add 17 hours

2007 MOON SIGN DATES—
NEW YORK TIME

JANUARY		FEBRUARY		MARCH	
Day Moon Enters		**Day Moon Enters**		**Day Moon Enters**	
1. Gemini		1. Leo	12:16 am	1. Leo	
2. Cancer	10:15 am	2. Leo		2. Virgo	4:33 pm
3. Cancer		3. Virgo	9:35 am	3. Virgo	
4. Leo	5:15 pm	4. Virgo		4. Virgo	
5. Leo		5. Libra	9:16 pm	5. Libra	4:26 am
6. Leo		6. Libra		6. Libra	
7. Virgo	1:19 am	7. Libra		7. Scorp.	5:18 pm
8. Virgo		8. Scorp.	10:11 am	8. Scorp.	
9. Libra	1:16 pm	9. Scorp.		9. Scorp.	
10. Libra		10. Sagitt.	10:02 pm	10. Sagitt.	5:36 am
11. Libra		11. Sagitt.		11. Sagitt.	
12. Scorp.	2:09 am	12. Sagitt.		12. Capric.	3:36 pm
13. Scorp.		13. Capric.	6:43 am	13. Capric.	
14. Sagitt.	1:12 pm	14. Capric.		14. Aquar.	9:53 pm
15. Sagitt.		15. Aquar.	11:36 am	15. Aquar.	
16. Capric.	8:50 pm	16. Aquar.		16. Aquar.	
17. Capric.		17. Pisces	1:31 pm	17. Pisces	12:31 am
18. Capric.		18. Pisces		18. Pisces	
19. Aquar.	1:17 am	19. Aries	2:07 pm	19. Aries	12:43 am
20. Aquar.		20. Aries		20. Aries	
21. Pisces	3:49 am	21. Taurus	3:04 pm	21. Taurus	12:16 am
22. Pisces		22. Taurus		22. Taurus	
23. Aries	5:53 am	23. Gemini	5:43 pm	23. Gemini	1:07 am
24. Aries		24. Gemini		24. Gemini	
25. Taurus	8:30 am	25. Cancer	10:49 pm	25. Cancer	4:50 am
26. Taurus		26. Cancer		26. Cancer	
27. Gemini	12:11 pm	27. Cancer		27. Leo	12:05 pm
28. Gemini		28. Leo	6:31 am	28. Leo	
29. Cancer	5:17 pm			29. Virgo	10:28 pm
30. Cancer				30. Virgo	
31. Cancer				31. Virgo	

Daylight saving time to be considered where applicable.

2007 MOON SIGN DATES—
NEW YORK TIME

APRIL Day Moon Enters		MAY Day Moon Enters		JUNE Day Moon Enters	
1. Libra	10:44 am	1. Scorp.	5:42 am	1. Sagitt.	
2. Libra		2. Scorp.		2. Capric.	10:10 am
3. Scorp.	11:37 pm	3. Sagitt.	5:49 pm	3. Capric.	
4. Scorp.		4. Sagitt.		4. Aquar.	6:16 pm
5. Scorp.		5. Sagitt.		5. Aquar.	
6. Sagitt.	11:58 am	6. Capric.	4:22 am	6. Aquar.	
7. Sagitt.		7. Capric.		7. Pisces	12:25 am
8. Capric.	10:37 pm	8. Aquar.	12:49 pm	8. Pisces	
9. Capric.		9. Aquar.		9. Aries	4:27 am
10. Capric.		10. Pisces	6:33 pm	10. Aries	
11. Aquar.	6:24 am	11. Pisces		11. Taurus	6:30 am
12. Aquar.		12. Aries	9:20 pm	12. Taurus	
13. Pisces	10:40 am	13. Aries		13. Gemini	7:25 am
14. Pisces		14. Taurus	9:49 pm	14. Gemini	
15. Aries	11:48 am	15. Taurus		15. Cancer	8:46 am
16. Aries		16. Gemini	9:35 pm	16. Cancer	
17. Taurus	11:12 am	17. Gemini		17. Leo	12:26 pm
18. Taurus		18. Cancer	10:39 pm	18. Leo	
19. Gemini	10:52 am	19. Cancer		19. Virgo	7:47 pm
20. Gemini		20. Cancer		20. Virgo	
21. Cancer	12:51 pm	21. Leo	2:58 am	21. Virgo	
22. Cancer		22. Leo		22. Libra	5:45 am
23. Leo	6:39 pm	23. Virgo	11:27 am	23. Libra	
24. Leo		24. Virgo		24. Scorp.	7:26 pm
25. Leo		25. Libra	11:17 pm	25. Scorp.	
26. Virgo	4:25 am	26. Libra		26. Scorp.	
27. Virgo		27. Libra		27. Sagitt.	7:25 am
28. Libra	4:46 pm	28. Scorp.	12:12 pm	28. Sagitt.	
29. Libra		29. Scorp.		29. Capric.	5:06 pm
30. Libra		30. Scorp.		30. Capric.	
		31. Sagitt.	12:06 am		

Daylight saving time to be considered where applicable.

2007 MOON SIGN DATES—
NEW YORK TIME

JULY		AUGUST		SEPTEMBER	
Day Moon Enters		**Day Moon Enters**		**Day Moon Enters**	
1. Capric.		1. Pisces		1. Taurus	12:36 am
2. Aquar.	12:25 am	2. Aries	3:44 pm	2. Taurus	
3. Aquar.		3. Aries		3. Gemini	2:31 am
4. Pisces	5:53 am	4. Taurus	6:17 pm	4. Gemini	
5. Pisces		5. Taurus		5. Cancer	6:09 am
6. Aries	9:58 am	6. Gemini	9:02 pm	6. Cancer	
7. Aries		7. Gemini		7. Leo	12:00 pm
8. Taurus	12:55 pm	8. Gemini		8. Leo	
9. Taurus		9. Cancer	12:37 am	9. Virgo	8:11 pm
10. Gemini	3:11 pm	10. Cancer		10. Virgo	
11. Gemini		11. Leo	5:43 am	11. Virgo	
12. Cancer	5:40 pm	12. Leo		12. Libra	6:32 am
13. Cancer		13. Virgo	1:04 pm	13. Libra	
14. Leo	9:44 pm	14. Virgo		14. Scorp.	6:38 pm
15. Leo		15. Libra	11:05 pm	15. Scorp.	
16. Leo		16. Libra		16. Scorp.	
17. Virgo	4:40 am	17. Libra		17. Sagitt.	7:22 am
18. Virgo		18. Scorp.	11:14 am	18. Sagitt.	
19. Libra	2:54 pm	19. Scorp.		19. Capric.	6:53 pm
20. Libra		20. Sagitt.	11:45 pm	20. Capric.	
21. Libra		21. Sagitt.		21. Capric.	
22. Scorp.	3:19 am	22. Sagitt.		22. Aquar.	3:19 am
23. Scorp.		23. Carpic.	10:21 am	23. Aquar.	
24. Sagitt.	3:31 pm	24. Capric.		24. Pisces	7:56 am
25. Sagitt.		25. Aquar.	5:36 pm	25. Pisces	
26. Sagitt.		26. Aquar.		26. Aries	9:24 am
27. Capric.	1:22 am	27. Pisces	9:35 pm	27. Aries	
28. Capric.		28. Pisces		28. Taurus	9:18 am
29. Aquar.	8:15 am	29. Aries	11:26 pm	29. Taurus	
30. Aquar.		30. Aries		30. Gemini	9:35 am
31. Pisces	12:42 pm	31. Aries			

Daylight saving time to be considered where applicable.

2007 MOON SIGN DATES
NEW YORK TIME

OCTOBER		NOVEMBER		DECEMBER	
Day Moon Enters		**Day Moon Enters**		**Day Moon Enters**	
1. Gemini		1. Leo		1. Virgo	
2. Cancer	11:58 am	2. Leo		2. Virgo	
3. Cancer		3. Virgo	7:46 am	3. Libra	1:02 am
4. Leo	5:26 pm	4. Virgo		4. Libra	
5. Leo		5. Libra	6:48 pm	5. Scorp.	1:32 pm
6. Leo		6. Libra		6. Scorp.	
7. Virgo	2:04 am	7. Libra		7. Scorp.	
8. Virgo		8. Scorp.	7:19 am	8. Sagitt.	2:12 am
9. Libra	12:59 pm	9. Scorp.		9. Sagitt.	
10. Libra		10. Sagitt.	8:00 pm	10. Capric.	1:52 pm
11. Libra		11. Sagitt.		11. Capric.	
12. Scorp.	1:14 am	12. Sagitt.		12. Capric.	
13. Scorp.		13. Capric.	8:02 am	13. Aquar.	12:02 am
14. Sagitt.	1:59 pm	14. Capric.		14. Aquar.	
15. Sagitt.		15. Aquar.	6:31 pm	15. Pisces	8:16 am
16. Sagitt.		16. Aqaur.		16. Pisces	
17. Capric.	2:04 am	17. Aquar.		17. Aries	1:54 pm
18. Capric.		18. Pisces	2:16 am	18. Aries	
19. Aquar.	11:52 am	19. Pisces		19. Taurus	4:39 pm
20. Aquar.		20. Aries	6:25 am	20. Taurus	
21. Pisces	6:03 pm	21. Aries		21. Gemini	5:15 pm
22. Pisces		22. Taurus	7:20 am	22. Gemini	
23. Aries	8:25 pm	23. Taurus		23. Cancer	5:19 pm
24. Aries		24. Gemini	6:30 am	24. Cancer	
25. Taurus	8:06 pm	25. Gemini		25. Leo	6:53 pm
26. Taurus		26. Cancer	6:08 am	26. Leo	
27. Gemini	7:12 pm	27. Cancer		27. Virgo	11:45 pm
28. Gemini		28. Leo	8:24 am	28. Virgo	
29. Cancer	7:51 pm	29. Leo		29. Virgo	
30. Cancer		30. Virgo	2:45 pm	30. Libra	8:38 am
31. Leo	11:49 pm			31. Libra	

Daylight saving time to be considered where applicable.

2007 PHASES OF THE MOON—
NEW YORK TIME

New Moon	First Quarter	Full Moon	Last Quarter
Dec. 20 ('06)	Dec. 27 ('06)	Jan. 3	Jan. 11
Jan. 18	Jan. 25	Feb. 2	Feb. 10
Feb. 17	Feb. 24	March 3	March 11
March 18	March 25	April 2	April 10
April 17	April 24	May 2	May 9
May 16	May 23	May 31	June 8
June 14	June 22	June 30	July 7
July 14	July 22	July 29	August 5
August 12	August 20	August 28	Sept. 3
Sept. 11	Sept. 19	Sept. 26	Oct. 3
Oct. 11	Oct. 19	Oct. 26	Nov. 1
Nov. 9	Nov. 17	Nov. 24	Dec. 1
Dec. 9	Dec. 17	Dec. 23	Dec. 31

Each phase of the Moon lasts approximately seven to eight days, during which the Moon's shape gradually changes as it comes out of one phase and goes into the next.

There will be a solar eclipse during the New Moon phase on March 18 and September 11.

There will be a lunar eclipse during the Full Moon phase on March 3 and August 28.

2007 FISHING GUIDE

	Good	Best
January	1-5-6-19-25	2-3-4-11-30-31
February	1-2-3-4-17-24-28	16-26-27
March	1-2-3-4-11-18-30-31	5-6-25-26
April	17-24-29	2-3-4-5-9-29-30
May	4-5-10-24-31	1-2-15-29-30
June	1-2-14-28-29	3-4-8-23-26-30
July	2-3-7-27-29-30-31	13-23-28
August	2-12-20-26-27-30-31	1-5-24-28-29
September	4-11-22-23-26-27-28	20-24-25-29
October	18-24-25-28-29	3-10-22-26-27
November	2-17-21-22-24-25	9-23-26-27
December	1-10-17-21-22-23-26-27	24-25-31

2007 PLANTING GUIDE

	Aboveground Crops	Root Crops
January	3-21-22-26-30-31	3-10-11-12-13-17-18
February	18-22-23-26-27	6-7-8-9-14
March	21-22-25-26	5-6-7-8-9-13-14-18
April	1-18-22-23-29-30	2-3-4-5-9-10-14
May	1-19-20-26-27-28-29-30	1-2-11-12-15-16
June	15-16-22-23-24-25-26	3-4-7-8-11-12-30
July	20-21-22-23-28	3-4-9-13-14
August	16-17-18-19-24-25	1-5-6-10-28-29
September	12-13-14-15-16-20-21-25	2-5-6-29
October	12-13-18-22-23	3-10-26-27-30-31
November	14-15-18-19-22-23	7-8-9-26-27
December	11-12-16-20	4-5-6-7-24-25-30

	Pruning	Weeds and Pests
January	3-12-13	6-7-8-15-16
February	9-10	2-3-4-11-16
March	8-17-18	4-10-11-15-16
April	4-5-14	7-8-12-16
May	2-11-12	4-5-9-13-14
June	7-8	5-6-9-10-14
July	4-5-13-14	2-3-7-11-12-30
August	10-29	3-7-8-12-30-31
September	5-6	3-4-8-9-10-11-27
October	2-3-30-31	1-5-6-7-8-28-29
November	9-26-27	1-2-3-4-25-29-30
December	6-7-24-25	1-2-9-26-27-28-29

MOON'S INFLUENCE OVER PLANTS

Centuries ago it was established that seeds planted when the Moon is in signs and phases called Fruitful will produce more growth than seeds planted when the Moon is in a Barren sign.

Fruitful Signs: Taurus, Cancer, Libra, Scorpio, Capricorn, Pisces
Barren Signs: Aries, Gemini, Leo, Virgo, Sagittarius, Aquarius
Dry Signs: Aries, Gemini, Sagittarius, Aquarius

Activity	Moon In
Mow lawn, trim plants	**Fruitful sign:** 1st & 2nd quarter
Plant flowers	**Fruitful sign:** 2nd quarter; best in Cancer and Libra
Prune	**Fruitful sign:** 3rd & 4th quarter
Destroy pests; spray	**Barren sign:** 4th quarter
Harvest potatoes, root crops	**Dry sign:** 3rd & 4th quarter; Taurus, Leo, and Aquarius

MOON'S INFLUENCE OVER YOUR HEALTH

ARIES   Head, brain, face, upper jaw
TAURUS   Throat, neck, lower jaw
GEMINI   Hands, arms, lungs, shoulders, nervous system
CANCER   Esophagus, stomach, breasts, womb, liver
LEO   Heart, spine
VIRGO   Intestines, liver
LIBRA   Kidneys, lower back
SCORPIO   Sex and eliminative organs
SAGITTARIUS   Hips, thighs, liver
CAPRICORN   Skin, bones, teeth, knees
AQUARIUS   Circulatory system, lower legs
PISCES   Feet, tone of being

Try to avoid work being done on that part of the body when the Moon is in the sign governing that part.

MOON'S INFLUENCE OVER DAILY AFFAIRS

The Moon makes a complete transit of the Zodiac every 27 days 7 hours and 43 minutes. In making this transit the Moon forms different aspects with the planets and consequently has favorable or unfavorable bearings on affairs and events for persons according to the sign of the Zodiac under which they were born.

When the Moon is in conjunction with the Sun it is called a New Moon; when the Moon and Sun are in opposition it is called a Full Moon. From New Moon to Full Moon, first and second quarter—which takes about two weeks—the Moon is increasing or waxing. From Full Moon to New Moon, third and fourth quarter, the Moon is decreasing or waning.

Activity	Moon In
Business: buying and selling new, requiring public support	Sagittarius, Aries, Gemini, Virgo 1st and 2nd quarter
meant to be kept quiet	3rd and 4th quarter
Investigation	3rd and 4th quarter
Signing documents	1st & 2nd quarter, Cancer, Scorpio, Pisces
Advertising	2nd quarter, Sagittarius
Journeys and trips	1st & 2nd quarter, Gemini, Virgo
Renting offices, etc.	Taurus, Leo, Scorpio, Aquarius
Painting of house/apartment	3rd & 4th quarter, Taurus, Scorpio, Aquarius
Decorating	Gemini, Libra, Aquarius
Buying clothes and accessories	Taurus, Virgo
Beauty salon or barber shop visit	1st & 2nd quarter, Taurus, Leo, Libra, Scorpio, Aquarius
Weddings	1st & 2nd quarter

Sagittarius

SAGITTARIUS

Character Analysis

People born under this ninth sign of the Zodiac are quite often self-reliant and intelligent. Generally, they are quite philosophical in their outlook on life. They know how to make practical use of their imagination.

There is seldom anything narrow about a Sagittarius man or woman. He or she is generally very tolerant and considerate. They would never consciously do anything that would hurt another's feelings. They are gifted with a good sense of humor and believe in being honest in relationships with others. At times Sagittarius is a little short of tact. They are so intent on telling the truth that sometimes they can be blunt.

Nevertheless, Sagittarius men and women mean well, and people who enjoy a relationship with them are often willing to overlook this flaw. Sagittarius may even tell people true things about themselves that they do not wish to hear. At times this can cause a strain in the relationship. Sagittarius often wishes that others were as forthright and honest as he or she is—no matter what the consequences.

Sagittarius men and women are positive and optimistic and love life. They often help others to snap out of an ill mood. Their joie de vivre is often infectious. People enjoy being around Sagittarius because they are almost always in a good mood.

Quite often people born under the sign of Sagittarius are fond of the outdoors. They enjoy sporting events and often excel in them. Like the Archer, the zodiacal symbol of the sign, Sagittarius men and women are fond of animals, especially horses and dogs.

Generally, the Archer is healthy—in mind and in body. They have pluck. They enjoy the simple things of life. Fresh air and good comradeship are important to them. On the other hand, they are fond of developing their minds. Many Sagittarius cannot read or study enough. They like to keep abreast of things. They are interested in theater and the arts in general. Some of them are quite religious. Some choose a religious life.

Because they are outgoing for the most part, they sometimes come in touch with situations that others are never confronted with. In the long run this tends to make their life experiences quite rich and varied. They are well-balanced. They like to be active. And they enjoy using their intellects.

It is important to the person born under this sign that justice prevails. They dislike seeing anyone treated unfairly. If Sagittarius feels that the old laws are out of date or unrealistic, he or she will fight to have them changed. At times they can be true rebels. It is important to the Archer that law is carried out impartially. In matters of law, they often excel.

Sagittarius are almost always fond of travel. It seems to be imbedded in their natures. At times, they feel impelled to get away from familiar surroundings and people. Faraway places have a magical attraction for someone born under this sign. They enjoy reading about foreign lands and strange customs.

Many people who are Sagittarius are not terribly fond of living in big cities; they prefer the quiet and greenery of the countryside. Of all the signs of the Zodiac the sign of Sagittarius is closest to mother nature. They can usually build a trusting relationship with animals. They respect wildlife in all its forms.

Sagittarius is quite clever in conversation. He or she has a definite way with words. They like a good argument. They know how to phrase things exactly. Their sense of humor often has a cheerful effect on their manner of speech. They are seldom without a joke.

At times, the Sagittarius wit is apt to hurt someone's feelings, but this is never intentional. A slip of the tongue sometimes gets the Archer into social difficulties. As a result, there can be argumentative and angry scenes. But Sagittarius men and women cool down quickly. They are not given to holding grudges. They are willing to forgive and forget.

On the whole, Sagittarius is good-natured and fun-loving. They find it easy to take up with all sorts of people. In most cases, their social circle is large. People enjoy their company and their parties. Many friends share the Sagittarius interest in the outdoor life as well as intellectual pursuits.

Sagittarius sometimes can be impulsive. They are not afraid of risk. On the contrary, they can be foolhardy in the way they court danger. But Sagittarius men and women are very sporting in all they that do. If they should wind up the loser, they will not waste time grieving about it. They are fairly optimistic—they believe in good luck.

Health

Often people born under the sign of Sagittarius are quite athletic. They are healthy-looking—quite striking in a robust way. Often they are rather tall and well-built. They are enthusiastic people and like being active or involved. Exercise and sports may interest them a great deal.

Sagittarius cannot stand not being active. They have to be on the go. As they grow older, they seem to increase in strength and physical ability. At times they may have worries, but they never allow them to affect humor or health.

It is important to Sagittarius men and women to remain physically sound. They are usually very physically fit, but their nervous system may be somewhat sensitive. Too much activity—even while they find action attractive—may put a severe strain on them after a time. The Archer should try to concentrate their energies on as few objects as possible. However, usually they have many projects scattered here and there, and can be easily exhausted.

At times, illnesses fall upon the Archer suddenly or strangely. Some Sagittarius are accident-prone. They are not afraid of taking risks and as a result are sometimes careless in the way they do things. Injuries often come to them by way of sports or other vigorous activities.

Sometimes men and women of this sign try to ignore signs of illness—especially if they are engaged in some activity that has captured their interest. This results in a severe setback at times.

In later life, Sagittarius sometimes suffers from stomach disorders. High blood pressure is another ailment that might affect them. They should also be on guard for signs of arthritis and sciatica. In spite of these possible dangers, the average Sagittarius manages to stay quite youthful and alert through their many interests and pastimes.

Occupation

Sagittarius is someone who can be relied upon in a work situation. They are loyal and dependable. They are energetic workers, anxious to please superiors. They are forward-looking by nature and enjoy working in modern surroundings and toward progressive goals.

Challenges do not frighten Sagittarius. They are flexible and can work in confining situations even though they may not enjoy it. Work that gives them a chance to move around and meet new people is well suited to their character. If they have to stay in one locale, they become sad and ill-humored. They can take orders but they would rather be in a situation where they do not have to. They are difficult to please at times, and may hop from job to job before feeling that it is really time to settle down. Sagittarius do their best work when they are allowed to work on their own.

Sagittarius individuals are interested in expressing themselves in the work they do. If they occupy a position that does not allow them to be creative, they will seek outside activities. Such hobbies or pastimes give them a chance to develop and broaden their talents.

Some Sagittarius do well in the field of journalism. Others make good teachers and public speakers. They are generally quite flexible and would do well in many different positions. Some excel as foreign ministers or in music. Others do well in government work or in publishing.

Men and women born under this ninth sign are often more intelligent than the average person. The cultivated Sagittarius knows how to employ intellectual gifts to their best advantage. In politics and religion, Sagittarius often displays brilliance.

The Sagittarius man or woman is pleasant to work with. They are considerate of colleagues and would do nothing that might upset the working relationship. Because they are so self-reliant, they often inspire teammates. Sagittarius likes to work with detail. Their ideas are both practical and idealistic. Sagittarius is curious by nature and is always looking for ways of expanding their knowledge.

Sagittarius are almost always generous. They rarely refuse someone in need, but are always willing to share what they have. Whether they are up or down, Sagittarius can always be relied upon to help someone in dire straits. Their attitude toward life may be happy-go-lucky in general. They are difficult to depress no matter what the situation. They are optimistic and forward-looking. Money always seems to fall into their hands.

The average Sagittarius is interested in expansion and promotion. Sometimes these concerns weaken their projects rather than strengthen them. Also, the average Sagittarius is more interested in contentment and joy than in material gain. However, they will do their best to make the most of any profit that comes their way.

When Sagittarius does get hooked on a venture, he or she is often willing to take risks to secure a profit. In the long run they are successful. They have a flair for carrying off business deals. It is the cultivated Sagittarius who prepares in advance for any business contingency. In that way he or she can bring knowledge and experience to bear on their professional and financial interests.

Home and Family

Not all Sagittarius are very interested in home life. Many of them set great store in being mobile. Their activities outside the home may attract them more than those inside the home. Not exactly homebodies, Sagittarius, however, can adjust themselves to a stable domestic life if they put their minds to it.

People born under this sign are not keen on luxuries and other displays of wealth. They prefer the simple things. Anyone entering their home should be able to discern this. They are generally neat.

They like a place that has plenty of space—not too cluttered with imposing furniture.

Even when they settle down, Sagittarius men and women like to keep a small corner of their life just for themselves. Independence is important to them. If necessary, they will insist upon it, no matter what the situation. They like a certain amount of beauty in the home, but they may not be too interested in keeping things looking nice. Their interests lead them elsewhere. Housekeeping may bore them to distraction. When forced to stick to a domestic routine, they can become somewhat disagreeable.

Children bring Sagittarius men and women a great deal of happiness. They are fond of family life. Friends generally drop in any old time to visit for they know they will always be welcomed and properly entertained. The Archer's love for their fellow man is well known.

The Sagittarius parent may be bewildered at first by a newborn baby. They may worry about holding such a tiny tot for fear of injuring the little one. Although some Sagittarius may be clumsy, they do have a natural touch with small children and should not worry about handling them properly. As soon as the infant begins to grow up and develop a definite personality, Sagittarius can relax and relate. There is always a strong tie between children and the Sagittarius parent.

Children are especially drawn to Sagittarius because they seem to understand them better than other adults.

One is apt to find children born under this sign a little restless and disorganized at times. They are usually quite independent in their ways and may ask for quite a bit of freedom while still young. They don't like being fussed over by adults. They like to feel that their parents believe in them and trust them on their own.

Social Relationships

Sagittarius enjoys having people around. It is not difficult for them to make friends. They are very sociable by nature. Most of the friends they make they keep for life.

Sagittarius men and women are broad-minded, so they have all sorts of pals and casual acquaintances. They appreciate people for their good qualities, however few a person might have. Sagittarius are not quick to judge and are usually very forgiving. They are not impressed by what a friend has in the way of material goods.

Sagittarius men and women are generally quite popular. They are much in demand socially. People like their easy disposition and good humor. Their friendship is valued by others. Quite often in spite of their chumminess, Sagittarius is rather serious. Light conversation may be somewhat difficult for them.

Sagittarius men and women believe in speaking their minds, in saying what they feel. Yet at times, they can appear quiet and retiring. It all depends on their mood. Some people feel that there are two sides to the Sagittarius personality. This characteristic is reflected in the zodiacal symbol for the sign—a double symbol: the hunter and the horse intertwined, denoting two different natures.

It may be difficult for some people to get to know a Sagittarius man or woman. In some instances Sagittarius employ silence as a sort of protection. When people pierce through, however, and will not leave him or her in peace, Sagittarius can become quite angry.

On the whole, Sagittarius is kind and considerate. Their nature is gentle and unassuming. With the wrong person, though, they can become somewhat disagreeable. They do become angry, but they cool down quickly and are willing to let bygones be bygones. Sagittarius individuals never hold a grudge against anyone.

Companionship and harmony in all social relationships is necessary for Sagittarius. They are willing to make some sacrifices for it. Any partner, friend, or mate must be a good listener. There are times when Sagittarius feel it necessary to pour their hearts out. They are willing to listen to someone's problems and want the same considerate treatment in return.

A partner, friend, or lover should also be able to take an interest in any hobbies, pastimes, or sports a Sagittarius wants to pursue. If not, Sagittarius men and women will be tempted to go their own way even more so than their nature dictates.

Sagittarius individuals do not beat around the bush. They do say what they mean. Being direct is one of their strongest qualities. Sometimes it pays off, sometimes it doesn't. They often forget that the one they love may be very sensitive and can take offhand remarks personally.

Sagittarius has a tendency to be too blunt and to reveal secrets, innocently or otherwise, that hurt people's feelings. A friend or partner may not be able to overlook this flaw or may not be able to correct it either in a subtle or direct way. When making jokes or casual comments, Sagittarius sometimes strikes a sensitive chord in a companion, which can result in a serious misunderstanding.

But the cultivated Sagittarius learns the boundaries of social behavior. They know when not to go too far. Understanding a partner's viewpoint is the first step toward assuring a good relationship down the road.

Love and Marriage

Sagittarius individuals are faithful to their loved ones. They are affectionate and not at all possessive. Love is important for them spiritually as well as physically. For some Sagittarius, romance is a chance to escape reality—a chance for adventure.

Quite often a mate or lover finds it difficult to keep up with Sagittarius—they are so active and energetic. When Sagittarius men and women fall in love, however, they are quite easy to handle.

Sagittarius do like having freedom. They will make concessions in a steady relationship. Still there will be a part of themselves that they keep from others. He or she is very intent on preserving their individual rights, no matter what sort of relationship they are engaged in. Sagittarius ideals are generally high, and they are important. Sagittarius is looking for someone with similar standards, not someone too lax or too conventional.

In love, Sagittarius men and women may be a bit childlike at times. As a result of this they are apt to encounter various disappointments before they find the one meant for them. At times he or she says things they really shouldn't, and this causes the end of a romantic relationship.

Men and women born under this sign may have many love affairs before they feel ready to settle down with just one person. If the person they love does not exactly measure up to their standards, they are apt to overlook this—depending on how strong their love is—and accept the person for what that person is.

On the whole, Sagittarius men and women are not envious. They are willing to allow a partner needed freedoms—within reason. Sagittarius does this so they will not have to jeopardize their own liberties. Live and let live could easily be their motto. If their ideals and freedom are threatened, Sagittarius fights hard to protect what they believe is just and fair.

They do not want to make any mistakes in love, so they take their time when choosing someone to settle down with. They are direct and positive when they meet the right one. They do not waste time.

The average Sagittarius may be a bit altar-shy. It may take a bit of convincing before Sagittarius agree that married life is right for them. This is generally because they do not want to lose their freedom. Sagittarius is an active person who enjoys being around a lot of other people. Sitting quietly at home does not interest them at all. At times it may seem that he or she wants to have things their own way, even in marriage. It may take some doing to get Sagittarius to realize that in marriage, as in other things, give-and-take plays a great role.

Romance and the Sagittarius Woman

The Sagittarius woman is kind and gentle. Most of the time she is very considerate of others and enjoys being of help in some way to

her friends. She can be quite active and, as a result, be rather difficult to catch. On the whole, she is optimistic and friendly. She
believes in looking on the bright side of things. She knows how to
make the best of situations that others feel are not worth salvaging.
She has plenty of pluck.

Men generally like her because of her easygoing manner. Quite
often she becomes friends with a man before venturing on to
romance. There is something about her that makes her more of a
companion than a lover. The woman Archer can best be described
as sporting and broad-minded.

She is almost never possessive. She enjoys her own freedom too
much to want to make demands on that of another person.

She is always youthful in her disposition. She may seem naive or
guileless at times. Generally it takes her longer really to mature
than it does others. She tends to be impulsive and may easily jump
from one thing to another. If she has an unfortunate experience in
love early in life, she may shy away from fast or intimate contacts
for a while. She is usually very popular. Not all the men who are
attracted to her see her as a possible lover, but more as a friend or
companion.

The woman born under the sign of the Archer generally believes
in true love. She may have several romances before she decides to
settle down. For her there is no particular rush. She is willing to
have a long romantic relationship with the man she loves before
making marriage plans.

The Sagittarius woman is often the outdoors type and has a
strong liking for animals—especially dogs and horses. Quite often
she excels in sports. She is not generally someone who is content to
stay at home and cook and take care of the house. She would rather
be out attending to her other interests. When she does household
work, however, she does it well.

She makes a good companion as well as a wife. She usually
enjoys participating with her husband in his various interests and
affairs. Her sunny disposition often brightens up the dull moments
of a love affair.

At times her temper may flare, but she is herself again after a few
moments. She would never butt into her husband's business affairs,
but she does enjoy being asked for her opinion from time to time.
Generally she is up to date on all that her husband is doing and can
offer him some pretty sound advice.

The Sagittarius woman is seldom jealous of her husband's interest in other people—even if some of them are of the opposite sex.
If she has no reason to doubt his love, she never questions it.

She makes a loving and sympathetic mother. She knows all the
sports news and probably has the latest board game to play with

her children. Her cheerful manner makes her an invaluable play-mate and encouraging guide.

Romance and the Sagittarius Man

The Sagittarius man is often an adventurer. He likes taking chances in love as well as in life. He may hop around quite a bit—from one romance to another—before really thinking about settling down. Many men born under this sign feel that marriage would mean the end of their freedom, so they avoid it as much as possible. Whenever a romance becomes too serious, they move on.

Many Sagittarius men are impulsive in love. Early marriages for some often end unpleasantly. A male Archer is not a very mature person, even at an age when most others are. He takes a bit more time. He may not always make a wise choice in a love partner.

He is affectionate and loving but not at all possessive. Because he is rather lighthearted in love, he sometimes gets into trouble.

Most Sagittarius men find romance an exciting adventure. They make attentive lovers and are never cool or indifferent. Love should also have a bit of fun in it for him too. He likes to keep things light and gay. Romance without humor can at times be difficult for him to accept. The woman he loves should also be a good sport. She should have as open and fun-loving a disposition as he has if she is to understand him properly.

He wants his mate to share his interest in the outdoor life and animals. If she is good at sports, she is likely to win his heart. The average Sagittarius generally has an interest in athletics of various sorts—from bicycling to baseball.

His mate must also be a good intellectual companion, someone who can easily discuss those matters which interest him. Physical love is important to him—but so is spiritual love. A good romance will contain these in balance.

His sense of humor may sometimes seem a little unkind to someone who is not used to being laughed at. He enjoys playing jokes now and again. It is the child in his nature that remains a part of his character even when he grows old and gray.

He is not a homebody. He is responsible, however, and will do what is necessary to keep a home together. Still and all, the best wife for him is one who can manage household matters single-handedly if need be.

He loves the children, especially as they grow older and begin to take on definite personalities.

Woman—Man

SAGITTARIUS WOMAN
ARIES MAN

In some ways, the Aries man resembles a wandering mountain sheep seeking high land. He has an insatiable thirst for knowledge. He's ambitious and is apt to have his finger in many pies. He can do with a woman like you—someone attractive, quick-witted, and smart.

He is not interested in a clinging vine for a mate. He wants someone who is there when he needs her, someone who listens and understands what he says, someone who can give advice if he should ever need it, which is not likely to be often.

The Aries man wants a woman who will look good on his arm without hanging on it too heavily. He is looking for a woman who has both feet on the ground and yet is mysterious and enticing, a kind of domestic Helen of Troy whose face or fine dinner can launch a thousand business deals if need be. That woman he's in search of sounds a little like you, doesn't she? If the shoe fits, put it on. You won't regret it.

The Aries man makes a good husband. He is faithful and attentive. He is an affectionate man. He'll make you feel needed and loved. Love is a serious matter for the Aries man. He does not believe in flirting or playing the field—especially after he's found the woman of his dreams. He'll expect you to be as constant in your affection as he is in his. He'll expect you to be one hundred percent his. He won't put up with any nonsense while romancing you.

The Aries man may be pretty progressive and modern about many things. However, when it comes to pants wearing, he's downright conventional: it's strictly male attire. The best role you can take in the relationship is a supporting one. He's the boss and that's that. Once you have learned to accept that, you'll find the going easy.

The Aries man, with his endless energy and drive, likes to relax in the comfort of his home at the end of the day. The good homemaker can be sure of holding his love. He'll watch a sports match with you from his favorite armchair. If you see to it that everything in the house is where he expects to find it, you'll have no difficulty keeping the relationship on an even keel.

Life and love with an Aries man may be just the medicine you need. He'll be a good provider. He'll spoil you if he's financially able.

The Aries father is young at heart and will spoil children every chance he gets. So naturally the kids will take to him like ducks to water. His quick mind and energetic behavior appeal to the young. His ability to jump from one thing to another will delight the kids and keep them active. You will have to introduce some rules of the game so that the children learn how to start things properly and finish them before running off elsewhere.

SAGITTARIUS WOMAN
TAURUS MAN

If you've got your heart set on a man born under the sign of Taurus, you'll have to learn the art of being patient. Taurus take their time about everything—even love.

The steady and deliberate Taurus man is a little slow on the draw. It may take him quite a while before he gets around to popping that question. For the woman who doesn't mind twiddling her thumbs, the waiting and anticipating almost always pays off in the end. Taurus men want to make sure that every step they take is a good one, particularly if they feel that the path they're on is one that leads to the altar.

If you are in the mood for a whirlwind romance, you had better cast your net in shallower waters. Moreover, most Taurus prefer to do the angling themselves. They are not keen on a woman taking the lead. Once she does, they might drop her like a dead fish. If you let yourself get caught in his net, you'll find that he's fallen for you—hook, line, and sinker.

The Taurus man is fond of a comfortable home life. It is very important to him. If you keep those home fires burning you will have no trouble keeping that flame in your Taurus mate's heart aglow. You have a talent for homemaking; use it. Your taste in furnishings is excellent. You know how to make a house come to life with colors and decorations.

Taurus, the strong, steady, and protective Bull, may not be your idea of a man on the move. Still he's reliable. Perhaps he could be the anchor for your dreams and plans. He could help you to acquire a more balanced outlook and approach to your life. If you're given to impulsiveness, he could help you to curb it. He's the man who is always there when you need him.

When you tie the knot with a man born under Taurus, you can put away fears about creditors pounding on the front door. Taurus are practical about everything including bill paying. When he carries you over that threshold, you can be certain that the entire house is paid for, not only the doorsill.

As a wife, you won't have to worry about putting aside your many interests for the sake of back-breaking house chores. Your Taurus husband will see to it that you have all the latest time-saving appliances and comforts.

The Taurus father has much love and affection for the children, and he has no trouble demonstrating his warmth. Yet he does not believe in spoiling the kids. The Taurus father believes that children have a place, and they should know their place at all times. He is an excellent disciplinarian and will see to it that the youngsters grow up to be polite, obedient, and respectful. You will provide mirth and fun to balance things out.

SAGITTARIUS WOMAN
GEMINI MAN

If opposites attract, as the notion goes, then Gemini and Sagittarius should be swell together. The fact that you two are astrologically related—being zodiacal partners as well as zodiacal opposites—does not automatically guarantee that you will understand each other, at least at first. Gemini is an air sign, you are a fire sign, so the initial contact between you should be warm and breezy.

The Gemini man is quite a catch. Many a woman has set her cap for him and failed to bag him. Generally, Gemini men are intelligent, witty, and outgoing. Many of them tend to be versatile.

On the other hand, some of them seem to lack that sort of common sense that you set so much store in. Their tendency to start a half-dozen projects, then toss them up in the air out of boredom may do nothing more than exasperate you.

One thing that causes a Twin's mind and affection to wander is a bore. But it is unlikely that the active Sagittarius woman would ever allow herself to be accused of dullness. The Gemini man who has caught your heart will admire you for your ideas and intellect—perhaps even more than for your athletic talents and good looks.

A strong-willed woman could easily fill the role of rudder for her Gemini's ship-without-a-sail. The intelligent Gemini is often aware of his shortcomings and doesn't mind if someone with better bearings gives him a shove in the right direction—when it's needed. The average Gemini doesn't have serious ego hang-ups and will even accept a well-deserved chewing out from his mate or girlfriend gracefully.

A successful and serious-minded Gemini could make you a very happy woman, perhaps, if you gave him half the chance. Although he may give you the impression that he has a hole in his head, the Gemini man generally has a good head on his shoulders and can make efficient use of it when he wants to. Some of them, who have learned the art of being steadfast, have risen to great heights in their professions.

Once you convince yourself that not all people born under the sign of the Twins are witless grasshoppers, you won't mind dating a few—to test your newborn conviction. If you do wind up walking down the aisle with one, accept the fact that married life with him will mean your taking the bitter with the sweet.

Life with a Gemini man can be more fun than a barrel of clowns. You'll never be allowed to experience a dull moment. But don't leave money matters to him, or you'll both wind up behind the eight ball.

Gemini men are always attractive to the opposite sex. You'll perhaps have to allow him an occasional harmless flirt. It will seldom amount to more than that if you're his ideal mate.

Gemini is your zodiacal mate, as well as your zodiacal opposite, so the Gemini-Sagittarius couple will make delightful parents together. Airy Gemini will create a very open, experimental environment for the kids. He loves them so much, he sometimes lets them do what they want. You will keep the kids in line and prevent them from running the household. But you and your Gemini mate's combined sense of humor is infectious, so the youngsters will naturally come to see the fun and funny sides of life.

SAGITTARIUS WOMAN
CANCER MAN

Chances are you won't hit it off too well with the man born under Cancer if your plans concern love. But then, Cupid has been known to do some pretty unlikely things. The Cancer man is very sensitive—thin-skinned and occasionally moody. You've got to keep on your toes—and not step on his—if you're determined to make a go of the relationship.

The Cancer man may be lacking in some of the qualities you seek in a man. But when it comes to being faithful and being a good provider, he's hard to beat.

The perceptive woman will not mistake the Crab's quietness for sullenness or his thriftiness for penny-pinching. In some respects, he is like that wise old owl out on a limb. He may look like he's dozing but actually he hasn't missed a thing.

Cancers possess a well of knowledge about human behavior. They can come across with some pretty helpful advice to those in trouble or in need. He can certainly guide you in making investments both in time and money. He may not say much, but he's always got his wits about him.

The Crab may not be the match or catch for a woman like you. At times, you are likely to find him downright dull. True to his sign, he can be fairly cranky and crabby when handled the wrong way. He is perhaps more sensitive than he should be.

If you're smarter than your Cancer friend, be smart enough not to let him know. Never give him the idea that you think he's a little short on brainpower. It would send him scurrying back into his shell. And all that ground lost in the relationship will perhaps never be recovered.

The Crab is most content at home. Once settled down for the night or the weekend, wild horses couldn't drag him any farther than the gatepost—that is, unless those wild horses were dispatched by his mother.

The Crab is sometimes a Momma's boy. If his mate does not put her foot down, he will see to it that his mother always comes first. No self-respecting wife would ever allow herself to play second fiddle, even if it's to her mother-in-law. With a little bit of tact, however, she'll find that slipping into that number-one position is as easy as pie (that legendary one his mother used to bake).

If you pamper your Cancer man, you'll find that mother turns up less and less, at the front door and in conversations.

Cancers make proud, patient, and protective fathers. But they can be a little too protective. Their sheltering instincts can interfere with a youngster's natural inclination to test the waters outside the home. Still, the Cancer father doesn't want to see his kids learning about life the hard way from the streets. Your qualities of optimism and encouragement and your knowledge of right and wrong will guide the youngsters along the way.

SAGITTARIUS WOMAN
LEO MAN

For the woman who enjoys being swept off her feet in a romantic whirlwind fashion, Leo is the sign of such love. When the Lion puts his mind to romancing, he doesn't stint. It's all wining and dining and dancing till the wee hours of the morning.

Leo is all heart and knows how to make his woman feel like a woman. The woman in constant search of a man she can look up to need go no farther: Leo is ten-feet tall—in spirit if not in stature. He's a man not only in full control of his faculties but in full control of just about any situation he finds himself in. Leo is a winner.

The Leo man may not look like Tarzan, but he knows how to roar and beat his chest if he has to. The woman who has had her fill of weak-kneed men finds in a Leo someone she can at last lean upon. He can support you not only physically but spiritually as well. He's good at giving advice that pays off.

Leos are direct people. They don't believe in wasting time or effort. They almost never make unwise investments.

Many Leos rise to the top of their professions. Through example, they often prove to be a source of great inspiration to others.

Although he's a ladies' man, Leo is very particular about his ladies. His standards are high when it comes to love interests. The idealistic and cultivated woman should have no trouble keeping her balance on the pedestal the Lion sets her on.

Leo believes that romance should be played on a fair give-and-take basis. He won't stand for any monkey business in a love relationship. It's all or nothing.

You'll find him a frank, off-the-shoulder person. He generally says what is on his mind.

If you decide upon a Leo man for a mate, you must be prepared to stand behind him full force. He expects it—and usually deserves it. He's the head of the house and can handle that position without a hitch. He knows how to go about breadwinning and, if he has his way (and most Leos do have their own way), he'll see to it that you'll have all the luxuries you crave and the comforts you need.

It's unlikely that the romance in your marriage will ever die out. Lions need love like flowers need sunshine. They're ever amorous and generally expect similar attention and affection from their mates. Leos are fond of going out on the town. They love to give parties, as well as to go to them. Because you, too, love to throw a party, you and your Leo mate will be the most popular host and hostess in town.

Leo fathers have a tendency to spoil the children—up to a point. That point is reached when the children become the center of attention, and Leo feels neglected. Then the Leo father becomes strict and insists that his rules be followed. You will have your hands full pampering both your Leo mate and the children. As long as he comes first in your affections, the family will be creative and joyful.

SAGITTARIUS WOMAN
VIRGO MAN

Although the Virgo man may be a bit of a fussbudget at times, his seriousness and dedication to common sense may help you to overlook his tendency to be too critical about minor things.

Virgo men are often quiet, respectable types who set great store in conservative behavior and levelheadedness. He'll admire you for your practicality and tenacity, perhaps even more than for your good looks. He's seldom bowled over by a glamour-puss. When he gets his courage up, he turns to a serious and reliable girl for romance.

The Virgo man will be far from a Valentino while dating. In fact, you may wind up making all the passes. Once he does get his motor running, however, he can be a warm and wonderful fellow—to the right lover.

He's gradual about love. Chances are your romance with him will start out looking like an ordinary friendship. Once he's sure you're no fly-by-night flirt and have no plans of taking him for a ride, he'll open up and rain sunshine all over your heart.

Virgo men tend to marry late in life. Virgo believes in holding out until he's met the right woman. He may not have many names in his little black book; in fact, he may not even have a black book. He's not interested in playing the field; leave that to men of the more flamboyant signs. The Virgo man is so particular that he may remain romantically inactive for a long period. His woman has to be perfect or it's no go.

If you find yourself feeling weak-kneed for a Virgo, do your best to convince him that perfect is not so important when it comes to love. Help him to realize that he's missing out on a great deal by not considering the near perfect or whatever it is you consider yourself to be. With your surefire perseverance, you will most likely be able to make him listen to reason and he'll wind up reciprocating your romantic interests.

The Virgo man is no block of ice. He'll respond to what he feels to be the right feminine flame. Once your love life with a Virgo man starts to bubble, don't give it a chance to fall flat. You may never have a second chance at winning his heart.

If you should ever break up with him, forget about patching it up. He'd prefer to let the pieces lie scattered. Once married, though, he'll stay that way—even if it hurts. He's too conscientious to try to back out of a legal deal of any sort.

The Virgo man is as neat as a pin. He's thumbs down on sloppy housekeeping. Keep everything bright, neat, and shiny. That goes for the children, too, at least by the time he gets home.

The Virgo father appreciates good manners, courtesy, and cleanliness from the children. He will instill a sense of order in the household, and he expects youngsters to respect his wishes. He can become very worried about scrapes, bruises, and all sorts of minor mishaps when the kids go out to play. Your easygoing faith in the children's safety will counteract Virgo's tendency to fuss and fret over them.

SAGITTARIUS WOMAN
LIBRA MAN

If there's a Libra in your life, you are most likely a very happy woman. Men born under this sign have a way with women. You'll always feel at ease in a Libra's company. You can be yourself when you're with him.

The Libra man can be moody at times. His moodiness is often puzzling. One moment he comes on hard and strong with declarations of his love, the next moment you find that he's left you like yesterday's mashed potatoes. He'll come back, though, don't worry. Libras are like that. Deep down inside he really knows what he wants even though he may not appear to.

You'll appreciate his admiration of beauty and harmony. If you're dressed to the teeth and never looked lovelier, you'll get a ready compliment—and one that's really deserved. Libras don't indulge in idle flattery. If they don't like something, they are tactful enough to remain silent.

Libras will go to great lengths to preserve peace and harmony—they will even tell a fat lie if necessary. They don't like showdowns or disagreeable confrontations. The frank woman is all for getting whatever is bothering her off her chest and out into the open, even if it comes out all wrong. To the Libra, making a clean breast of everything seems like sheer folly sometimes.

You may lose your patience while waiting for your Libra friend to make up his mind. It takes him ages sometimes to make a decision. He weighs both sides carefully before committing himself to anything. You seldom dillydally, at least about small things. So it's likely that you will find it difficult to see eye-to-eye with a hesitating Libra when it comes to decision-making methods.

All in all, though, he is kind, considerate, and fair. He is interested in the real truth. He'll try to balance everything out until he has all the correct answers. It's not difficult for him to see both sides of a story.

He's a peace-loving man. Even a rough-and-tumble sports event, and certainly a violent one, will make Libra shudder.

Libras are not show-offs. Generally, they are well-balanced, modest people. Honest, wholesome, and affectionate, they are serious about every love encounter they have. If Libra should find that the woman he's dating is not really suited to him, he will end the relationship in such a tactful manner that no hard feelings will come about.

The Libra father is patient and fair. He can be firm without exercising undue strictness or discipline. Although he can be a harsh judge at times, with the youngsters he will radiate sweetness and light in the hope that they will grow up to imitate his gentle manner. To balance the essential refinement the children will acquire from their Libra father, you will teach them a few rough-and-ready ways to enjoy recreation.

SAGITTARIUS WOMAN
SCORPIO MAN

Scorpio shares at least one trait in common with Sagittarius. You both are blunt. But Scorpio, who can be vengeful and vindictive, intends an insult as an insult, not just a thoughtless comment. Many find Scorpio's sting a fate worse than death. When his anger breaks loose, you better clear out of the vicinity.

The average Scorpio may strike you as a brute. He'll stick pins into the balloons of your plans and dreams if they don't line up with what he thinks is right. If you do anything to irritate him—just anything—you'll wish you hadn't. He'll give you a sounding out that would make you pack your bags and go back to Mother—if you were that kind of woman.

The Scorpio man hates being tied down to home life. He would rather be out on the battlefield of life, belting away at whatever he feels is a just and worthy cause, instead of staying home nestled in a comfortable armchair with the evening paper. If you have a strong homemaking streak, don't keep those home fires burning too brightly too long; you may just run out of firewood.

As passionate as he is in business affairs and politics, the Scorpio man still has plenty of fire and light stored away for the pursuit of romance and lovemaking.

Most women are easily attracted to him—perhaps you are no exception. Those who allow a man born under this sign to sweep them off their feet quickly find that they're dealing with a pepper pot of seething excitement. The Scorpio man is passionate with a capital P, you can be sure of that. When you two meet on the playing field of love, Scorpio will be much more intense and competitive than you.

If you can match his intensity and adapt to his mood swings, you are fair game. If you're the kind of woman who can keep a stiff upper lip, take it on the chin, turn a deaf ear, and all of that, because you feel you are still under his love spell in spite of everything—lots of luck.

If you have decided to take the bitter with the sweet, prepare yourself for a lot of ups and downs. Chances are you won't have as much time for your own affairs and interests as you'd like. The Scorpio's love of power may cause you to be at his constant beck and call.

Scorpios like fathering large families. He is proud of his children, but often he fails to live up to his responsibilities as a parent. In spite of the extremes in his personality, the Scorpio man is able to transform the conflicting characteristics within himself when he becomes a father. When he takes his fatherly duties seriously, he is a powerful teacher. He believes in preparing his children for the hard knocks life sometimes delivers. He is adept with difficult youngsters because he knows how to tap the best in each child.

SAGITTARIUS WOMAN
SAGITTARIUS MAN

The woman who has set her cap for a man born under the sign of Sagittarius may have to apply an awful amount of strategy before she can get him to drop down on bended knee. Although some Sagittarius may be marriage-shy, they're not ones to skitter away from romance. A high-spirited woman may find a relationship with a Sagittarius—whether a fling or the real thing—a very enjoyable experience.

As you know, Sagittarius are bright, happy, and healthy people. You all have a strong sense of fair play. You all are a source of inspiration to others. You're full of ideas and drive.

You'll be taken by the Sagittarius man's infectious grin and his lighthearted friendly nature. If you do wind up being the woman in his life, you'll find that he's apt to treat you more like a buddy than the love of his life. It's just his way. Sagittarius are often chummy instead of romantic.

You'll admire his broad-mindedness in most matters—including those of the heart. If, while dating you, he claims that he still wants to play the field, he'll expect you to enjoy the same liberty. Once he's promised to love, honor, and obey, however, he does just that.

Marriage for him, once he's taken that big step, is very serious business.

A woman who has a keen imagination and a great love of freedom will not be disappointed if she does tie up with the Archer. The Sagittarius man is often quick-witted. Men of this sign have a genuine interest in equality. They hate prejudice and injustice.

If he does insist on a night out with the boys once a week, he won't scowl if you decide to let him shift for himself in the kitchen once a week while you pursue some of your own interests. He believes in fairness.

He's not much of a homebody. Quite often he's occupied with faraway places either in his dreams or in reality. He enjoys—just as you do—being on the go or on the move. He's got ants in his pants and refuses to sit still for long stretches at a time. Humdrum routine, especially at home, bores him. So the two of you will probably go out a lot or throw lots of parties at home.

He likes surprising people. He'll take great pride in showing you off to his friends. He'll always be a considerate mate; he will never embarrass or disappoint you intentionally.

He's very tolerant when it comes to friends, and you'll most likely spend a lot of time entertaining people—which suits you party animals royally.

The Sagittarius father, unlike you, may be bewildered and made utterly nervous by a newborn. He will dote on any infant son or daughter from a safe distance because he can be clumsy and frightened handling the tiny tot. The Sagittarius dad usually becomes comfortable with youngsters once they have passed through the baby stage. As soon as they are old enough to walk and talk, he will encourage each and every visible sign of talent and skill.

SAGITTARIUS WOMAN
CAPRICORN MAN

A with-it woman like you is likely to find the average Capricorn man a bit of a drag. The man born under this sign is often a closed up person and difficult to get to know. Even if you do get to know him, you may not find him very interesting.

In romance, Capricorn men are a little on the rusty side. You'll probably have to make all the passes.

You may find his plodding manner irritating and his conservative, traditional ways downright maddening. He's not one to take a chance on anything. If it was good enough for his father, it's good enough for him. Capricorn can be habit-bound. He follows a way that is tried and true.

Whenever adventure rears its tantalizing head, the Goat will turn the other way. Unlike you, he is not prone to taking risks.

He may be just as ambitious as you are, perhaps even more so. But his ways of accomplishing his aims are more subterranean than yours. He operates from the background a good deal of the time. At a gathering you may never even notice him. But he's there, taking everything in, sizing everyone up, planning his next careful move.

Although Capricorns may be intellectual to a degree, it is not generally the kind of intelligence you appreciate. He may not be as quick or as bright as you. It may take him ages to understand a joke, and you love jokes.

If you do decide to take up with a man born under the sign of the Goat, you ought to be pretty good in the cheering up department. The Capricorn man often acts as though he's constantly being followed by a cloud of gloom.

The Capricorn man is most himself when in the comfort and privacy of his own home. The security possible within four walls can make him a happy man. He'll spend as much time as he can at home. If he is loaded down with extra work, he'll bring it home instead of finishing it up at the office.

You'll most likely find yourself frequently confronted by his relatives. Family is very important to the Capricorn—his family that is. They had better take an important place in your life, too, if you want to keep your home a happy one.

Although his caution in most matters may all but drive you up the wall, you'll find that his concerned way with money is justified most of the time. He'll plan everything right down to the last penny.

The Capricorn father is a dutiful parent and takes a lifelong interest in seeing that his children make something of themselves. He may not understand their hopes and dreams because he often tries to put his head on their shoulders. The Capricorn father believes that there are certain goals to be achieved, and there is a traditional path to achieving them. He can be quite a scold if the youngsters break the rules. Your easygoing, joyful manner will moderate Capricorn's rigid approach and will make things fun again for the children.

SAGITTARIUS WOMAN
AQUARIUS MAN

Aquarius individuals love everybody—even their worst enemies sometimes. Through your love relationship with an Aquarius you'll find yourself running into all sorts of people, ranging from near genius to downright insane—and they're all friends of his.

As a rule, Aquarius are extremely friendly and open. Of all the signs, they are perhaps the most tolerant. In the thinking department, they are often miles ahead of others.

You'll most likely find your relationship with this man a challenging one. Your high respect for intelligence and imagination may be reason enough for you to set your heart on a Water Bearer. You'll find that you can learn a lot from him.

In the holding-hands phase of your romance, you may find that your Water Bearer friend has cold feet. Aquarius take quite a bit of warming up before they are ready to come across with that first goodnight kiss. More than likely, he'll just want to be your pal in the beginning. For him, that's an important first step in any relationship—love included.

The poetry and flowers stage—if it ever comes—will come later. Aquarius is all heart. Still, when it comes to tying himself down to one person and for keeps, he is almost always sure to hesitate. He may even try to get out of it if you breathe down his neck too heavily.

The Aquarius man is no Romeo, and he wouldn't want to be. The kind of love life he's looking for is one that's made up mainly of companionship. He may not be very romantic, but still the memory of his first romance will always hold an important position in his heart. So in a way he is like Romeo after all. Some Aquarius wind up marrying their childhood sweethearts.

You won't find it difficult to look up to a man born under the sign of the Water Bearer, but you may find the challenge of trying to keep up with him dizzying. He can pierce through the most complicated problem as if it were simple math. You may find him a little too lofty and high-minded. But don't judge him too harshly if that's the case. He's way ahead of his time.

If you marry this man, he'll stay true to you. Don't think that once the honeymoon is over, you'll be chained to the kitchen sink forever. Your Aquarius husband will encourage you to keep active in your own interests and affairs. You'll most likely have a minor tiff now and again but never anything serious.

The Aquarius father has an almost intuitive understanding of children. He sees them as individuals in their own right, not as extensions of himself or as beings who are supposed to take a certain place in the world. He can talk to the kids on a variety of subjects, and his knowledge can be awe-inspiring. Your dedication to learning and your desire to educate the children will be bolstered by your Aquarius mate. And your love of sports and games, the fun physical activities in life, will balance the airy Aquarius intellectualism.

SAGITTARIUS WOMAN
PISCES MAN

The man born under Pisces is quite a dreamer. Sometimes he's so wrapped up in his dreams that he's difficult to reach. To the average, active woman, he may seem a little passive.

He's easygoing most of the time. He seems to take things in his stride. He'll entertain all kinds of views and opinions from just about everyone, nodding or smiling vaguely, giving the impression that he's with them one hundred percent while that may not be the case at all. His attitude may be why bother when he's confronted with someone wrong who thinks he's right. The Pisces man will seldom speak his mind if he thinks he'll be rigidly opposed.

The Pisces man is oversensitive at times. He's afraid of getting his feelings hurt. He'll sometimes imagine a personal affront when none's been made. Chances are you'll find this complex of his maddening. At times you may feel like giving him a swift kick where it hurts the most. It wouldn't do any good, though. It would just add fuel to the fire of his complex.

One thing you'll admire about this man is his concern for people who are sickly or troubled. He'll make his shoulder available to anyone in the mood for a good cry. He can listen to one hard-luck story after another without seeming to tire. When his advice is asked, he is capable of coming across with some words of wisdom. He often knows what is bothering someone before that person is aware of it. It's almost intuitive with Pisces.

Still, at the end of the day, this man will want some peace and quiet. If you've got a problem when he comes home, don't unload it in his lap. If you do, you are apt to find him short-tempered. He's a good listener but he can only take so much.

Pisces are not aimless although they may seem so at times. The positive sort of Pisces man is quite often successful in his profession and is likely to wind up rich and influential. Material gain, however, is never a direct goal for a man born under this sign.

The weaker Pisces are usually content to stay on the level where they find themselves. They won't complain too much if the roof leaks or if the fence is in need of repair.

Because of their seemingly laissez-faire manner, people under the sign of the Fishes—needless to say—are immensely popular with children. For tots the Pisces father plays the double role of confidant and playmate. It will never enter the mind of a Pisces to discipline a child, no matter how spoiled or incorrigible that child becomes.

Man—Woman

SAGITTARIUS MAN
ARIES WOMAN

The Aries woman is quite a charmer. When she tugs at the strings of your heart, you'll know it. She's a woman who's in search of a knight in shining armor. She is a very particular person with very high ideals. She won't accept anyone but the man of her dreams.

The Aries woman never plays around with passion. She means business when it comes to love.

Don't get the idea that she's a dewy-eyed damsel. She isn't. In fact, she can be practical and to the point when she wants to be. She's a dame with plenty of drive and ambition.

With an Aries woman behind you, you can go far in life. She knows how to help her man get ahead. She's full of wise advice; you only have to ask. The Aries woman has a keen business sense. Many of them become successful career women. There is nothing passive or retiring about her. She is equipped with a good brain and she knows how to use it.

Your union with her could be something strong, secure, and romantic. If both of you have your sights fixed in the same direction, there is almost nothing that you could not accomplish.

The Aries woman is proud and capable of being quite jealous. While you're with her, never cast your eye in another woman's direction. It could spell disaster for your relationship. The Aries woman won't put up with romantic nonsense when her heart is at stake.

If the Aries woman backs you up in your business affairs, you can be sure of succeeding. However, if she only is interested in advancing her own career and puts her interests before yours, she can be sure to rock the boat. It will put a strain on the relationship. The overambitious Aries woman can be a pain in the neck and make you forget you were in love with her once.

The cultivated Aries woman makes a wonderful wife and mother. She has a natural talent for homemaking. With a pot of paint and some wallpaper, she can transform the dreariest domicile into an abode of beauty and snug comfort. The perfect hostess— even when friends just happen by—she knows how to make guests feel at home.

You'll also admire your Aries because she knows how to stand on her own two feet. Hers is an independent nature. She won't break down and cry when things go wrong, but will pick herself up and try to patch up matters.

The Aries woman makes a fine, affectionate mother. Although she is not keen on burdensome responsibilities, like you she relishes the joy that children bring. The Aries woman is skilled at juggling both career and motherhood, so her kids will never feel that she is an absentee parent. In fact, as the youngsters grow older, they might want some of the liberation that is so important to her. One of your roles is to encourage the children's quest for independence.

SAGITTARIUS MAN
TAURUS WOMAN

The woman born under the sign of Taurus may lack a little of the sparkle and bubble you often like to find in a woman. The Taurus woman is generally down to earth and never flighty. It's important to her that she keep both feet flat on the ground. She is not fond of bounding all over the place, especially if she's under the impression that there's no profit in it.

On the other hand, if you hit it off with a Taurus woman, you won't be disappointed in the romance area. The Taurus woman is all woman and proud of it, too. She can be very devoted and loving once she decides that her relationship with you is no fly-by-night romance. Basically, she's a passionate person. In sex, she's direct and to the point. If she really loves you, she'll let you know she's yours—and without reservations.

Better not flirt with other women once you've committed yourself to her. She's capable of being very jealous and possessive.

She'll stick by you through thick and thin. It's almost certain that if the going ever gets rough, she won't go running home to her mother. She can adjust to the hard times just as graciously as she can to the good times.

Taurus are, on the whole, pretty even-tempered. They like to be treated with kindness. Beautiful things and aesthetic objects make them feel loved and treasured.

You may find her a little slow and deliberate. She likes to be safe and sure about everything. Let her plod along if she likes. Don't coax her, but just let her take her own sweet time. Everything she does is done thoroughly and, generally, without mistakes.

Don't deride her for being a slowpoke. It could lead to a tirade of insults that could put even your blunt manner to shame. The Taurus woman doesn't anger readily but when prodded often enough, she's capable of letting loose with a cyclone of ill will. If you treat her with kindness and consideration, you'll have no cause for complaint.

The Taurus woman loves doing things for her man. She's a whiz in the kitchen and can whip up feasts fit for a king if she thinks they'll be royally appreciated. She may not fully understand you, but she'll adore you and be faithful to you if she feels you're worthy of it.

The Taurus woman makes a wonderful mother. She knows how to keep her children loved, cuddled, and warm. She may have some difficult times with them when they reach adolescence, and start to rebel against her strictness. You can inject a sense of adventure even in the most mundane of household responsibilities, so you will moderate your Taurus mate's insistence on discipline.

SAGITTARIUS MAN
GEMINI WOMAN

You may find a romance with a woman born under the sign of the Twins a many-splendored thing. In her you can find the intellectual companionship you often look for in a friend or mate.

Gemini, your astrological mate, can appreciate your aims and desires because she travels pretty much the same road as you do intellectually. At least she will travel part of the way. She may share your interests, but she will lack your tenacity.

She suffers from itchy feet. She can be here, there, all over the place and at the same time, or so it would seem. Her eagerness to move around may make you dizzy. Still, you'll enjoy and appreciate her liveliness and mental agility.

Geminis have sparkling personalities. You'll be attracted by her warmth and grace. While she's on your arm, you'll probably notice that many male eyes are drawn to her. She may even return a gaze or two, but don't let that worry you. All women born under this sign have nothing against a harmless flirt once in a while. They enjoy this sort of attention. If Gemini feels she is already spoken for, however, she will never let such attention get out of hand.

Although she may not be as handy as you'd like in the kitchen, you'll never go hungry for a filling and tasty meal. The Gemini woman is always in a rush. She won't feel like she's cheating by breaking out the instant mashed potatoes or the frozen peas. She may not be much of a good cook but she is clever. With a dash of this and a suggestion of that, she can make an uninteresting TV dinner taste like a gourmet meal.

Then, again, maybe you've struck it rich and have a Gemini lover or mate who finds complicated recipes a challenge to her intellect. If so, you'll find every meal an experiment—a tantalizing and mouth-watering surprise.

When you're beating your brains out over the Sunday crossword puzzle and find yourself stuck, just ask your Gemini partner. She'll give you all the right answers without batting an eyelash.

Like you, she loves all kinds of people. You may even find that you're a bit more particular than she. Often all that a Gemini requires is that her friends be interesting—and stay interesting. One thing she's not able to abide is a dullard.

Leave the party organizing to your Gemini sweetheart or mate, and you'll never have a chance to know a dull moment. She'll bring out the swinger in you if you give her half the chance.

The Gemini mother has a youthful streak that guides her in bringing up children through the various stages. She enjoys her kids, which can be the most sincere form of love. Like you—and like them—the Gemini mother is often restless, adventurous, and easily bored. She will never complain about the children's fleeting interests because she understands how they will change as they mature. Gemini-Sagittarius parents, being true zodiacal mates as well as zodiacal opposites, can encourage variety and experience in life so the kids really get to know what the world is like.

SAGITTARIUS MAN
CANCER WOMAN

If you fall in love with a Cancer woman, be prepared for anything. Cancer is sometimes difficult to understand when it comes to love. In one hour, she can unravel a whole gamut of emotions that will leave you in a tizzy. She'll undoubtedly keep you guessing.

You may find her a little too uncertain and sensitive for your liking. You'll most likely spend a good deal of time encouraging her, helping her to erase her foolish fears. Tell her she's a living doll a dozen times a day, and you'll be well loved in return.

Be careful of the jokes you make when in her company. Don't let any of them revolve around her, her personal interests, or her family. If you do, you'll most likely reduce her to tears. She can't stand being made fun of. It will take bushels of roses and tons of chocolates—not to mention the apologies—to get her to come back out of her shell.

In matters of money managing, she may not easily come around to your way of thinking. Money will never burn a hole in her pocket. You may get the notion that your Cancer sweetheart or mate is a direct descendent of Scrooge. If she has her way, she'll hang onto that first dollar you earned. She's not only that way with money, but with everything right on up from bakery string to jelly jars. She's a saver. She never throws anything away, no matter how trivial.

Once she returns your love, you'll find you have an affectionate, self-sacrificing, and devoted woman for life. Her love for you will never alter unless you want it to. She'll put you high upon a pedestal and will do everything—even if it's against your will—to keep you up there.

Cancer women love home life. For them, marriage is an easy step. They're domestic with a capital D. The Cancer woman will do her best to make your home comfortable and cozy. She, herself, is more at ease at home than anywhere else. She makes an excellent hostess. The best in her comes out when she is in her own environment, one she has created to meet her own and her family's needs.

Cancer women make the best mothers. Each will consider every complaint of her child a major catastrophe. With her, children always come first. If you're lucky, you'll run a close second. You'll perhaps see her as too devoted to the children. You may have a hard time convincing her that her apron strings are a little too tight.

SAGITTARIUS MAN
LEO WOMAN

If you can manage a woman who likes to kick up her heels every now and again, then the Lioness was made for you. You'll have to learn to put away jealous fears when you take up with a woman born under the sign of Leo. She's often the kind that makes heads turn and tongues wag. You don't have to believe any of what you hear. It's most likely jealous gossip or wishful thinking.

The Leo woman has more than a fair share of grace and glamour. She knows it, and she knows how to put it to good use. Needless to say, other women in her vicinity turn green with envy and will try anything to put her out of the running.

If she's captured your heart and fancy, woo her full force—if your intention is eventually to win her. Shower her with expensive gifts and promise her the moon, if you're in a position to go that far. Then you'll find her resistance beginning to weaken. It's not that she's such a difficult cookie. She'll probably pamper you once she's decided you're the man for her. But she does enjoy a lot of attention. What's more, she feels she's entitled to it. Her mild arrogance, however, is becoming.

The Leo woman knows how to transform the crime of excessive pride into a very charming misdemeanor. It sweeps most men—or rather, all men—right off their feet. Those who do not succumb to her leonine charm are few and far between.

If you've got an important business deal to clinch and you have doubts as to whether you can bring it off as you should, take your Leo mate along to the business luncheon. It will be a cinch that you'll have that contract—lock, stock, and barrel—in your pocket before the meeting is over. She won't have to say or do anything, just be there at your side. The grouchiest oil magnate can be transformed into a gushing, obedient schoolboy if there's a Leo woman in the room.

If you're rich and want to see to it that you stay that way, don't give your Leo spouse a free hand with the charge accounts and credit cards. When it comes to spending, Leo tends to overdo. If you're poor, you have no worries because the luxury-loving Leo will most likely never recognize your existence—let alone consent to marry you.

A Leo mother can be so proud of her children that she is sometimes blind to their faults. Yet when she wants them to learn and take their rightful place in the social scheme of things, the Leo mother can be strict. She is a patient teacher, lovingly explaining the rules the youngsters are expected to follow. Easygoing and friendly, like you are, she loves to pal around with the kids and show them off on every occasion. Your family will be a bundle of joy.

SAGITTARIUS MAN
VIRGO WOMAN

The Virgo woman may be a little too difficult for you to understand at first. Her waters run deep. Even when you think you know her, don't take any bets on it. She's capable of keeping things hidden in the deep recesses of her womanly soul—things she'll only release when she's sure that you're the man she's been looking for.

It may take her some time to come around to this decision. Virgo women are finicky about almost everything. Everything has to be letter-perfect before they're satisfied. Many of them have the idea that the only people who can do things right are Virgos.

Nothing offends a Virgo woman more than slovenly dress, sloppy character, or a careless display of affection. Make sure your tie is not crooked and that your shoes sport a bright shine before you go calling on this lady. The typical Sagittarius male should keep the off-color jokes for the locker room. She'll have none of that. Take her arm when crossing the street. Don't rush the romance. Trying to corner her in the back of a cab may be one way of striking out. Never criticize the way she looks. In fact, the best policy would be to agree with her as much as possible.

Still, there's just so much a man can take. All those dos and don'ts you'll have to observe if you want to get to first base with a Virgo may be just a little too much to ask of you. After a few dates, you may come to the conclusion that she just isn't worth all that trouble.

However, the Virgo woman is mysterious enough, generally speaking, to keep her men running back for more. Chances are you'll be intrigued by her airs and graces.

If lovemaking means a lot to you, you'll be disappointed at first in the cool ways of your Virgo partner. However, under her glacial facade there lies a hot cauldron of seething excitement. If you're patient and artful in your romantic approach, you'll find that all that caution was well worth the trouble. When Virgos love, they don't stint. It's all or nothing as far as they're concerned. Once they're convinced that they love you, they go all the way, tossing all cares to the wind.

One thing a Virgo woman can't stand in love is hypocrisy. They don't give a hoot about what the neighbors say if their hearts tell them to go ahead. They're very concerned with human truths. So if their hearts stumble upon another fancy, they will be true to that new heartthrob and leave you standing in the rain.

The Virgo woman is honest to her heart and will be as true to you as you are with her, generally. Do her wrong once, however, and it's farewell.

The Virgo mother has high expectations for her children, and she will strive to bring out the very best in them. They usually turn out just as she hoped, despite her anxiety about health and hygiene, safety and good sense. You must step in and ease her fears when she tries to restrict the kids at play or at school. The Virgo mother is more tender than strict, though, and the children will sense her unconditional love for them.

SAGITTARIUS MAN
LIBRA WOMAN

You'll probably find that the woman born under the sign of Libra is worth more than her weight in gold. She's a woman after your own heart.

With her, you'll always come first—make no mistake about that. She'll always be behind you 100 percent, no matter what you do. When you ask her advice about almost anything, you are likely to get a very balanced and realistic opinion. She is good at thinking things out and never lets her emotions run away with her when clear logic is called for.

As a homemaker she is hard to beat. She is very concerned with harmony and balance. You can be sure she'll make your house a joy to live in. She'll see to it that the home is tastefully furnished and decorated. A Libra cannot stand filth or disarray or noise. Anything that does not radiate harmony, in fact, runs against her orderly grain.

She is chock-full of charm and womanly ways. She can sweep just about any man off his feet with one winning smile. When it comes to using her brains, she can outthink almost anyone and, sometimes, with half the effort. She is diplomatic enough, though, never to let this become glaringly apparent. She may even turn the conversation around so that you think you were the one who did all the brainwork. She couldn't care less, really, just as long as you wind up doing what is right.

The Libra woman will put you up on a pretty high pedestal. You are her man and her idol. She'll leave all the decision making, large or small, up to you. She's not interested in running things and will only offer her assistance if she feels you really need it.

Some find her approach to reason masculine. However, in the areas of love and affection the Libra woman is all woman. She'll literally shower you with love and kisses during your romance with her. She doesn't believe in holding out. You shouldn't, either, if you want to hang onto her.

She is the kind of lover who likes to snuggle up to you in front of the fire on chilly autumn nights, the kind who will bring you breakfast in bed on Sunday. She'll be very thoughtful about anything that concerns you. If anyone dares suggest you're not the grandest guy in the world, she'll give that person what-for. She'll defend you till her dying breath. The Libra woman will be everything you want her to be.

The Libra mother will create a harmonious household in which young family members can grow up as equals. She will foster an environment that is sensitive to their needs. The Libra mother understands that children need both guidance and encouragement. With your enthusiastic input, the youngsters will never lack for anything that could make their lives easier and richer.

SAGITTARIUS MAN
SCORPIO WOMAN

The Scorpio woman can be a whirlwind of passion, perhaps too much passion to suit you casual types. When her temper flies, you'd better lock up the family heirlooms and take cover. When she chooses to be sweet, you're overcome with joy. When she uses sarcasm, she can shock even a blunt Sagittarius.

The Scorpio woman can be as hot as a tamale or as cool as a cucumber, but whatever mood she's in, she's in it for real. She does not believe in posing or putting on airs.

The Scorpio woman is often sultry and seductive. Her femme fatale charme can pierce through the hardest of hearts like a laser ray. She may not look like Mata Hari (quite often Scorpios resemble the tomboy next door) but once she's fixed you with her tantalizing eyes, you're a goner.

Life with the Scorpio woman will not be all smiles and smooth sailing. When prompted, she can unleash a gale of venom. Generally, she'll have the good grace to keep family battles within the walls of your home. When company visits, she's apt to give the impression that married life with you is one great big joyride. It's just one of her ways of expressing her loyalty to you, at least in front of others. She may fight you tooth and nail in the confines of your living room, but at a party or during an evening out, she'll hang onto your arm and have stars in her eyes.

Scorpio women are good at keeping secrets. She may even keep a few buried from you if she feels like it.

Never cross her up on even the smallest thing. When it comes to revenge, she's an eye-for-an-eye woman. She's not one for forgiveness, especially if she feels she's been wronged unfairly. You'd be well-advised not to give her any cause to be jealous, either. When the Scorpio woman sees green, your life will be made far from rosy. Once she's put you in the doghouse, you can be sure that you're going to stay there awhile.

You may find life with a Scorpio woman too draining. Although she may be full of extreme moods, it's quite likely that she's not the kind of woman you'd like to spend the rest of your natural life with. You'd prefer someone gentler and not so hot-tempered, someone who can take the highs with the lows and not complain, someone who is flexible and understanding. A woman born under Scorpio can be heavenly, but she can also be the very devil when she chooses.

The Scorpio mother is protective yet encouraging. The opposites within her nature mirror the very contradictions of life itself. Under her skillful guidance, the children learn how to cope with extremes and grow up to become many-faceted individuals.

SAGITTARIUS MAN
SAGITTARIUS WOMAN

You are in sync with your zodiacal sister born under the sign of Sagittarius. This good-natured gal is full of bounce and good cheer. Her sunny disposition seems almost permanent and can be relied upon even on the rainiest of days.

Women born under the sign of the Archer are almost never malicious. If ever they seem to be, it is only seeming. Sagittarius are often a little short on tact and say literally anything that comes into their heads, no matter what the occasion is. Sometimes the words that tumble out of their mouths seem downright cutting and cruel.

Still, no matter what the Sagittarius woman says, she means well. Lover or spouse, she is quite capable of losing some of your friends through a careless slip of the lip.

On the other hand, you will appreciate her honesty and good intentions. To you, qualities of this sort play an important part in life. With a little patience and practice, you can probably help cure your Sagittarius partner of her loose tongue. In most cases, you both will have to use better judgment, and you both will have to practice what you preach.

Chances are, she'll be the outdoors type of woman who likes sports, recreation, and exercise. Long hikes, fishing trips, and white-water canoeing will most likely appeal to her. She's a busy person. No one could ever call her a slouch. She sets great store in mobility. She won't sit still for one minute if she doesn't have to.

The Sagittarius woman is great company most of the time and, generally, lots of fun. Even if your buddies drop by for poker and beer, she won't have any trouble fitting in.

On the whole, she is a very kind and sympathetic woman. If she feels she's made a mistake, she'll be the first to call your attention to it. She's not afraid to own up to her own faults and shortcomings.

You might lose your patience with her once or twice. After she's seen how upset her shortsightedness or carelessness with money has made you, she'll do her best to straighten up.

The Sagittarius woman is not the kind who will pry into your business affairs. But she'll always be there, ready to offer advice if you need it.

The Sagittarius woman is seldom suspicious. Your word will almost always be good enough for her.

The Sagittarius mother is a wonderful and loving friend to her children. She is not afraid if a youngster learns some street smarts along the way. In fact, both of you Sagittarius parents may compete playfully in teaching the children all about the world from your various and combined experiences. You both will see to it that the kids get the best education and recreation money can buy.

SAGITTARIUS MAN
CAPRICORN WOMAN

If you are not a successful businessman or, at least, on your way to success, it's quite possible that a Capricorn woman will have no interest in entering your life. Generally, she is a very security-minded female. She'll see to it that she invests her time only in sure things.

Men who whittle away their time with one unsuccessful scheme or another seldom attract a Capricorn. Men who are interested in getting somewhere in life and keep their noses close to the grindstone quite often have a Capricorn woman behind them, helping them to get ahead.

Although she can be an opportunist and a social climber, she is not what you could call cruel or hard-hearted. Beneath that cool, seemingly calculating exterior, there is a warm and desirable woman. She happens to think that it is just as easy to fall in love with a rich or ambitious man as it is with a poor or lazy one. She's practical.

The Capricorn woman may be interested in rising to the top, but she'll never be aggressive about it. She'll seldom step on someone's feet or nudge competitors away with her elbows. She's quiet about her desires. She sits, waits, and watches. When an opening or opportunity does appear, she'll latch onto it.

For an on-the-move man, an ambitious Capricorn wife or lover can be quite an asset. She can probably give you some very good advice about business matters. When you invite the boss and his wife for dinner, she'll charm them both and make you look good.

The Capricorn woman is thorough in whatever she does: cooking, cleaning, making a success out of life. Capricorns are excellent hostesses as well as guests. Generally, they are very well-mannered and gracious, no matter what their backgrounds are. They seem to have a built-in sense of what is right. Crude behavior or a careless faux pas can offend them no end.

If you should marry a woman born under Capricorn, you need never worry about her going on a wild shopping spree. Capricorns are careful with every cent that comes into their hands. They understand the value of money better than most women and have no room in their lives for careless spending.

The Capricorn woman is usually very fond of family—her own, that is. With her, family ties run very deep. Don't make jokes about her relatives; she won't stand for it. You'd better check her family out before you get down on bended knee. After your marriage, you'll undoubtedly be seeing a lot of her relatives.

The Capricorn mother is very ambitious for her children. She wants them to have every advantage and to benefit from things she perhaps lacked as a child. She will train her youngsters to be polite and kind and to honor traditional codes of conduct.

SAGITTARIUS MAN
AQUARIUS WOMAN

If you find that you've fallen head over heels for a woman born under the sign of the Water Bearer, you'd better fasten your safety belt. It may take you quite a while actually to discover what this woman is like. Even then, you may have nothing to go on but a string of vague hunches.

Aquarius is like a rainbow, full of bright and shining hues. She's like no other woman you've ever known. There is something elusive about her—something delightfully mysterious. You'll most likely never be able to put your finger on it. It's nothing calculated, either. Aquarius do not believe in phony charm.

There will never be a dull moment in your life with this Water Bearer woman. She seems to radiate adventure and magic. She'll most likely be the most open-minded and tolerant woman you've ever met. She has a strong dislike for injustice and prejudice. Narrow-mindedness runs against her grain.

She is very independent by nature and quite capable of shifting for herself if necessary. She may receive many proposals of marriage from all sorts of people without ever really taking them seriously. Marriage is a very big step for her; she wants to be sure she knows what she's getting into. If she thinks that it will seriously curb her independence and love of freedom, she might return the engagement ring—if indeed she's let the romance get that far.

The line between friendship and romance is a pretty fuzzy one for an Aquarius. It's not difficult for her to remain buddy-buddy with an ex-lover. She's tolerant, remember? So, if you should see her on the arm of an old love, don't jump to any hasty conclusions.

She's not a jealous person herself and doesn't expect you to be, either. You'll find her pretty much of a free spirit most of the time. Just when you think you know her inside out, you'll discover that you don't really know her at all, though.

She's a very sympathetic and warm person. She can be helpful to people in need of assistance and advice.

She'll seldom be suspicious even if she has every right to be. If she loves a man, she'll forgive him just about anything. If he allows himself a little fling, chances are she'll just turn her head the other way. Her tolerance does have its limits, however, and her man should never press his luck.

The Aquarius mother is bighearted and seldom refuses her children anything. Her open-minded attitude is easily transmitted to her youngsters. They have every chance of growing up as respectful and tolerant individuals who feel at ease anywhere. You will appreciate the lessons of justice and equality that your Aquarius mate teaches the children.

SAGITTARIUS MAN
PISCES WOMAN

Many a man dreams of an alluring Pisces woman. You're perhaps no exception. She's soft and cuddly and very domestic. She'll let you be the brains of the family; she's contented to play a behind-the-scenes role in order to help you achieve your goals. The illusion that you are the master of the household is the kind of magic that the Pisces woman is adept at creating.

She can be very ladylike and proper. Your business associates and friends will be dazzled by her warmth and femininity. Although she's a charmer, there is a lot more to her than just a pretty exterior. There is a brain ticking away behind that soft, womanly facade. You may never become aware of it—that is, until you're married to her. It's no cause for alarm, however; she'll most likely never use it against you, only to help you and possibly set you on a more successful path.

If she feels you're botching up your married life through careless behavior or if she feels you could be earning more money than you do, she'll tell you about it. But any wife would, really. She will never try to usurp your position as head and breadwinner of the family.

No one had better dare say one uncomplimentary word about you in her presence. It's likely to cause her to break into tears. Pisces women are usually very sensitive beings. Their reaction to adversity, frustration, or anger is just a plain, good, old-fashioned cry. They can weep buckets when inclined.

She can do wonders with a house. She is very fond of dramatic and beautiful things. There will always be plenty of fresh-cut flowers around the house. She will choose charming artwork and antiques, if they are affordable. She'll see to it that the house is decorated in a dazzling yet welcoming style.

She'll have an extra special dinner prepared for you when you come home from an important business meeting. Don't dwell on the boring details of the meeting, though. But if you need that grand vision, the big idea, to seal a contract or make a conquest, your Pisces woman is sure to confide a secret that will guarantee your success. She is canny and shrewd with money, and once you are on her wavelength you can manage the intricacies on your own.

Treat her with tenderness and generosity and your relationship will be an enjoyable one. She's most likely fond of chocolates. A bunch of beautiful flowers will never fail to make her eyes light up. See to it that you never forget her birthday or your anniversary. These things are very important to her. If you let them slip your mind, you'll send her into a crying fit that could last a considerable length of time.

If you are patient and kind, you can keep a Pisces woman happy for a lifetime. She, however, is not without her faults. Her sensitivity may get on your nerves after a while. You may find her lacking in practicality and good old-fashioned stoicism. You may even feel that she uses her tears as a method of getting her own way.

The Pisces mother has, as you do, great joy and utter faith in the children. She makes a strong, self-sacrificing mother through all the phases from infancy to young adulthood. She will teach her youngsters the value of service to the community while not letting them lose their individuality.

SAGITTARIUS
LUCKY NUMBERS 2007

Lucky numbers and astrology can be linked through the movements of the Moon. Each phase of the thirteen Moon cycles vibrates with a sequence of numbers for your Sign of the Zodiac over the course of the year. Using your lucky numbers is a fun system that connects you with tradition.

New Moon	First Quarter	Full Moon	Last Quarter
Dec. 20 ('06)	Dec. 27 ('06)	Jan. 3	Jan. 11
0 6 8 3	6 4 1 0	3 5 7 9	9 4 0 2
Jan. 18	Jan. 25	Feb. 2	Feb. 10
2 8 8 2	9 6 7 0	6 3 5 9	9 0 7 4
Feb. 17	Feb. 24	March 3	March 11
4 8 5 3	9 1 4 6	8 8 3 7	0 1 7 2
March 18	March 25	April 2	April 10
2 5 5 2	3 6 8 1	1 5 0 3	3 9 4 7
April 17	April 24	May 2	May 9
7 5 2 9	3 5 7 2	5 6 9 6	6 1 4 2
May 16	May 23	May 31	June 8
2 8 9 2	4 6 1 5	0 8 5 9	9 3 1 0
June 14	June 22	June 30	July 7
7 8 2 4	6 3 2 0	3 2 6 9	9 7 4 5
July 14	July 22	July 29	August 5
5 8 1 3	3 7 0 4	9 5 8 6	6 3 4 7
August 12	August 20	August 28	Sept. 3
7 9 2 6	6 1 8 5	4 3 1 0	7 8 2 4
Sept. 11	Sept. 19	Sept. 26	Oct. 3
4 6 1 0	5 8 5 1	7 2 8 9	9 3 5 7
Oct. 11	Oct. 19	Oct. 26	Nov. 1
7 2 6 9	9 6 1 7	5 2 3 6	6 8 1 5
Nov. 9	Nov. 17	Nov. 24	Dec. 1
5 0 3 9	9 4 7 8	2 5 6 9	2 4 8 3
Dec. 9	Dec. 17	Dec. 23	Dec. 31
0 6 3 7	7 1 8 0	3 2 5 7	9 4 0 8

SAGITTARIUS
YEARLY FORECAST 2007

*Forecast for 2007 Concerning Business
and Financial Affairs, Job Prospects,
Travel, Health, Romance and Marriage
for Persons Born with the Sun
in the Zodiacal Sign of Sagittarius.
November 23–December 20*

For those born under the influence of the Sun in the zodiacal sign
of Sagittarius, ruled by Jupiter, the planet of wisdom and good fortune, 2007 will be a year of new beginnings. Jupiter is now settled in
your own sign of Sagittarius, increasing your luck, opening more
doors for you, and improving opportunities for advancement in
most areas of life. There is often a touch of the guru in Sagittarius
folk. With your first house of self and personality being strongly
activated by Jupiter and Pluto throughout most of 2007, there is a
tendency to intuitively know as well as anticipate current trends.
This will be especially helpful if you need to make major career or
business decisions. It is the right time to take action and rid yourself of attitudes, emotions, or aspects of life that are not relevant or
are no longer working. Free of these, you can then move on.

Negative qualities that you need to guard against this year are an
overly generous tendency and self-indulgence. Do all that you can
to avoid mishandling both physical and financial resources. Your
fire can be smothered slightly from early April until early August,
when Jupiter moves into retrograde motion. This will decrease
motivation and optimism for personal plans and also lead to fluctu-
ating weight gain or loss. However, this period can be an excellent
time to reevaluate the way you are leading your life. Also reexam-

ine your current skills and expertise to determine if further education would help you achieve personal aspirations.

With taskmaster Saturn remaining in the regal sign of Leo until early September, abundant patience will be available to enhance a hobby or creative pursuit that involves research or probing deeply into a topic of interest. Long-distance travel for the purpose of education, business, or career advancement is more likely than for pleasure, although many travelers will figure out a way to combine both. Legal problems could be a source of concern as delays and mistakes take their toll for periods throughout the year. However, a positive settlement is likely eventually.

Returning to academic study might appeal if you are eager to increase your knowledge base and broaden your horizons. Potential students need to be discerning with topics selected for study. Only choose those that you have a true interest in since much work and effort will have to be applied to get good grades. Learning a second language could help if you regularly deal with people from overseas. Knowing the language can assist with personal contact and help in importing and exporting products. There may be some serious commitment involving caring for an older family member. This might impinge on your personal freedom, causing possible resentment.

From September 2 into year 2010, Saturn will be visiting Virgo, your house of vocation and business affairs. This should increase your workplace responsibilities as well as helping career-minded Sagittarius move further up the ladder of success. Accompanying an increase in status and recognition, you may be required to put in more effort and hours on the job. Remuneration should be in line with your extra effort.

Unconventional Uranus in Pisces continues to activate your home and family zone, bringing changes within the home and family mix. There is a likelihood of relocation if you hope to expand your horizons either interstate or abroad. Or you might decide to upgrade your living conditions. Adult children could decide to take up residence once more with parents after deciding that home is where the heart is. New members might come into the family through birth or marriage, while a few could leave in order to relocate.

Compassionate friends may become a surrogate family for Sagittarius folk living away from loved ones. Inspiring Neptune continues to move through Aquarius, your house of communication, transportation, and neighborhood matters throughout the year. This will assist creative expression, adding exceptional color and vision to artistic pursuits, writing, and speaking. Returning to school, an interest in having your work published, public relations, or advertising could set new directions for you.

Pluto is still moving through your personality sector, with the result that you may experience a transformation and exhibit a new image to the world. This may have come at a personal cost but positive trends should be evident.

Pluto also continues to affect your health, with negative behavior patterns being replaced by more constructive habits. Exercise and physical fitness will be important as well as getting out into the great outdoors to inhale plenty of clean fresh air. Eat wisely, drink less caffeine, and drink more water to protect your liver, which can be an area of weakness for those born under the sign of the Archer. Include plenty of physical activity, such as workouts, playing sports, dancing, and walking. With Jupiter also gracing your first house of physical body, self-indulgent tendencies may be more evident. The result will be a weight gain if a vigilant approach is not taken. Following a practical diet and health regime throughout 2007, although challenging if you prefer a high-calorie diet, will be worthwhile. A totally new lifestyle program can change your life. For the typical Sagittarius, being depressed is not a usual trait. This year, however, you may at least be more serious and pensive than normal. This is not necessarily a bad thing providing you do not let negativity become a regular occurrence.

Cooperation and compromise are the key to maintaining harmony on the home front. New love stands an excellent chance of lasting. A past love that is rekindled might also be enduring. From late July to early September, coinciding with the retrograde motion of Venus, be ready for changes. Romantic relationships that are on the rocks could finally fizzle out completely unless extra effort is devoted to restoring mutual affection. Romantic involvement could lead to emotional upset if both parties are not considerate of each other's feelings. However, many long-term partnerships will experience greater appreciation and respect for each other. Ensure that romantic spontaneity is part of your routine. Singles are likely to experience numerous romantic encounters throughout 2007. A walk down the aisle or moving in together is very possible since you will prefer being part of a couple, adding increased security and stability to your emotional life. The birth of a child will be a most welcome addition.

In December expansive Jupiter enters Capricorn, your house of finances, possessions, and values, marking a new twelve-year cycle. This can be a beneficial period with improved potential to generate more income and increase material possessions and wealth. Negatively, this transit of Jupiter confers a more reckless attitude toward financial resources, with a tendency for wastefulness. Speculation should be avoided or kept to a minimum. Secure investments would be the best course of action to protect finances. There is an increased need to be extra prudent about borrowing money, ensuring that a loan taken out now can be comfortably repaid. Take stock of your situation and align your spending with your long-term vision.

Tracking the Moon phases around the zodiac each month can assist in planning your activities to ensure successful outcomes. When there is a New Moon, this is a perfect time to start fresh projects. Finishing projects that are already in progress is easier under the influence of a Full Moon.

During the year's three Mercury retrograde periods, expect holdups, malfunctions, and crossed wires to occur. These Mercury retrogrades periods are February 14 to March 8, June 15 to July 10, and October 12 to November 1. These can be times of delays commuting back and forth to work, communication mix-ups, and computer malfunctions. It is recommended to postpone signing of contracts, purchasing major assets, and making important life decisions. But success can come throughout these retrograde time frames by rethinking decisions made in the past, reevaluating current goals, and resolving any issues you have with others.

Sagittarius, your rewards can come in the same measure you exert effort throughout the year 2007.

SAGITTARIIUS DAILY FORECAST

January–December 2007

JANUARY

1. MONDAY. Lively. Happy New Year, Sagittarius! You are likely to remain in a party mood whether you went to bed early or in the wee hours of the morning. If you celebrated at home, organize the cleaning up brigade early while motivation and enthusiasm are high. Energy will begin to flag later in the day. If you overspent during the festive season, opt for free or inexpensive entertainment if looking for amusement today. Arguments between you and your mate or partner are likely when the current state of the bank account is made known. It would be wiser to defer financial discussions until everyone is feeling more refreshed.

2. TUESDAY. Uneven. A power struggle or a disagreement that you could do without may erupt if you are up and about early this morning. Rather than engage in a battle with your mate or partner, extend your stay in bed until the last possible moment. This strategy will diffuse possible emotional upsets as well as helping you find more relaxing pursuits to keep you occupied. By midmorning cosmic energies are smiling again, making this an excellent day for shopping and replenishing household supplies. A new budget or investment idea is likely to get the go-ahead from your significant other providing you can demonstrate that your plan is practical and stands a good chance of being successful.

3. WEDNESDAY. Manageable. You might wonder why everyone around you seems so demonstrative all of a sudden. Emotions rise to the surface quickly when the Moon is full and round as it is today. The Cancer Full Moon highlights both of your financial houses, possibly bringing an urgent need to review the current state of your credit cards or an overdue account. This in turn could lead to cutting back on any unnecessary spending. Keep a tight hold on your own purse strings. Also try to stop family indulgences from interfering with the practical reality of meeting day-to-day household expenses. In this way you should begin to make headway toward balancing income with expenditures.

4. THURSDAY. Enjoyable. The planet Venus has now entered your erratic Aquarius third sector of movement and short travels, heralding a pleasant period for Sagittarius. This signals a shift in energy that encourages experimentation, thinking outside the box, and utilizing unusual or unconventional techniques and processes. Communicating with and visiting friends is likely to increase, with some supplying unusual or unexpected influences in your life. Expect to be more involved in local activities as well as sharing your ideas and interests with those you see daily. Unattached Sagittarius should look closer to home for an encounter of the romantic kind. Be ready for anything.

5. FRIDAY. Stimulating. As a Sagittarius, visiting as many far-flung places on the world globe as possible always interests your free spirit. If vacation plans are beckoning, talk to the boss about specific time off, examine current travel trends and likely destinations, and sit down with your mate or partner or friend to outline your trip. Entertaining friends and family members with amusing information on your return will be as important as having fun, so be sure to include historical or unusual sites in your plans. Also take plenty of photos, or buy lots of postcards. Grasp any opportunity to advance your education. Even if the available course selection isn't as interesting as you would like, sign up if it will further your career potential.

6. SATURDAY. Sparkling. Your concentration should be at a high level, making this an excellent time to study a complex topic, conduct in-depth research, or take an exam that needs focus and attention to detail. If you have some free time, attending a conference or seminar can bring you into contact with like-minded people who share your passion for a particular interest or hobby. Sagittarius teachers, lecturers, and public speakers who are experts in their subject matter are also favorably assisted under current cosmic energies. You should receive warm applause and appreciation from your audience. Seek entertainment this evening that provides mental stimulation as well as a pleasant diversion from the usual.

7. SUNDAY. Constructive. This is an excellent day for the career-oriented Sagittarius to review all that is going on. Consider where you are headed and if you are moving in the direction of choice. If current employment is not offering sufficient challenge or opportunity for advancement, settle down with the Sunday newspaper and check out the job vacancies. Circle those of interest, update your resume, and look forward to making progressive changes to your life and income. Your ability to communicate effectively and with just the right amount of humor ensures that your presence will be welcome at any social gathering or other event.

8. MONDAY. Useful. Today's efficient and organized atmosphere will help if you need to perform detailed or complex work. The promise of future progress, a promotion, or a salary increase might also be on your mind at this time. Important decisions relating to business or vocational matters can be made. Listen to what other people have to say and think about what you have learned. This information could make a difference to your future. Sagittarius folk setting off on travels for career or business purposes should have an exciting adventure. Expect lots of interesting developments that have the potential to expand your networking and opportunities.

9. TUESDAY. Changeable. Don't throw a tantrum if changes have to be made to your plans this morning. Even if this arouses instant annoyance, it could work out better for you in the long term. Take care if dealing with people in authority. Misunderstandings are likely, causing confusion and upsets. You may also struggle to concentrate on anything for a long period of time. Ideally you should plan a day with plenty of diversity so boredom doesn't set in. If you are planning to visit a local tourist destination that you have not been to before, make sure you take along a map so that you don't become geographically misplaced in your own locale.

10. WEDNESDAY. Helpful. There is a certain amount of luck floating around, especially where your ambitions are concerned. Let other people know that you are eager to pursue some special aims. Support could be forthcoming from where you least expect it. An enthusiastic friend might try to involve you in one of their favorite activities or persuade you to join a group that they belong to. If you don't have any other plans, go along with their suggestions. This could eventually lead to more exciting or pleasant developments in the future. You can still have a great time by exercising moderation and resisting the temptation to overindulge when socializing tonight.

11. THURSDAY. Disconcerting. Mixed trends prevail throughout the day. Although strange to the outgoing and talkative Sagittarius nature, you could find it difficult to verbalize your thoughts or ideas to other people. As a result it would be better to write them down on paper or send an e-mail. Counteract any tendency toward a pessimistic attitude by surrounding yourself with positive-thinking people who make you laugh and lift your spirits. Even though you may not feel overly social, it is important to put recreational time to good use. Planning some future fun activities with a group of friends will give you something worthwhile to anticipate.

12. FRIDAY. Enjoyable. Even though you might prefer to stay in the background today, this is unlikely. Your ruler, jolly Jupiter, is happily connected to charming Venus, attracting people to you based on your generosity of spirit, warmth, and good humor. If you need a special favor or have an important request, ask and it should be granted. Love and romance are highlighted on the schedule for both singles and couples. If you have a partner, arrange a romantic dinner to finish the day on a high note. A pleasant romantic surprise could be in store for Sagittarius singles who make the effort to socialize with neighbors or a sibling this evening.

13. SATURDAY. Challenging. Constructive celestial energies that could also prove challenging greet you today with the merging of active Mars and passionate Pluto. Power struggles and disagreements could arise if you are overly domineering or aggressive. You are apt to feel particularly energized, which will be of great assistance if you have a heavy workload to get through. Taking advantage of the post-festive sales and venturing out to shop should be on your must-do list if you want to expand your winter wardrobe at significant savings. There is a great deal of fire and passion in romance, making for fun times providing that any possessive inclinations are kept at bay.

14. SUNDAY. Manageable. Keep alert today. Someone might hint rather loudly that some of your ideas and opinions are a bit narrow-minded or outdated. This could come as a shock, especially if you think that you are always fair and have a broad outlook on life. It would be wise to analyze your views and establish for yourself if you are being hasty or judgmental in interpreting a current situation. If hosting friends or relatives from overseas you could find that the cost skyrockets well over the amount you budgeted for entertaining expenses. Use the local newspaper or Internet to find places of interest that suit your budget and still adequately fill the days.

15. MONDAY. Innovative. You begin the new workweek with the planetary movement of Mercury, messenger to the gods, entering into your Aquarius third sector. This increases activity and motion in your working environment, areas of communication, and social interaction with friends and other people who are close to you. Ways to increase income from business and career efforts should be in abundance as new and unique ideas rush into your mind. Over the next three weeks don't feel guilty if you are unable to make snap decisions since your mind will be highly stimulated at that time. Also be prepared for your opinions and viewpoints to be changing, sometimes even on a whim.

16. TUESDAY. Assertive. With a number of planets occupying your first house of self, a great deal of physical energy and motivation will be available to you this morning. Personal ambitions and plans will be uppermost in your mind, with success coming from whatever area you decide to focus on. Fiery Mars moves into your personal monetary house of Capricorn, bringing a more practical trend when it comes to spending and overall finances. From now until February 25, hard work should produce plenty of rewards. This is the right time to begin the process of reaping what you have been sowing. It is also a period to find ways to make money and resources work more effectively and efficiently for you.

17. WEDNESDAY. Spirited. A restless atmosphere pervades the air, although this is unlikely to prove too disruptive for the Sagittarius who prefers to live on the edge. You might be required to make some financial adjustments, but even this should not be worrisome. Budgetary relief is likely when you cut some expenses down to a more manageable size. If responsible for handling any type of tricky transaction, use all of your creative powers to find a middle ground. Once you work out the major details, remaining negotiations should fall easily into place. Prepare for unexpected visitors to descend on you, brightening up the evening hours but keeping you up much later than usual.

18. THURSDAY. Beneficial. Tonight's New Moon in your Capricorn second house of personal possessions and money brings in a fresh annual cycle that will help you use financial resources more wisely. This can be especially useful if you have been spending wildly recently. Consider purchasing something that will grow in value over the years as well as provide you with pleasure, such as property of precious jewelry. Effort expanded into increasing income from career or business activities should also pay big dividends if you are willing to take the initiative or be more aggressive. You could also be on the receiving end of a pay increase in the guise of a bonus, commission check, or parking perk.

19. FRIDAY. Inspiring. With inspirational Neptune happily connecting with the love goddess Venus, romance and some seriously good times are high on your agenda over the next few days. Dress to impress. Love at first sight is very possible for Sagittarius singles. This could happen at the bus stop, in class, or at the local supermarket. Creative and talented Sagittarius will also be inspired, seeing beauty in many things and especially in items that those less gifted might never notice or would consider unappealing. This is not the best time to sign any important financial document unless you have first consulted a legal expert.

20. SATURDAY. Dynamic. With the Sun now shining in your third sector of eccentric Aquarius, the next four weeks are likely to be anything but boring. Excitement and chaos will be the norm, keeping you truly on your toes. This is a great time to be spontaneous, to put your plans into perspective, and to express yourself in an honest and upfront manner. All this fits in well with the Sagittarius personality. With four planets in your house of communication, you can now begin writing the great novel if you have always wanted to be an author, to give that first lecture if public speaking appeals, or to begin sharing your wisdom if teaching is your passion.

21. SUNDAY. Misleading. Once all the household chores are out of the way, focus on having fun with the family. Plan daytime activities that stimulate the mind as well as being enjoyable. Tonight just relax at home with a good book and that special person in your life. Celestial influences convey confusing energy, suggesting that it would be better to keep activities simple and straightforward so that your blood pressure doesn't rise higher than normal. Ignore any matters involving money right now. This is not a good time to trust other people with personal resources and assets because there is a strong possibility of being misled now.

22. MONDAY. Uncertain. Be prepared for surprises to come your way. You might be thrown for a loop by some of the day's events. It is not usual for Sagittarius to feel bound by rigid rules and regulations, but this is apt to be the case now. Bending them even slightly could prove more difficult than you envision. Expressing yourself honestly and saying precisely what is on your mind is important. Once you speak out, you must be willing to make the appropriate commitments and take action needed to back up your words. Although your thoughts include some clever ideas, steer clear of complex tasks that demand total concentration.

23. TUESDAY. Variable. Excitement and adventure are calling, which won't be very helpful if you need to concentrate on earning a living. Although your ruler, jovial Jupiter, is making an inharmonious aspect to erratic Uranus, you could be in for some luck. Don't hesitate to invest in a lottery ticket or a raffle chance and hope for the best. You cannot lose very much, and you might gain a small windfall. Be prepared for a phone call to inform you about sudden changes involving domestic arrangements, especially if you share living quarters with people who are unrelated to you. Having to look for another place to live or advertise for a new roommate is likely to be annoying and time consuming but also necessary.

24. WEDNESDAY. Exciting. Look forward to a happy day ahead. If you are able to mix business with pleasurable activities much can be accomplished. For the self-employed running a small business enterprise, the bottom line could gain from increased networking. If heading for the shopping mall you might feel a strong pull toward antiques or a store that includes a good range of secondhand items. Don't ignore the opportunity. You might make a major find that rewards you in the form of a significant profit or personal happiness. If unattached you might meet a very unusual person with whom you fall in love at first sight.

25. THURSDAY. Guarded. Actions of youngsters could prove disruptive this morning if you are a parent or are in charge of children. Implement some major corrective action sooner rather than later so peace can be restored and the display of bad behavior is not ongoing. There is a strong possibility that personal frustrations could take the form of excessive eating or drinking if you are not careful. Also watch your weight and get some exercise. As a Sagittarius you are well known for quick wit, which sometimes borders on sarcasm. You need to tone this down now, especially in regard to anyone you consider annoying.

26. FRIDAY. Creative. A dash of inspiration is added to today's mix as chatty Mercury connects with dreamy Neptune in your house of communication and writing. Sit down and start composing romantic poetry, a love song, or a book for children or the young at heart. Your creative juices are flowing freely. This aspect also may do funny things to your memory, causing you to forget things you would normally remember or remember what you yearn to forget. Venus, the goddess of love, is happily harmonizing with passionate Pluto, so be sure to set aside plenty of leisure time to spend with someone you find irresistible.

27. SATURDAY. Changeable. Minor annoyances are foreseen involving financial issues with a relative. Extra effort will be needed to control your anger or frustration. Direct your energy toward a physical activity or pursuit that is both educational and interesting. Venus, the lady of love, prepares to move into your Pisces zone of home and family concerns this evening. This will increase your opportunity to benefit financially through real estate, home building, renovations, or redecorating. This is also a time when home entertaining should be extremely enjoyable. Parties and celebrations will bring together family members and friends, creating joyous memories for all to share.

28. SUNDAY. Difficult. Pessimism could overwhelm even those Sagittarius not prone to negative thinking or a gloomy attitude. Remaining on the go will help keep this to a minimum. Make sure your day has lots of variety and entertainment so that you stay fully occupied and amused. Sagittarius travelers are likely to encounter some bad weather which causes frustrating delays. Make sure you have good reading material on hand if traveling by public transportation. Plans to upgrade living conditions could preoccupy many householders. Spend a few pleasurable hours with your mate or partner drawing up plans for renovations, rearranging furniture, or freshening up the walls with a new paint job.

29. MONDAY. Good. The morning hours are apt to more productive than later in the day. A legal or financial issue, perhaps involving establishment of a new business partnership, could require a lot of tedious paperwork. Although time consuming, irritating, and boring, completing this is essential for your peace of mind as well as to get the ball rolling. Early afternoon may bring conflict with a business or personal partner unless you keep the lines of communication wide open. Even if you do not see eye-to-eye on a particular matter, find a suitable compromise until a true resolution is found. A night spent at home with family members should be the most relaxing leisure pursuit.

30. TUESDAY. Important. This is a good time to study investment strategies that could help increase your long-term financial prospects. To aid relaxation, include plenty of greenery and healthy plants in your home or office decor. If indoor plants are currently suffering due to your lack of a green thumb, consult a garden expert or purchase a book on how to maintain and grow healthier specimens. If cleaning out the attic, garage, or your closet, carefully sort through everything to see if there are any useful items that you no longer want but would be of value to those less well-off than you. Donate them and get a tax receipt.

31. WEDNESDAY. Fruitful. Speculating in property could be a profitable way to steadily increase your net worth. Before committing to anything, make sure that it is the right type of investment for you. Otherwise you might end up with something that is more of a stone around your neck than an asset. If unsure about where you want to live permanently, or if you are having trouble deciding on a specific location, consider becoming a house sitter for a short period. In this way you not only receive payment but have the added benefit of free rent while deciding on the area that offers the services and amenities that you seek.

FEBRUARY

1. THURSDAY. Stimulating. Like your Gemini cousins you usually excel in the art of writing or speaking. Today this ability is increased, imparting the ease of communicative skills and expertise. This will be of great assistance to those who need to push a product for sale, to sell personal services, or to convince others that a plan or idea has merit. Be wary of challenging someone's spiritual and philosophical views unless you are an expert in the field or have a strong knowledge of the topic. An urge for variety could tempt you to take time off from boring work and look for more diversity through leisure activities.

2. FRIDAY. Useful. A Full Moon in your fellow fire sign of Leo is followed by the entry of messenger Mercury, joining Venus and

Uranus in your Pisces fourth zone of property and family concerns. With all of these planetary influences to liven up the day, your travel house is also activated. This is a perfect period to complete vacation arrangements or business travel plans that are already in the pipeline. Inspirational ideas and thoughts are likely to flow freely. These will help if you need to change living conditions by implementing minor home renovations or drawing up plans for a major extension to the family dwelling.

3. SATURDAY. Delightful. The stars are rallying round to ensure that today is eventful as well as happy. Luck is also on your side, especially if you intend to purchase or sell property. If seeking your dream home is your number-one priority, get ready to start looking. Before you begin, research locations, consider how much of a mortgage and down payment you can afford, and write all the things you would like the property to contain. Positive developments are also likely in matters connected to an event that will require you to travel to attend. Or an educational goal may move closer to reality, with increased financial benefits likely to come your way.

4. SUNDAY. Uneasy. Although it is not usually in the Sagittarius nature to be picky or pedantic, this could occur today due to the influence of the Moon sitting at the top of your chart in Virgo, the sign of perfection. This negative tendency coupled with restless energy could cause dissension with other household members unless you are on the move or involved in a constructive project that is absorbing as well as interesting. Even if you are tempted to cancel attending a social occasion or family gathering, make the effort to comply with what you promised to do. In the long run you will probably be glad that you did. A long soak in a warm bath filled with relaxing aromatherapy oils is the perfect end to weekend activities.

5. MONDAY. Alert. Keep your ear to the ground and you could hear important information relating to career or business activities. This can give you an advantage or offer a valuable opportunity. Important decisions that have been on your mind for some time should be made now rather than later. You are entering a period when clear thinking may be at a lower level than usual. Sagittarius singles should take extra care with appearance and grooming, even if at home over the next few days. Love could appear unexpectedly at your front door, when you are out shopping, or while visiting family members or friends. Take extra care if handling sharp or hot objects this evening.

6. TUESDAY. Uncertain. Today's influences indicate that it is unlikely to be plain sailing. Just when you thought that things were settled, minor mishaps or changes in circumstances are likely to jolt you out of your comfort zone. Fortunately, remaining relaxed with the ability to go with the flow should not present a problem for those born under the sign of Sagittarius. You are very aware that becoming upset does not solve anything and often makes matters worse. Discussions with family members regarding an upcoming social event are unlikely to be productive. Defer them until everyone is in a more agreeable mood.

7. WEDNESDAY. Pleasant. Although a happy period ahead, vagueness and confusion are likely to bother you for the next few days. Keep complex tasks to a minimum in order to avoid errors in your work. A friend who has been missing from your social scene could come back into the fold if you make the effort. A friendly phone call or e-mail might be all it takes for a reunion to take place soon. That first glance of a new romantic potential could make your heart beat faster than usual if you are single and looking. Do what you can to bring love into your life. A family gathering could be the venue for a pleasing encounter with someone recently divorced or widowed. Don't be shy about coming forward.

8. THURSDAY. Creative. Make notes if you need to remember important dates or tasks since your memory is likely to fail. Take along an up-to-date road map if setting off on a journey by car. You are bound to have moments of confusion about what direction to take to reach your destination. Sagittarius with a creative talent are likely to excel in writing, sculpting, painting, or drawing. Imaginative ideas should flow freely, providing you with inspiration and artistic thoughts. Romance at home remains strong. You and your significant other can now create plenty of pleasurable memories that will sustain you through the good and not so good times ahead.

9. FRIDAY. Fair. As vixen Venus, the goddess of love, challenges your ruler Jupiter, planet of abundance, your love life or lack thereof is brought into focus. A former love might reappear on the scene, opening up old wounds as well as creating new excitement. Under current influences it might be wise to quell rising feelings and emotions and stay emotionally neutral. Becoming involved with this person once again could bring a repeat performance of past negative experiences. Confess to any error that you might have made but don't become a martyr about it. Nor should you take responsibility for mistakes that have nothing to do with you. This is not the best day to shop for household appliances because you are likely to go way over your budget.

10. SATURDAY. Chancy. As a Sagittarius you are inclined to bury your head in the sand rather than face up to making a difficult decision today. Instead, take the practical approach. Try to relax so you can keep things in true perspective. Sinking into the doldrums will not help you come up with the best choices. Your coping mechanism is strong as you realize that everyone experiences occasional difficult periods throughout life. Use your natural optimistic attitude and watch worries melt away. An invitation later in the day could nurture your romantic desires. Don't sit home waiting for the phone to ring. Get out and mingle with your close friends, finishing the day on a high note.

11. SUNDAY. Tricky. This is another day when you need to focus on the positive aspects of your life and try to ignore the negative. The Moon is zooming through your own sign of Sagittarius, providing a chance to be more daring than usual. If your bank balance can tolerate a little retail therapy, visit the nearest shopping mall. This will give you and your attire a new lift. You will feel better for it, and other people are likely to comment on your fresh appearance. Your love life should remain good providing you do not try to shock your mate or steady date with some outrageous comments. Singles remain in a period when love could appear in the most unexpected places.

12. MONDAY. Spirited. Creative forces are strong, although Sagittarius people involved in the entertainment industry might need to work a little harder to impress the powers that be. You will come out on top if you exude confidence and passion in making a presentation. Formulating changes in your personal life and improving your health and lifestyle can produce long-term benefits. Make an appointment this week with a beautician, naturopath, dentist, or podiatrist to ensure that your overall well-being remains in top form. Listening to music, writing poetry, researching photographs, or enjoying an artistic field would be excellent relaxation this evening.

13. TUESDAY. Romantic. Love is in the air as adorable Venus cuddles up to excitable Mars. If currently unattached, make sure you do not confuse passionate feelings with deep and lasting love. Sagittarius couples can make the most of this happy connection by spending an evening at home, preferably just the two of you. Mercury, messenger of the gods, is moving backward, highlighting the domestic sphere from tonight until March 8. Throughout this period it is more important to complete outstanding projects rather than begin new ones. Do not purchase major household products or computer equipment unless guaranteed with no restocking fee. The discovery of faults could find you returning goods for a refund.

14. WEDNESDAY. Cautious. Pace yourself throughout the day. Your energy could be at low ebb, but you need to be full of vim and vitality if you have big plans for this evening's Valentine celebration. If currently experiencing money worries, face up to your obligations no matter how unpleasant this may be, endeavoring to sort out your finances. Once you make a start, relief coupled with motivation should return. Positive results are likely to be the result of your effort. Be wary if you are involved in a fund-raising event right now. Someone who claims to be in need might be inclined to take advantage of your generous nature.

15. THURSDAY. Distracting. Whatever you attempt today, take it slow. Keep in mind that minor errors can become major problems while Mercury is retrograde. If mistakes made by you are uncovered, try not to judge yourself too harshly. Other people will not cast blame if you show that you are doing the best that you possibly can. A neighbor or a relative might make certain demands that are more than you are willing to fulfill. Don't hesitate to speak up in a straightforward but tactful manner. Explain that you are unable to take on any extra commitments or financial outlays right now, but may reconsider at a later date.

16. FRIDAY. Helpful. Morning influences might bring minor concerns, but these should clear up quickly and be replaced by more positive events. Guard against a propensity to continually change your mind from one decision to the next. In the end you might not remember what you liked, disliked, wanted to do, or didn't want to do. If this seems to be happening, take time out to focus, collect yourself, and then slowly and sensibly review your options. Love and money should flow happily, with Sagittarius couples displaying mutual accord in these areas. Sagittarius singles could meet romantic luck at a place associated with music or the arts.

17. SATURDAY. Supportive. Your communication skills should receive a boost during the next two weeks thanks to today's New Moon in the eccentric sign of Aquarius. You'll be chatting more, which should especially assist salespeople, public speakers, and debt collectors. In general this is an excellent period to begin new projects and enterprises. However, the tension carried by Mercury in retrograde warns against starting endeavors that you want to last a long time. A fresh beginning is possible with a friend you recently argued with and should be a positive experience. It is up to you to make the first move to restore your good relations.

18. SUNDAY. Empowering. The Sun is now visiting your Pisces sector until March 20, increasing the already strong emphasis on your zone of home and domestic affairs. A number of opportunities are likely to open up. As well, there is the possibility of a change of residence, providing a more stable and secure environment. Sagittarius with a flair for home decorating and renovating should make steady progress with this venture while increasing home comforts and improving living conditions. With your eye for a bargain, purchasing antique furniture or artwork could add considerable value to your assets.

19. MONDAY. Sparkling. Home sweet home will appeal strongly to the usually outgoing Sagittarius. You may even decide to take the day off from work or normal routine duties to focus on pressing family issues or domestic matters. Make constructive use of this energy to improve your space, even if this only involves simple tasks like getting the car washed, catching up on ironing, or cleaning out a closet. Over the next few days celestial influences will bring turbulent and passionate times in the romance department. Jealousy may erupt for Sagittarius people experiencing insecurity in an intimate relationship. Couples in a stable love relationship can look forward to increased emotional intensity.

20. TUESDAY. Active. Look forward to this interesting day ahead. The focus is on things of a romantic nature. Call to confirm the likely arrival time if you are waiting for movers, a taxi, or a friend from out of town. Otherwise you might waste half the day hanging around waiting. Although this is not the right time to sign a contract, it is an excellent period for business proprietors to contact a landlord to review a current lease, especially if the aim is to renegotiate a better deal. Mingle with a crowd this evening if you are seeking some fun and excitement, but don't stay out too late. Someone you meet from another city or state could soon be your special friend.

21. WEDNESDAY. Rewarding. Venus, goddess of love and good times, travels into enterprising Aries, spotlighting the romantic part of your solar chart from now until March 17. More fun, frivolity, loving, and adventure are in store for you. Increase your vitamin intake so you can keep up and take advantage of the many opportunities that are coming your way. One of your children or a younger relative could set off on a wonderful journey which in the future will provide many blessings for other family members. For the unattached Archer, a love affair may develop into all you ever wanted and possibly even more.

22. THURSDAY. Constructive. Extra mental stability conveyed by the Sun merging with Mercury provides the chance to totally concentrate or to act on tasks that you normally find tedious. An efficient approach will help if you are arranging a special activity or making important advance preparations. Your communication skills are excellent, so organize thoughts so you know exactly what, when, and how to express whatever you feel needs to be said. Cleaning up clutter from around your home of office could result in finding some unused space that you can take advantage of right away.

23. FRIDAY. Accomplished. Self-nurturing instincts are strong. With your ruler Jupiter in your sign impacting your physical body, you could be involved in battling a seemingly ever-expanding waistline. Considering the best way to improve your health and well-being might be overdue, especially if work and family commitments have eroded time you normally spend on personal activities. Implementing an exercise regime, a healthier diet, or finding time for a full-body massage can help to bring your body back to more robust fitness. Make the most of today's practical mood, especially if your plans include accomplishing plenty of work on the job.

24. SATURDAY. Useful. The Moon in your opposite sign of Gemini highlights the partnership sector throughout the weekend. This provides an opportunity to focus on relationship issues for open, honest discussion. This can be beneficial for long-term happiness, particularly if recent differences have caused arguments or distress. With competitive urges strong, Sagittarius athletes or those involved in any sporting activity can make considerable progress. Just be sure to follow the rules of the game and use sensible precautions to protect yourself against possible injury. Don't be afraid to relax and have fun this evening.

25. SUNDAY. Mixed. Mars, the planet that provides drive, enthusiasm, and energy, has now shifted into your Aquarius sector of information, communication, and movement. Sagittarius folk don't usually require much encouragement to get out and mingle, which is just as well because you may not have much spare time from now until April 6. Thinking faster and smarter will be positive attributes of this planetary placement. However, impulsive action and speaking before giving due consideration to what you are about to say could be a recipe for disaster. Love and affection provide an enjoyable climax to this evening. Be quick to respond to a special request.

26. MONDAY. Positive. Mercury, the planet that governs the mind, slips back into your Aquarius third sector, urging a review of ideas that are very different from the norm but seem innovative and worth considering. By revisiting your ideas you can ascertain if they are realistic with a good chance of success or are based more on wishful thinking. Property management, joint finances, and assets owned in conjunction with other people, as well as business and partnership resources, are strongly in focus now and will benefit from your energetic input. Examining ways to get a better return from investments you already own can also make a big impact on your long-term financial stability.

27. TUESDAY. Significant. If you have lost something important around your home, search today. Chances of finding the missing item are excellent, and you could also turn up a long forgotten treasure. Monetary matters involving other family members, such as drawing up a more manageable household budget or a list of home maintenance requirements, might take more time than you allocated. Either start the discussion earlier or wait until later in the week when everyone has more free time available. Relax with a good mystery story that will keep you entertained and intrigued this evening.

28. WEDNESDAY. Variable. This is a day of mixed trends as realistic Saturn challenges the dreams and illusions of dreamy Neptune. Expect some confusion, misunderstandings, and mix-ups when communicating with other people. This is also a time to pay close attention to what others have to say. Just be on your guard because some of what is conveyed might not be relevant or true, and should not be taken as gospel. Profound thinking is enhanced. Being able to think on your feet means you don't have to write everything down ahead of time if involved in discussions or meetings. You will be able to easily remember facts and figures. Dig out your tools and begin work on a creative project, applying self-discipline to get the best result.

MARCH

1. THURSDAY. Bewildering. Confusing influences prevail, hindering your ability to think clearly. If the urge for an overseas escapade is getting stronger, research likely destinations. For now this will suit your sense of adventure as well as your wallet and give you lots of exciting options from which to choose. Once Mercury begins trekking forward, reservations can be made, deposits paid, and passport paperwork filled out. Avoid becoming entangled in legal issues. Glossing over the small print of a contract is likely to have disastrous consequences. Instead, leave matters in the hands of a trustworthy lawyer to take care of issues that you might not totally comprehend.

2. FRIDAY. Demanding. Convincing a skeptic that your ideas have merit could prove extremely challenging. It might be wiser to save your breath and let time prove that your decisions were correct. Although this should be the end of the working week, an unexpected order or uncompleted work may mean that you will have to stay late to catch up. Putting in a few extra hours on the job this evening could save you from having to cut into your weekend leisure activities. Steer clear of quarrels between siblings. Taking a neutral stance when they come to you telling stories will ensure that you do not become enmeshed in their disputes.

3. SATURDAY. Sensitive. Today's eclipsed Virgo Full Moon connects your career activities with home and family matters, bringing changes or completion to one or both of these areas. If traveling to your place of employment every day is becoming too time consuming, consider moving closer to work. Renting or purchasing larger living quarters could also improve your living conditions, resulting in a happier family life. If you have a house for sale you could receive good news about the chance of selling your property. An interested party may now be eager to negotiate a price. Enter into discussions, but defer signing on the dotted line until next Wednesday, when Mercury moves into direct motion.

4. SUNDAY. Lively. Motivation will only emerge if you are engaged in tasks that fully occupy your mind and are enjoyable. Allowing plenty of time for rest and relaxation can help to remove built-up stress and calm frazzled emotions stemming from yesterday's Full Moon influences. Choose your company carefully if socializing. A relative could trump you in the tactless department. They may mean well, however, so be diplomatic and ignore any poorly chosen words or harsh criticism. Take in a musical or a comedy show tonight. Sharing laughter and good times with a few good friends can make this a night to remember.

5. MONDAY. Fortunate. Enjoy this excellent day which combines romance and good fortune. Plenty of excitement is coming your way. Lucky Sagittarius can look forward to an unexpected surprise in the form of fortunate news or a chance windfall. An ambition or desire that you have had for a long time could also begin to move to fruition, giving you heightened anticipation. Turn to friends if you need advice or support, especially if this involves purchasing a home or property. They may have inside knowledge that can help you cut a few corners. Setting aside some private time to spend with your mate or partner should be rewarding.

6. TUESDAY. Popular. With your popularity on the rise and your energy increasing, the urge to get out and about will be dominant. A romantic relationship should continue to bubble along nicely, so make the most of this happy time. Realizing that your feelings of affection for that special person run deeper than you were consciously aware of could come as a delightful surprise. Insight and a new understanding of where you are heading are likely once you admit the depth of your feelings. Budding Sagittarius authors should send off a manuscript even if previously rejected. This time you could get the byline or publicity you deserve.

7. WEDNESDAY. Lucky. You have entered a lucky period. The two planets of wealth, bountiful Jupiter which is your ruler and income-attracting Venus, are forming a fortunate association over the next few days. Benefits range from a gift bestowed by a lover, a lottery win, or a financial windfall coming your way through a sports event. Accept an invitation to attend a social gathering or recreational activity. Gains will far outweigh any inconvenience of staying out late when you have to work in the morning. The thinking planet Mercury begins to move forward in the Aquarius sector of transportation and information, making this a favorable time to take your car in for mechanical servicing.

8. THURSDAY. Artistic. Creative urges are strongly enhanced. In addition, you now have heightened ability to stimulate other people in a range of diverse topics from educational aims and philosophical issues to artistic endeavors. Combining business and pleasure should bring positive long-term implications if you want to build a network of retail or commercial contacts. Sometimes dreams can just seem too far off and not really obtainable. However, the future belongs to those who are proactive. If travel, beginning a new venture, and buying your own home are cherished desires on your current wish list, your efforts may now be realized as one of your dreams moves closer to reality.

9. FRIDAY. Sincere. A love affair that has been more about fun and good times could now achieve a new level of commitment, prompting serious analysis of your feelings. For Sagittarius singles, the matchmaking antics of a friend who relishes this type of activity could be a winner this time around. Go along with their plans. You have nothing to lose and everything to gain if you find your lifetime partner. Ask and you should receive today. The chances are good of a favor being granted by an authority figure or one of your relatives. Creative energies are at full strength, increasing your enjoyment in the finer things of life.

10. SATURDAY. Cautious. Don't allow other people to take advantage of your easygoing nature. Insist that all members of the household help with routine weekend chores. Teenage children may have to be reminded that tasks have to be completed before they venture out to socialize. Otherwise you will be left to do their work. Participate in leisure pursuits that are pleasant, relaxing, and not overly strenuous since your vim and vitality are lower than normal. If going out to socialize or to grace the party scene this evening, be extra cautious of how much food and alcohol you consume. Otherwise digestion problems could develop, spoiling your fun.

11. SUNDAY. Auspicious. Make a physical workout or exercise from walking or riding a bike part of your daily routine now to increase fitness. Without feeling pressured, give serious consideration to a new offer even if it carries a small risk. Future dividends could more than compensate. As a typical Sagittarius you value your freedom and independence, and this is a time to do something special just for yourself. If you are obligated to care for an elderly parent or relative, asking someone else to take over for a little while can give you a needed break. This will restore motivation and make you feel alive and free again, even if only for a short period.

12. MONDAY. Important. Focus on a more responsible attitude toward finances and personal possessions. If you are owed money by someone who has consistently failed to pay you back or always comes up with lame excuses, confront them. Ask why they are so tardy with repaying the money and when they intend to do so. Don't be put off by any more excuses. Insist that a repayment plan be worked out and strictly adhered to. For currently single Sagittarius, wonderful romantic opportunities could spring up when least expected. Partnered Sagittarius can look forward to strengthened ties of affectionate.

13. TUESDAY. Changeable. Events occurring this morning could produce petty annoyances. There is not much you can do but go with the flow and allow the day to unfold. Mechanical problems could force you to dig deep into your wallet to pay for service and repairs that have escalated above the original price quote. Don't stress too much about this. Fortunately you could be on the receiving end of cash coming from an unexpected source, which will help relieve financial pressure. Hidden aspects of a love affair could come to light. Or someone might reveal their true feelings for you, bringing surprise, delight, and a possible proposal.

14. WEDNESDAY. Industrious. Make sure you have a healthy breakfast before setting out for this very busy day. Running errands, commuting, and trying to stay on top of your heavy load will keep you constantly on the move. Although you might feel the need for a little variety in your life, there may be more than you want today. You may be consumed by thoughts spinning round and round in your mind, hindering your ability to focus on anything in particular. Stay in contact with your home or office, checking your messages frequently or you might miss important information or a lucrative lead.

15. THURSDAY. Mixed. If outdated technology is holding you back, consider upgrading computer equipment or purchasing new software to make your job easier. Call and obtain price estimates. You are likely to find just what you are looking for, and at an affordable price. Sagittarius students presenting a paper or taking an exam should be pleasantly surprised by the results. There is a good possibility this evening of losing your cool with a family member, an act that is not usual in your nature. Try to keep a lid on your feelings to quell irritation. Otherwise it can take on a life of its own, leading to a display of bad temper and escalating tension that you will regret.

16. FRIDAY. Intense. Matters relating to a short trip or transportation issues could lead to scouring the newspaper in search of a new or more reliable set of wheels. These may range from a bicycle or scooter to a car or even a plane. If you intend purchasing any means of transportation, wait until after midmorning. Planetary influences are then more supportive, allowing you to negotiate a better deal. Romantic Venus is forming a harmonious pattern with sexy Pluto, intensifying the love life of all Sagittarius. This configuration will convey feelings of emotional satisfaction for those in a stable partnership. This could also put the emphasis on possessive traits, which need to be kept under control if you want your relationship to remain on an even keel.

17. SATURDAY. Positive. Determination and willpower to improve your health and lifestyle, with the aim of slowing down the aging process, receives a boost now that Venus has entered her own sign of Taurus. This accentuates your sixth house of health, work, and daily routine. There is also a chance to update your work wardrobe so that you stand out on the job. If you are on a housing list you might soon move right to the top, improving your comfort and conditions. For Sagittarius singles, a special person could be attracted to you, possibly a new colleague or someone otherwise connected to your place of employment.

18. SUNDAY. Revitalizing. Today's New Moon eclipse in the sign of Pisces indicates an ending of one cycle with a significant fresh one beginning. This provides a perfect chance to embark on a new chapter in your life. Changes may come through a family member, domestic link, or relocation to new living quarters. It is also the perfect time to entertain loved ones or just enjoy the companionship of family members and loved ones. For those who recently moved into a new home, organizing a housewarming party within the next two weeks should ensure that all your guests will have a good time.

19. MONDAY. Lucky. Good fortune through a sports event or game could come your way, possibly providing enough cash for a down payment on a new home or apartment. If you hope to become a home owner, investigate alternate financing. Having the knack of efficiently handling problems raised by the boss or another authority figure is your key to career advancement. Just refrain from exhibiting a know-it-all attitude. Instead display confidence and go about your job quietly. Those in charge are then bound to be pleased with your work. A good dose of cooperation and compromise might be needed to avoid disharmony at home this evening.

20. TUESDAY. Dynamic. Life should be much more animated now that the Sun is shining in adventurous Aries, spotlighting your leisure and pleasure sector. Sagittarius with artistic talent should be bursting with inspiration. Ideas will flow freely. Creative plans that you have been formulating in your mind are now ready to be put into action. If you have been experiencing some lack in your love life, it should now begin to improve. Your popularity is increasing and social invitations are on the rise. A hobby or pastime that you feel passionate about could bring you a measure of fame as well as financial gain.

21. WEDNESDAY. Eventful. Impatience could surface because you are likely to resent the behavior or manner of a coworker or family member who insists on trying to change your mind or attitude. Smile, stay cool, and relax. Annoying issues can be resolved without too much drama or tension. Sagittarius animal lovers are under excellent cosmic influences. There is a possibility that your favorite pet could beat the other competition and take a blue ribbon. Consider joining a social gym class. Not only will your health and fitness improve, your circle of friends will also expand. Don't forget to return a phone call.

22. THURSDAY. Emotional. Controlling anger requires tolerance and fortitude since your temper is prone to erupt quickly. Conversely, holding in feelings of resentment and annoyance can be just as damaging. If your emotions reach a point where you are about to burst, don't make a public spectacle of yourself. Instead, head for a place where you can release your feelings in private. Pace yourself over the next few days. Mars, planet of physical resources, forms an unhappy alliance with restrictive Saturn, eroding energy and causing possible difficulties if you are employed in strenuous manual tasks. Although patience is limited, chores that require a meticulous effort or a steady hand can progress favorably.

23. FRIDAY. Cheerful. Rekindled energy and a return of some motivation and enthusiasm greet you this morning, providing something to be happy about. Finding yourself the center of attraction at a social gathering can be a pleasant surprise for the friendly Archer. Make the most of opportunities of a personal or professional nature. A talent for photography can be utilized over the weekend, capturing family exploits and adventures at a family gathering. Record the event for future generations to enjoy. Or you may want to use it in a documentary to further career advancement in the realm of movie making. Today's project is to check all your photography equipment and be sure you have needed supplies.

24. SATURDAY. Fortunate. Although not as fortunate as yesterday, good luck is still gracing your chart. There is a need to be extremely creative in order to work out some of today's problems. This is unlikely to faze you for very long, as you realize that traditional methods are not the answer now. You might need to suspend the flood of cash being spent on a social engagement or leisure pursuit for you or for a child. Review how much more money will be required so that it doesn't become an endless flow of cash. For Sagittarius singles a promising encounter brings delight, with the possibility of an enduring love affair.

25. SUNDAY. Fair. There will not be a lot of energy for strenuous activities. However, a few hours spent cleaning can help refresh the household. Remove possessions or clothing that you or family members no longer wear or need. Donating to a worthwhile charity can give you a good feeling knowing that other people can benefit from your discards. For health reasons check the expiration date on food in the pantry and the fridge, discarding whatever is long out of date. Mars merging with Neptune emphasizes replacing ideas and plans that are now worn out with ones that have a better likelihood of success. You need to do away with the old to make way for the new.

26. MONDAY. Useful. A carefree approach toward financial matters could be regretted at a later date. Call a creditor if you envision problems paying an account on time. Having something repossessed or a vital service cut off could be embarrassing as well as inconvenient. Maintain a responsible attitude toward monetary matters. Keep abreast of the ups and downs of stocks, bonds, or other investments. Follow the trends and take action when needed. Your talents and skills may lead to receiving an award of some sort for original work. This will bolster pride in your work and yourself.

27. TUESDAY. Active. Even though you are very popular at the moment, try not to schedule too much. You will get more satisfaction giving quality time to social engagements and friends who matter rather than scattering your energies far and wide. You might consider becoming a travel guide, combining your passion for travel with your talent for teaching. As a Sagittarius you are used to handling your own affairs and are more likely to give advice than receive it. Right now, however, you could be the one who needs some assistance or wise counsel. You might need to go away in order to get things straightened out in your head. Today is a good time to plan a short vacation or a weekend getaway.

28. WEDNESDAY. Beneficial. A short trip for business or educational purposes will bring a sense of liberation. As a Sagittarius you do not like standing still for very long. Studying new concepts and beliefs is also favored. Your ability to understand abstract ideas and your desire to obtain more knowledge are strong. Just be wary of entering into arguments or debates. There is a tendency to try to force your views on other people. Later in the day your ability to go with the flow will be stretched to the limit. Household matters become pressure-packed, with the possibility of having to deal with criticism regarding the way you are handling domestic responsibilities.

29. THURSDAY. Empowering. Eating regular meals, participating in physical exercise, and getting plenty of sleep are all important components. Be especially good to yourself if you are a student hoping to be successful or if you are studying for an important exam. Misunderstandings can arise between loved ones. Keeping your cool and reflecting on all that you love about the other person will give you a more stable perspective that enables you to find the middle ground. Be particularly careful midmorning, which is a period when disagreements could erupt. A new love affair might take you to unknown places and make you forget all about your responsibilities.

30. FRIDAY. Productive. There is not much happening in the universe to impede progress on the job, making it possible for you to get twice the amount of work done if you remain focused. There could be some good news regarding revenue from a business. Or a work-related issue might lead to a raise, bonus, or larger than expected commission check. An older relative could be experiencing problems that are your main concern at the moment. Visit or call them to let them know how much you care. Say whatever is on your mind. They might be relieved to finally get things out in the open.

31. SATURDAY. Pleasant. This is a fortunate day regarding romance and monetary matters. However, this does not guarantee that you are going to win in love or get the jackpot, but it can be fun trying. All dealings with authority figures need to be treated with extra caution and a degree of diplomacy. The aggressive side of your personality could be on display, which is unlikely to help your cause. Even if you prefer low-key entertainment, don't stay home watching television. Immerse your senses in creative exploration. Or make a point of experiencing something different, even if it is just going for a walk or a drive to somewhere you haven't been before.

APRIL

1. SUNDAY. Exciting. You begin the new month with Pluto, the small planet of powerful influences, turning retrograde in the skies. This accentuates your house of personal appearance and projects. Over the next few months temper flare-ups could increase unless you use this energy constructively. This is also a time to rid yourself of an outmoded look and replace it with a trendy new image that reflects your current thinking. In addition, review, rethink, and revise personal plans, philosophies, and interests. Expect the unexpected and be prepared to act spontaneously. Doors might suddenly open up, providing opportunities you never dreamed would be coming your way.

2. MONDAY. Sensitive. Romantic involvement could lead to emotional upsets if you and your partner are not considerate of each other's feelings. The Full Moon in gentle Libra increases the importance of finding a balance in all of your relationships. Compromise on minor matters. Try not to demand too much over the next two weeks or you might discover that people dig their heels in and refuse to even give an inch. Although your creative energies may seem blocked, increased effort and hard work will lead to success.

A volunteer organization can inspire you to join in and donate your skills, time, or money to a worthy cause.

3. TUESDAY. Promising. Your enthusiastic and optimistic attitude makes you a welcome addition to any circle, lightening up the sober atmosphere of the day. If you have something to prove to yourself or to other people, this could be an opportunity to link up with those who are seriously intent about moving forward. Together you can accomplish whatever needs to be done. Even though your talents are vast, best results will come from not exaggerating or underestimating your own abilities. Be wary when it comes to making decisions. Friends are your greatest allies, so don't hesitate to lean on people who care about you.

4. WEDNESDAY. Confusing. Take sanctuary in a quiet place, working alone and preferably from home. Confusing influences prevail. Take care or you could easily misunderstand or misconstrue something that is stated in ambiguous terms. Forgetting an appointment, overlooking significant details, or making mistakes on the job is also possible if your concentration begins to lapse. Sagittarius singles are likely to prefer staying home instead of having to deal with the superficial social circuit. However, if you do decide to mingle with other people, remove your rose-colored glasses to avoid deception in a romantic situation.

5. THURSDAY. Variable. Ensure that your reputation remains intact by keeping personal and confidential matters to yourself. Not everyone in your family or social circle is completely trustworthy today. The loyalty as well as individualism shown by a pet can be a source of inspiration for animal-loving Sagittarius. If you have room at home and feel drawn to a particular dog, cat, or even fish, consider bringing one home so that you can share your affection with the pet. Someone in your work environment could be openly flirtatious with you. Although flattering, you might need to back off if either of you is already romantically involved with someone else.

6. FRIDAY. Changeable. The emotional atmosphere from the last few days now lightens up as the Moon gallops into your sign of Sagittarius, bringing welcome relief. Change is also in the air as Mars, planet of action, moves into your Pisces sector of domestic concerns. Mars in a water sign can diffuse energy, bringing a need to pace both yourself and the activities you participate in so that you do not run out of steam. This is only a temporary situation.

Take some time out, slow down, and relax more. If employed in a job requiring strenuous physical labor, ask your boss to schedule some time off to conserve your physical resources.

7. SATURDAY. Lucky. A fortunate period continues for those born under the lucky sign of Sagittarius. This is a very favorable time for enhancing your appearance by going for a new hair style or purchasing new clothes. With your ruler Jupiter retrograde in your first house along with Pluto, diet is emphasized. Those who are inclined to suffer from weight fluctuation will need to eat less if weight needs to come off, or eat more if a weight gain is required. A romantic person could make a welcome appearance in your life at this time. Don't get nervous or uptight. Just be yourself; that is what was appealing in the first place.

8. SUNDAY. Fruitful. Your heightened sense of responsibility combined with a good dose of luck provide the impetus and confidence to launch a new venture or tackle something that you have never tried before. It will be fun to push yourself harder or further than usual, or to embark upon an ambitious venture. First listen to your intuition, and don't jump unless it feels right. If you are searching for an activity that is interesting and can add to your net financial worth, check out antique, junk, and thrift shops. You might find a bargain that you can bring home, restore, and then sell for a handsome profit.

9. MONDAY. Motivating. You should be feeling energetic, motivated, and willing to act on or follow through with all of your commitments. Professional Sagittarius sportspeople will be rewarded for hard work and perseverance with training. It is starting to pay off, and you are apt to be selected for the team. This ensures a healthy boost to your future income from sponsors. Even amateur athletes will find that a superior fitness level increases sporting prowess. A child may need help with a creative endeavor. Working jointly can draw you closer together. Plan to go out for a special treat when you have completed tasks as you will deserve a little indulgence.

10. TUESDAY. Intense. Refrain from taking impulsive action regarding your financial assets. Subsequent proceedings might not turn out the way you envision. Instead give yourself time to assess the situation, then react based on factual knowledge. Control your tongue. Today Mercury, the communication planet, enters your assertive Aries house of creative expression and also squares off with passionate Pluto. Friends, neighbors, or siblings might feel especially fragile, perhaps with explosive emotions. Do not initiate intense communications or a debate. However, the evening is perfect for a romantic date with your mate or lover.

11. WEDNESDAY. Eventful. Although you may prefer to relax and take it easy, you might need to make a number of short journeys throughout the day. You probably have a lot of errands to run as well as projects that require attention. If you are trying to decide on a gift for a special someone, asking a family member could give you a few clues. Or you could decide to trust your own judgment, which should prove to be right on the mark. Expressing yourself through reciting your own poetry, acting in a local drama group, or performing in a variety act can produce an adrenaline rush and put your name up in lights.

12. THURSDAY. Mixed. You will be better off keeping to yourself as much as possible if feeling sad or depressed. It is best to work through these feelings on your own. Other people are not apt to be too sympathetic to your situation. Don't judge yourself harshly. Give yourself a pep talk to provide motivation, then go out and create new goals or complete those already in the pipeline. A neighborhood project might capture your imagination and rope you into working side by side for the betterment of your community. If you think you don't have the time to participate, it would be worth rearranging your schedule.

13. FRIDAY. Interesting. There is no need to worry too much about today's date. Cosmic influences lean toward positive situations occurring today. Sagittarius shoppers should be able to find lots of bargains, especially at garage sales and auctions. It also wouldn't hurt to check classified ads. Travelers seeking to pick up a few exotic souvenirs can purchase items that offer good memories. Be sure to haggle over the price, which is often half the enjoyment for both buyer and seller overseas. If at loose ends you could host an impromptu theme party and invite a few friends to share a casual buffet dinner.

14. SATURDAY. Fair. Anticipate a certain amount of forgetfulness or confused thinking. This will heighten annoyance and cause tolerance for other people to disappear. You need to find balance if you want peace and harmony to reign on the home front. If continually bothered by something that is old, tired, or damaged and needs to be replaced, remove it from sight as soon as possible. Even if you are unable to afford replacing it right now, the energy will lift once the object is removed. An evening on the dance floor with that special person in your life could be the exercise and therapy you need to unwind and destress after the busy week.

15. SUNDAY. Joyous. Take time out today for romance, music, art, or any of the more pleasurable aspects of life. Relationships can be delightful, although they take effort and resourcefulness if you're hoping for a long-term association. Being too easygoing with a child may cause more problems in the long run. Instead, be firm and fair in all of your dealings and you will gain love and respect in return. Sports-minded Sagittarius singles will gain opportunities for romance by attending a game. Expect surprises this evening, such as visitors arriving just as you are about to sit down to a romantic candlelit dinner. Be gracious about changing plans.

16. MONDAY. Empowering. A stroke of luck or a fortunate change is highly probable. Successful speculation could be the turning point for you. Your childhood recollections could prove interesting to someone researching how times have changed, and you will find it pleasant to reminisce about people and places from the past. Someone might try to coerce you into a new financial plan to ensure future stability. Although this is not a bad thing and they mean well, you are apt to resent the interference. To keep the peace, listen and learn but don't commit to anything. With your strong feelings for your romantic partner, this is an excellent time to show your affection by taking the initiative.

17. TUESDAY. Lucrative. If you have an offer to present or accept, don't hesitate to act. The positive influences of the Aries New Moon makes this one of the best possible astrological cycles to begin a new venture. Important decisions that affect your romantic life, such as saying yes to a marriage proposal, can be made providing you are certain that your judgment is correct. Whatever you decide now is likely to be enduring. You may discover new interests or hobby pursuits as you feel the urge to widen your scope. This could eventually be the source of a rewarding part-time business. Matters of the heart bring a smile to the face of singles who are seeking a new love.

18. WEDNESDAY. Starred. A strong sense of dedication will help you advance toward your aims. However, if boredom and disinterest overtake you, you will be distracted from the main goal. New methods of operation could come to your attention, possibly involving modern technology. This can accelerate processes, increase the bottom line for your boss or organization, and flow on to you through a pay raise. If you are going on an important job interview you should be successful. Your Sagittarius charisma and enthusiasm make you larger than life. A love of your work may take you away from home and family more than they like. You need to make some compromises for the sake of harmony; talk it out with them for the best result.

19. THURSDAY. Encouraging. Initiate contact with other people in your line of work or reach out to those who can offer career assistance. Different ideas regarding your life's direction need to be ironed out between you and your mate or partner. Find time to discuss this. Treat your loved one's concerns as important and you will be able to work out problems amicably and cooperatively. It is vital to get grievances out in the open so that tension does not build to an unmanageable level. Some relief now comes with Saturn, the planet of testing situations, again moving forward, which should free up tricky situations that have been stalled or stuck.

20. FRIDAY. Manageable. Mixed trends prevail throughout the day. Irritations and conflicts are likely with those you see on a regular basis. And generalized feelings of intolerance or edginess are other possible manifestations of the current cosmic energy. Relationship difficulties need a fair amount of patience and understanding before you can expect to arrive at a satisfactory resolution. The Sun shimmies into the money-oriented sign of Taurus, urging Sagittarius to prepare for possible changes over the next four weeks regarding health, domestic life, or employment conditions. If you hold a steady job, consider asking the boss for a wage increase if one is overdue and deserved.

21. SATURDAY. Focused. You are likely to be more focused than usual, determined to accomplish whatever you set out to do. Although those born under the sign of Sagittarius are known as a freedom-loving party animal, you also know how to work. Your dream of travel, education, or a larger home looms large now, leading to working harder than ever to realize these goals. A personal or business partner may try your patience with some bullying tactics this morning. The best response for a peaceful outcome is not to be drawn into a dispute. Put off trying to resolve the problem until the afternoon hours; otherwise you might come out on the losing end.

22. SUNDAY. Energizing. This is another day when extra effort brings better than expected rewards. An insurance or legal matter may involve charging a friend, leaving you feeling a little guilty. However, if your friend is adequately covered, this situation should end up being beneficial to both of you. Fill out the necessary paperwork the same as if you were dealing with a stranger rather than someone you know. Restlessness ensures that you remain on the go. You might opt for the fresh air and the wide open spaces, or you might prefer to focus on a pet project at home. If in need of retail therapy, a trip to the shopping mall will be right up your alley, although you are bound to spend more than you intend.

23. MONDAY. Challenging. You could decide to seek counseling because of a negative pattern that keeps recurring in your life. With help you can overcome unconscious triggers and remain on the right path. Consideration and assistance shown to a colleague are likely to be repaid at a later time. Right now, however, the reward will be their ability to efficiently handle work tasks and the inner knowledge that you have the skill to be a successful tutor. Issues with your significant other could occur due to today's clash between Venus and Mars. This can cause conflict at home as relationship values are challenged. Organize fun activities to keep love on fire and arguments at bay.

24. TUESDAY. Helpful. The typical Sagittarius displays a general tendency of curiosity, always reading and researching to gain more knowledge and wisdom regarding diverse topics. Today, however, finding an interest that keeps you stimulated might prove difficult. Unless you are determined to waste time browsing bookshops, websites, or the local library, it might be wise to become involved in more practical activities. The feeling of being lucky increases the possibility of overestimating your abilities to handle a particular task. Be careful not to pledge too much now. Doing so could make you look foolish when you are unable to deliver on all of your promises.

25. WEDNESDAY. Industrious. Duty and responsibility are the key to career success, overshadowing other issues. Your ability to concentrate on business and occupational matters is excellent, making this the time to attend to details and handle practical concerns designed to make your life more stable and secure. If you are not yet in a vocation of choice, work with a volunteer organization will suit you and also let you gain extra skills that aid your career decision. Taking the plunge in love requires you to walk the talk. If you are ready to make a commitment, surprise the love of your life with a heartfelt proposal.

26. THURSDAY. Exciting. Your increased powers of concentration and stronger communication skills convey a renewed sense of self-confidence and assurance. If you are dissatisfied with a current situation, concerns can be articulately voiced to the appropriate people who might be able to sort out unresolved issues. An urge to be more active on the social scene, seeking new contacts and interests, may lead to parties or venues where other singles congregate. There is a possibility of a surprising romantic encounter that makes your heart soar. If you are half of a couple, keeping your love life exciting will keep your mate or partner committed.

27. FRIDAY. Stabilizing. You are now highly focused and goal oriented, giving other people cause to marvel at your innate sense of timing. Your ability to draw on little used skills and expertise is very useful now with the entrance of adaptable Mercury joining the Sun in your solar Taurus house of work and service. If business and retail sales or orders have been slower than usual, expect this to change. Increased interest in your wares is likely. If you are the boss, implementing new work practices or installing more advanced technology and equipment will provide improvements on the job, increasing productivity as well as raising staff morale.

28. SATURDAY. Slow. Today you can't escape a number of cosmic influences as well as the opposition between your ruler, jovial Jupiter, and Venus, lover of luxury. This is apt to make you prone to laziness. Since it is a day off for many, take full advantage by slowing down and relaxing. A child's spending habits might cause an argument between you and your mate or partner. Try not to become emotional. Stay practical and avoid getting into the blame game or you will get nowhere. Don't place yourself in situations where temptation lurks since self-discipline is unlikely to be very strong.

29. SUNDAY. Unpredictable. Being able to fulfill your current hopes and desires depends more on hard work than good fortune right now. You are likely to experience a dash of luck to help you on your way. Over the next few days aggressive Mars challenges excessive Jupiter, your Sun sign ruler, indicating that self-control is likely to be in short supply. As a result you need to plan your activities to avoid wasting energy and resources on nonproductive ventures. Home renovators should be especially careful of beginning a project that involves plumbing and pipes. Make sure that drains are thoroughly checked before impulsively starting any work.

30. MONDAY. Variable. Although the day has a dreamy atmosphere, there is also the chance of arguments arising at the drop of a hat. Today's celestial influences encourage focusing on developing your creative skills. Channel your inspirational thoughts into writing a story, music, or poetry. Or follow through with an artistic pursuit where imagination but not aggression can take free rein. An irritating problem at home can be solved through sheer persistence. Traveling to or reading about a place less fortunate than your country of birth might spark your compassion and start you thinking about what you as an individual can do to help in a direct way.

MAY

1. TUESDAY. Lackluster. If possible, work from home today or take the day off if you have some sick leave or vacation days due you. You are apt to feel totally drained. Trying to revitalize your energy could prove challenging even for the most motivated Sagittarius. An unresolved emotional issue that has been kept under wraps might be the reason for ongoing lethargy. Addressing the problem by clearing the air sooner rather than later could be the answer to relieving stress and returning you to vim and vitality. Minor injuries can happen to even the most safety-conscious Sagittarius unless you watch what you are doing and don't try to hurry a task.

2. WEDNESDAY. Uneasy. Making changes to your everyday routine is not easy under the intense influence of the current Scorpio Full Moon. If you want positive developments to occur in your life, this is the time to end something that has been hanging around for some time, especially something you have put off deciding. Hoping for divine intervention or for the situation to miraculously disappear, although optimistic, is an unrealistic approach. Even if making the break causes initial sadness, take the step to improve your overall life. Be wary of an influential person who could be giving you bad advice, possibly intentionally to serve their own purposes.

3. THURSDAY. Busy. With the Moon in Sagittarius, the focus shifts to your personal wants and needs. Go that extra mile and spoil yourself a little. Personal accomplishment is also important. This is a period when projects can be started that you have had in mind for a while but haven't had the time, energy, or motivation to do something about. Protect your interests against computer or electrical failures by making sure all data that you do not have a copy of is backed up. Missing the bus, train, or an important appointment is foreseen. Keep your renowned good humor intact and you will keep stress to a minimum. Don't forget an important family member's birthday or anniversary.

4. FRIDAY. Distracting. You could be preoccupied with everything that you shouldn't be and focus on nothing of much importance. With the weekend looming ahead, you might be in a relaxed mood from first thing this morning. Concentration will be needed quickly if you hope to complete outstanding responsibilities. Sagittarius employers may experience frustration due to a staff shortage or inefficiency on the job. Meeting a commitment and completing or delivering urgent orders might only occur with a hands-on approach, joining your staff to get the work done. Music can have a healing effect this evening, even stimulating your creative urges.

5. SATURDAY. Changeable. Be ready to adapt to possible changes occurring around the home front. A roommate or older child could decide that now is the right time to move into their own apartment and establish a household of their own. This is an excellent period to make essential renovations and adjustments to your living quarters while Mars activates your domestic concerns. However, care must be taken if you are handling these tasks yourself. Be sure to call the gas company or an electrician if these areas are part of maintenance or renovations this weekend. Amusement that is interesting and stimulates the mind might be the preferred option for evening entertainment.

6. SUNDAY. Passionate. Your ability to do several things at once is an asset that will come in handy unless you act impulsively. An old grievance, possible one that relates to money, may provoke tension at a family gathering. Use your superb negotiation skills to defuse an argument and smooth over lingering tension. If personal finances are tight right now, be discriminating with how you manage monetary affairs. This will help your bank balance to grow, putting you back on track quicker than expected. Prepare for abundant passion and love with your mate or partner if you are in an intense romantic situation. If currently solo, beware of jealous tendencies that could end an affair.

7. MONDAY. Exhausting. An unrelenting workload could be weighing heavily on you, making it difficult to concentrate on what you should be doing. Learning more about time management can take the pressure out of meeting your busy schedule and alleviate stress from your working day. Another option is to reschedule or delegate less important appointments or domestic matters so that you have extra hours to complete urgent obligations. Although time consuming, personally check for errors and verify that all paperwork is authentic. There is a likelihood of inaccurate data, so double-checking could save a lot of effort in the long term.

8. TUESDAY. Promising. Venus, the planet of attraction, moves into your Cancer house of other people's money. This will support plans to get an enterprise off the ground. If you are looking for financial backing, it should be forthcoming if you approach the right people with the appropriate facts and figures. If experiencing monetary hassles, consider tightening your budget. If you have already implemented a strict financial plan, obtaining one loan to cover all the smaller loans and accounts could make it easier for you to repay. Romance could blossom for Sagittarius singles with someone on the job. Dress to impress when meeting clients and associates.

9. WEDNESDAY. Uncertain. Changes to your work hours, job description, employment conditions, or implementation of new technology might appear to be positive. However, you may not have been told the full story. Additional responsibility, increased overtime, and effort to make the new reforms work efficiently are some of the issues that might be kept hidden. An after-hours get-together with coworkers or other people you see on a regular basis is unlikely to be lively and could end up being a flop. You might be better off heading home and spending time with a relative. Or leave in order to study or to watch an interesting current affairs program. You can keep informed without being physically present.

10. THURSDAY. Testing. The challenging aspect between your ruler, over-the-top Jupiter, and erratic Uranus could encourage you to seek a larger residence or move to a more upscale location. Being patient is not one of your endearing qualities, so if mortgage money is an issue consider changing your furniture or decor or adding an extra room to provide more living space instead of actually moving. Sudden demands could catch you off guard, but don't let this irritate you. Instead, take everything in stride even if you are fuming inside. Other people will be impressed by your ability to accept a challenge without the accompaniment of loud moans and complaints.

11. FRIDAY. Fair. This is another day when self-discipline needs to be in full force. Maintaining productivity is important despite increasing anticipation of a big event over the weekend. This must not be allowed to interfere with your daily functioning. Change is as good as a vacation. You are likely to still be considering moving or purchasing a property. Talkative Mercury now moves into your Gemini seventh house of relationships, assisting your ability to improve understanding and to cooperate with others. If an honest, open discussion is needed to clear the air with a business or professional partner, this is the time to begin such a discussion.

12. SATURDAY. Bumpy. Feeling low probably has more to do with the confusing celestial influences that are depleting your vitality rather than anything serious to worry about. On top of a number of sagas that you might experience throughout the day, domestic repairs or breakdowns could make you totally exasperated, as if nothing will ever go right again. However, don't despair. Life is bound to appear brighter in a day or two. If you cannot afford to purchase a necessary new replacement, a local charity shop may have an inexpensive used item that will do until you can afford to purchase a new product.

13. SUNDAY. Risky. You are likely to experience high voltage as well as some restless energy. This needs careful handling in order for you to make the most of the day. You are in an accident-prone period, so take special care when working around home base. If you are inclined to manage your own home repairs and maintenance, beware of standing on or under a ladder and reaching up to high places. A simmering personal matter might cause you to issue or accept a challenge, but think about this first. Rash or impulsive action could land you in trouble. Solo Sagittarius looking for romance should be alert to an unexpected opportunity for a passionate encounter. Just be sure to stay away from dangerous people or locations.

14. MONDAY. Frustrating. Frustrating stars are out again today, which could force a change in your schedule. Try hard to take this in stride. Fretting about delays or alterations will not help and will only end up increasing your stress. If setting off on a vacation trip or work journey be proactive in order to cope with a change of circumstances. Leave home early if driving. If traveling by public transportation, call a taxi in advance or catch an earlier bus, train, or ferry to take you to your destination in plenty of time to make connections. A teenage child needs your guidance as opposed to discipline, plus extra thought for their emotional state. You'll remember how it was.

15. TUESDAY. Constructive. Mars is now settling into his own sign of Aries, in your solar fifth sector. This indicates that you are now in the mood for adventure, challenge, and especially for love if currently single. A good way to get a relationship fired up is to take immediate action. Pick up the phone, and making a date with that new romantic interest will bring rewards. Although you are on a winning streak, a sensible attitude and avoidance of foolish risks are required if you are to come through this period unscratched. A creative project can both energize and inspire all your actions, instilling them with a love of life and exploration. Entertaining or hosting a special party or event is bound to be successful.

16. WEDNESDAY. Rejuvenating. This afternoon's Taurus New Moon in your sixth house of health and work brings opportunities to take the initiative and implement plans for a grand new project or financial enterprise. Investigating a new employment option or attending a job interview should also produce desired results. Catching up with boring routine tasks such as balancing your checkbook, paying bills, or organizing your filing cabinet or desk drawers can be emotionally satisfying. Beginning a new diet or fitness program, or hiring a personal trainer for those with little personal willpower, can lead to big improvements to your overall health and well-being.

17. THURSDAY. Supportive. Computers may have made your life less stressful as well as making it easier to obtain knowledge and record data. However, don't become so entrenched sitting in front of the screen that you use this to escape reality and forget about sharing your company with loved ones. The harmony of relating with other people is necessary for personal growth and is essential to maintain healthy relationships. Analyze your work performance or your staff's to see if you are operating at peak efficiency or if improvements can be implemented. If you are the boss be sure to congratulate staff members if a special deadline is met and perhaps give a few hours off as a reward.

18. FRIDAY. Talkative. Once you catch up on all your outstanding e-mails, phone calls, and general correspondence you will feel like a load has been taken off your back. As a Sagittarius you like to talk a lot more than you like to listen. Reverse that trend today and you may hear something to your benefit. Early this evening a nagging issue with your mate or partner could get under your skin. This might wind up as a dispute over something minor. Rather than attack or withdraw, try to find common ground to resolve the issue. A creative plan or project could be improved by making significant revisions or adjustments, so don't mull it over for too long. Just get on with the changes and you will be happy with the outcome.

19. SATURDAY. Difficult. The stars are not in the best position for this weekend. Endeavor to keep a low profile. Otherwise you could overreact to what someone says. Or perhaps one of your own comments will trigger an intense response, causing unnecessary stress and tension. Watch your spending, especially if you share an account with someone else. The tendency to go overboard is strong, which could deplete your bank balance to a dangerously low level. Feelings that you are trying hard to fulfill responsibilities but are not receiving needed support should be expressed and not concealed. If you are planning on entertaining or socializing, after dinner should be the most enjoyable part of the day.

20. SUNDAY. Trying. This is another day when an uneasy atmosphere prevails. A friend could put you on the spot by asking to borrow one of your prized possessions or a sum of money. It would be wise to politely say no, but you may feel generous and give in. It is not a good idea to loan money and items to anyone outside your immediate family because you might not see it or them again. Some relevant paperwork could be missing, so don't finalize any contract until you double-check all the facts, figures, and other information. With carelessness and a tendency to overlook details enhanced, it might be wise to enjoy the day off and catch up with outstanding work tomorrow.

21. MONDAY. Fortunate. This is an excellent day to schedule a vacation to begin in the second week of June, when Venus, the planet of good times, will support your travel plans. Marriage and other partnerships are positively accentuated with the movement of the shining Sun entering into your opposing sign of informative Gemini. Sales presentations, lectures, or training seminars should be highly successful, with positive accolades coming from your peers. Public life is also set to change. You may become the face of an advertising program or take over a corporate department or entire organization.

22. TUESDAY. Productive. This is a favorable period for study and research. If you are not currently a student and have little interest in furthering your formal education, you might get involved with genealogy, self-awareness, or spiritual topics. In-laws might want to take your child on a vacation and all you think about is your child's safety instead of the adventure they could experience. If you are in need of time out and are still researching possible destinations for your summer holiday, don't ignore cut-price package deals. If you are low on funds, consider special rates for off-season travel. You can still enjoy yourself and see the sights, and you won't have to worry about crowds.

23. WEDNESDAY. Helpful. Creativity and imagination are intensified now. Business meetings will be successful, and international affairs can be conducted agreeably. For parents, this is a time to lend support to a youngster's school, team, or religious class. Sponsoring a special activity for a good cause or giving a few hours of your time to train or coach a team will be well worth the effort and will be appreciated by those who benefit the most. If inclined to spendthrift behavior, your tastes might not suit your budget at the moment. Reappraise your spending habits and come up with some thrifty alternatives.

24. THURSDAY. Misleading. There is a good chance of missing an important appointment or meeting unless you check your calendar early this morning. Neptune, planet of confusing influences and creative urges, moves backward now, bringing past issues with siblings or neighbors to the surface for review and reexamination. Make appropriate overtures if this analysis reveals that you have made hasty judgments of a recent situation. Defer purchasing expensive musical equipment because you might decide on the first one you see instead of looking around for the best price. If shipping gifts or items overseas, be sure to get adequate insurance to guard against loss.

25. FRIDAY. Happy. An eventful day is assured for those intent on making inroads in the corporate world. Sagittarius in a committed partnership should take advantage of today's romantic trends and do something different to escape normal routine. This will put excitement back into your life. Slipping off for a romantic getaway or exploring a new locality can give you a new lease on life. Financing for home renovations or to purchase property can be unexpectedly approved, providing happiness to the whole household. Friends are likely to drop by unexpectedly this evening, so stock up on food and drink and enjoy an evening of fun and good company.

26. SATURDAY. Pleasurable. If you begin to experience a need for greater freedom and autonomy, follow these feelings. You might be able to find a way to make money by working from home, therefore becoming your own boss and creating flexible working hours. Other people will pay attention to your ideas and opinions. You can come up with a realistic solution to a perplexing family situation. If socializing outside the home does not appeal, recharge your batteries and tune into a latent creative skill. Or begin to get into a stimulating activity that has been dormant or put on hold for some time. You might prefer to invite guests over for a casual dinner, swapping stories over a leisurely meal.

27. SUNDAY. Inquisitive. You are in a probing mood, ready to dig out facts, figures, and secrets. Rather than sticking your nose in other people's business, even if unintentional, use this ability in a way that helps rather than hinders you. Check your bank statement and bills for errors, research a topic of interest, or begin writing a fictional story. This will keep you happily occupied in an industrious and worthwhile project. Sagittarius is about truth and fair play, so it might go against the grain today if you are asked to tell a little white lie. Figure out what is in the best interests for all concerned before making your decision. If a minor untruth is for the right reasons and no one will be hurt by it, go along.

28. MONDAY. Guarded. Harsh words spoken today could lead to a power struggle if steps are not taken to cool down touchy emotions and reduce the tension in the air. Some inside information could tempt you to speculate. Just make sure you can trust your source and that the investment will be secure. Intellectual Mercury now moves into your canny Cancer eighth house of joint monetary affairs and tax matters. Extra insight regarding fiscal concerns will be provided, so make sure you are alert over the next three weeks. Feelings of being taken for granted by your mate or partner are likely to bring discontentment, increasing stress and pressure.

29. TUESDAY. Sensitive. Your sensitivities are higher than usual, making you more impressionable and moody. Please yourself first, and don't wait for other people to do it for you. People are apt to grate on your nerves, so working alone or behind the scenes is the most suitable way to spend the day. This is also a favorable time to get some counseling to free yourself from unconscious drives that are holding you back. Someone from the past might want to reenter your life. The choice is yours, but you will first need to ensure that this time communication is going to be open and honest and that no issues will be kept hidden from you.

30. WEDNESDAY. Useful. Although you may not be antisocial, this is another day when you prefer to stay in the background, away from distractions and people. Lock your door and concentrate on finishing ongoing tasks and obligations. Don't begin a new project until you have a clean slate and an empty in basket. If spending the day away from work and in need of some social interaction, visit friends you rarely see or a relative who is confined to bed or sick in the hospital. Take along flowers or fruit, and stay for a long chat that will surely cheer them up and make you feel that you have done something worthwhile with your day.

31. THURSDAY. Energetic. The recent tendency to withdraw from contact with other people now disappears as the Moon slides into your own sign of Sagittarius. You should feel reenergized and enthusiastic, willing to follow through on a variety of specific commitments. This is a good time to initiate activity. Be aware of your instincts and first impressions. Social life continues to be full, but now you should feel more like participating and enjoying the company of loved ones, friends, and your significant other. When confronted with choices or decisions, think of your own needs as well as family obligations, then go for the options that mean the most to you.

JUNE

1. FRIDAY. Uplifting. Celestial influences are mainly positive as the Moon glides through Sagittarius, shining light on you and your personal plans and aspirations. If you are enamored with someone special, let your feelings be known in a subtle and discreet manner. Then the object of your affection can reject or accept your advances in the same discreet fashion. New clothes for work can add to the excitement of the day providing you spend your money wisely. Opt for an outfit that accentuates your style, not one that is merely current fashion fad that you might only wear once or twice. This is a good time to make a decision about whether you have time to take on a volunteer commitment or other nonpaying position.

2. SATURDAY. Useful. Whatever you have planned for the day, be prepared for last-minute changes which could throw you into a tailspin. Someone may let you down or have a change of heart about attending a social function without realizing or worrying about the inconvenience this creates for you. Rather than moping around, take advantage of the extra time to catch up on something you keep putting off. An older relative who does not normally interfere in your affairs could oppose one of your current ideas or plans and even become argumentative about it. Take this as an indication that they care a lot about you and listen to their words, which probably have merit.

3. SUNDAY. Disquieting. Dealing with money matters will be annoying but necessary for the spendthrift Archer. If your finances are not as healthy as you would like, reworking your household budget can enable you to save up for a trip that will give you much pleasure. With the high cost of gas these days, plan your route efficiently if setting off on a long journey by car. Be alert to mood swings if socializing. Keep financial and social matters separate to avoid arguments and gossip. Your own jealous feelings might be difficult to control. You may not be able to resist a confrontation if given the slightest cause to suspect the loyalty and trustworthiness of your mate or partner. Looks can be deceiving.

4. MONDAY. Bright. On this Monday morning you are ready to get down to business. This focus coupled with your tendency to be optimistic will begin to open new doors for you. If you cannot wait any longer to acquire a long-desired object, you should have little trouble obtaining a higher limit on your credit card now providing monthly payments have always been made on time. Your significant other might call with some terrific news regarding a career promotion, negotiating a lucrative deal, or some other professional success. Don't hide your pride. Go out and celebrate the achievement together even if you have to reschedule your own evening plans.

5. TUESDAY. Fortunate. A friend, sibling, or neighbor could encourage you to join in a fun social activity. Go along if you don't have any other pressing commitments. You might be surprised how enjoyable the day turns out to be. With Venus now in Leo transiting your sector of long-distance journeys and academic achievements, organizing an overseas vacation or applying for school will be attractive. Being born under the sign of Sagittarius makes you a natural lifelong learner. Airline travelers might receive a pleasant surprise as reservations to fly economy class are upgraded to a more expensive seat, making the journey much more comfortable. Or your compact rental car may be upgraded to a luxury sedan.

6. WEDNESDAY. Variable. News you were expecting regarding a legal matter might not come through again today, increasing frustration and anxiety. Although patience is not usually one of your virtues, it is necessary now. Paperwork might be held up by the court or one of the lawyers but should be delivered to you soon. Ties with friends or relatives living at a distance can grow stronger if you use Internet technology to have regular long chats. What you learn now can prove most helpful in furthering your career options. If you cannot decide where to obtain new skills, check a local community college for classes in new computer or communications expertise.

7. THURSDAY. Helpful. The day is likely to fly by quickly whether you are puttering around at home or have lots of little jobs to keep you fully occupied at work. Changing a few things can brighten the environment with a fresh new look. Optimism and big plans might set you on a collision course with reality, especially if you are considering home renovations. Hiring a professional might be the wisest action if you are new to do-it-yourself activities. Just be sure to thoroughly review all references and credentials before going ahead and hiring someone. For Sagittarius singles, romantic activity could come in the form of a short fling with a casual acquaintance.

8. FRIDAY. Promising. A change of profession or relocating to another area might be the answer to current dissatisfaction or unhappiness about your current work. However, before proceeding too far with your plans, make sure that family members who may be affected by the choices are also involved in the decision-making process. Be quick to accept an unexpected chance to move into the limelight even though what is expected of you might not be straightforward and could be quite difficult. As a Sagittarius you love a challenge, and stepping up now could have future benefits. If the pace has been hectic lately, try to relax and slow down tonight, spending time with loved ones.

9. SATURDAY. Fruitful. Creativity is stimulated, indicating that challenging activities and amusements that are out of the ordinary are required to keep you pleasantly occupied. A hobby or leisure pursuit could also be a source of extra income on a part-time basis. This is a good time for solo Sagittarius to make connections with new people, which could lead to more than just casual conversation. Your social life may be causing resentment because your partner feels neglected and in need of reassurance. Bring harmony back into your romantic life by trying to spend more time with the person you love and less time with your friends and colleagues.

10. SUNDAY. Smooth. The generous and caring side of your nature shines through, which could tempt you to give a lot of time and attention to helping others. This is very noble providing you also have sufficient time to spend with your nearest and dearest. If single, someone who conveys an air of authority and self-confidence, or wears a uniform, could appeal to your romantic side. Don't panic if you cannot afford to purchase an expensive present if you are going to attend a special celebration. It is the thought that counts, and costly gifts are not always necessary. Sometimes a simple, carefully bought present is worth far more for its sentimental value.

11. MONDAY. Active. Your Sagittarius optimism is at a high on this first day of the working week. Your judgment is sound, with the ability to take care of business in an orderly manner. You may amaze yourself by how much work you manage to get through. A superior might make suggestions that point the way toward a more fulfilling and prosperous career path. Although this could involve a huge change as well as challenge, it would be worth doing some research to see whether this is something you could easily slot into. Make plans for a weekend away or a recreational break so you have something special to look forward to.

12. TUESDAY. Volatile. Today's influences do not flow as smoothly as yesterday's. Irritation, conflicts with the people you relate to on a daily basis, and generalized feelings of impatience or agitation are possible issues you will have to address. For less energetic Archers, tending to indoor plants, the garden, or a pet might be the only activity required. If your mate or partner is receiving some type of recognition or honor, don't be shy about basking in the reflected glory. Your sacrifice and moral support undoubtedly contributed to their ability to reach this milestone. Your own get-up-and-go can be restored if you make changes to develop a healthier way of living.

13. WEDNESDAY. Peaceful. Today you are more sensitive to the beauty of your surroundings as well as to the emotions and needs of your loved ones. Spiritual values take on more importance than material possessions. Daily writing in a diary would be advantageous, giving you a chance to explain your own thoughts and feelings and then to reread what you have written and mull over what you are telling yourself. Family members are very supportive now, so make sure you involve them in any and all decisions. Dancing, singing, or listening to favorite music offers the perfect way to relax and escape tonight.

14. THURSDAY. Constructive. This evening's Gemini New Moon in your seventh house boosts the chance of a successful outcome in any venture that you undertake. In particular, this is a positive period to begin a new business partnership, implement an advertising program, or open a retail store providing you have already done the research and preparation. If you have not done advance preparation, it would be wiser to wait until the completion of the Mercury retrograde period. Relationships that need healing or more compromise and cooperation to restore mutual affection can benefit greatly from effort applied by both parties. If in a long-term stable relationship, review accomplishments so far this year and redefine your goals to ensure that shared aims still remain the same.

15. FRIDAY. Manageable. If monetary worries have come to a head, approach your financial institution to find exactly where you stand with them. Covering up any important details or falsifying any records will only bring you trouble in the future. From now until July 10 Mercury moves backward through the zodiac, warning Sagittarius to take care if involved in financial and business activity with other people. If employed in a job where money belonging to other people is handled frequently, check and recheck your work often. Mistakes are likely to slip by unnoticed, possibly proving costly or at least embarrassing in the future.

16. SATURDAY. Encouraging. If you have been considering going for a palm or astrology reading to help you to understand an ongoing inner conflict, make an appointment today. If you don't know a qualified person who would meet your needs, call your local metaphysical bookstore and ask for a referral. The advice you receive is bound to be helpful. Seek cooperation from household members with domestic chores, and avoid taking on more than your fair share of responsibilities. Find a quiet sanctuary at a beach, lake, or pool where you can swim or paddle. This will help clear your mind of all thoughts, even if only for an hour or two.

17. SUNDAY. Tricky. Don't procrastinate with your aims and aspirations once you know what you must do, especially if this concerns education or anything designed to assist your long-range plans. Your circle of friends might be interested in doing something similar, so propose a gathering to discuss subjects that appeal to the group. If a few of you go together, interest is unlikely to wane as it could if you go it alone. Steering clear of drama involving other loved ones won't be easy, but getting involved isn't very smart either. Get up early, pack a picnic lunch, and head for the great outdoors to escape a potential family uproar.

18. MONDAY. Empowering. Gaining understanding and wisdom is one of the most enjoyable activities for Sagittarius. Expansion of knowledge and broadening of horizons will come through travel, work, or just mingling with like-minded people. Sagittarius students might discover a hidden talent for debate and start to consider a political career. Professional Archers need to take care not to step on the wrong toes when climbing up the ladder of success. Otherwise you might get bumped down a rung or two. Relationships can quickly turn sour if your ego becomes enlarged. Settle in with a good book tonight rather than watching television.

19. TUESDAY. Positive. Relationships may be challenged, but try to stay united as you ride out the storm. If you are having trouble expressing yourself, consider getting some professional help. This is a very favorable time for a spiritual retreat. Carrying out research and investigation into a pet project is also favored. Foreign affairs become important, either through contact with immigrants or travel abroad. Your criticism of global affairs and the solutions you think best might be wiser than you thought. Silence is often golden. A special connection could be broken if you are unable to keep a confidence entrusted to you.

20. WEDNESDAY. Confusing. Over the next two weeks serious Saturn and nebulous Neptune are moving to an opposition. This will bring restrictions and confusion to your thought processes, hindering your ability to study and to think clearly. Someone may be pulling the wool over your eyes, perhaps because your Sagittarius nature is to trust others. The unpleasant realization could now surface that you have been fooled or duped. Finding out might be a difficult pill to swallow, but at least you will know what has been going on and can then put an end to deceit. If involved in writing for a living, or wishfully so, your productivity will increase by applying self-discipline and organizing a daily routine. Love swirls around you, so enjoy the moment.

21. THURSDAY. Renewing. Finding a more equitable balance between family life and career responsibilities is greatly emphasized and necessary if harmony is to reign on the home front. The summer solstice occurs today with the entry of the Sun joining Mercury in your Cancer eighth house of shared financial resources. Business associates provide the best avenue for financial gain. This is the time to get serious about your investments, to check your pension, send off paperwork relating to taxes, and make sure that all of your valuable possessions are adequately insured. Lessons and learning come through challenges, so welcome these without fear.

22. FRIDAY. Insightful. Expanding your mind remains a priority, whether through taking an educational course, attending a lecture, or interacting with a special-interest group. This is a good time to decide on what you no longer need around your home or work. Aim to remove clutter and unimportant items. Buried sentiments and feelings could rise to the surface. These need to be examined and dealt with so you can move on without any emotional baggage cluttering up your thoughts and life. An expected financial settlement could be further delayed, causing disappointment. However, don't look upon this as totally negative because a delay now could work in your favor.

23. SATURDAY. Diverse. Uranus, the planet of friends and unexpected events, turns retrograde in your sector of home and family affairs. Prepare for past issues to resurface for a second airing before finally being resolved. A difference of opinion between you and a friend doesn't have to destroy your friendship, but you might see each other through new eyes from now on. Irrational mood swings or temper tantrums could flare up easily over the next few months. Try to take issue with matters that are worthwhile and not frivolous. Otherwise you might be better off staying quiet or putting your energies into more constructive activities.

24. SUNDAY. Motivating. By completing old projects as your main priority you will make more room on your agenda. This will let you begin new ventures in a few days when the Moon sails through your sign of Sagittarius. If you are experiencing apprehension and stress at your current place of employment, get involved in daily physical exercise. The passage of Mars through your Taurus sixth house of health and working conditions increases pressure and anxiety on the job from now until August 7. Reorganize your filing system, read technical journals relating to work, catch up on household chores, and do whatever gives you a sense of accomplishment on a day-by-day basis.

25. MONDAY. Satisfying. Your imagination is disciplined and can be utilized positively, although energy may be at a lower level. A confusing matter might suddenly become clearer. However, there could be so much going on in your head you will be glad of the chance to work behind the scenes or by yourself. Withdrawal from social contact often occurs when the Moon is gliding through your Scorpio twelfth house each month. This is the time to take a deep breath, relax, and unwind. If time permits go out for a walk. You may stumble on a peaceful garden or a park where you can stay for a while enjoying the serene calm.

26. TUESDAY. Tricky. Today more than ever you are inclined to slip into a fantasy world of dreams and imagination to compensate for any dreary situation in which you find yourself. Some problems will be of your own making. Private plans will only succeed if willingness is shown and effort applied. You are unlikely to move along your chosen path if you make decisions and then fail to follow through. Drink ample water if you are out and about or you run the risk of becoming overheated or dehydrated. A New Age center or bookstore could be a setting for a potential romantic encounter for singles.

27. WEDNESDAY. Varied. For most of the day you will feel optimistic and upbeat. A little glamour could come into your life, leading to buying a new outfit for a wedding or other special celebration. If your role will be more high-profile than most of the guests, and if you don't like current fashion trends, stick to what suits your style and age. Don't allow anyone to sway you or you will not feel comfortable when socializing. A contentious legal or financial matter is about to end. Although you might have been dreading the outcome, you could find that the decision is not as bad as you thought it would be.

28. THURSDAY. Active. Plenty is happening right now and, providing you set your sights at a realistic level, a lot can be achieved. Just maintain your focus. Problems could arise if you experience difficulties keeping your mind on what you are doing, and it will tend to keep wandering off in all directions. Hold back if you need to make a major decision. Changing your mind several times a minute is likely, which could frustrate you as much as everyone around you. Consider yourself honored if someone chooses to confide a happy secret to you, but be sure to keep this information quiet until they are ready to make it public knowledge.

29. FRIDAY. Demanding. Dealing with those who speak a language you are unable to understand could be frustrating, especially if you have to talk on the phone. Use this as a learning experience in the art of tolerance. If contact is to be a regular occurrence, consider learning some basic words and phrases. You may be expected to give extra hours of your free time to a group activity, reducing time for personal projects. This might start you thinking about how many hours you spend in volunteer service and whether you are receiving enough emotional fulfillment to continue or whether it is time for a change.

30. SATURDAY. Deceptive. Confusing times surround the emotional life of partnered Sagittarius, especially if you have placed your mate on a pedestal or are viewing your love life through rose-colored glasses. If single and looking for a partner, be careful. A deceptive atmosphere surrounds you when it comes to romance. It would be wiser to enjoy what comes along but to remain uncommitted. A Capricorn Full Moon heralds the warning to pay attention to all matters relating to joint affairs, legacies, taxes, and savings. Complications could arise with a business transaction involving family members. Seek expert advice before proceeding any further.

JULY

1. SUNDAY. Productive. Be proactive and sort out your monetary affairs early in the day if you need to know the current state of your finances. Eliminating waste and inefficiency is vital. You might have to contact your parents or in-laws for help or advice. Be prepared to go humbly with your hat in your hand. The advice you receive will be based on wisdom and experience and should be very valuable. This is an excellent time for Sagittarius singles to formally make an engagement announcement, apply for a marriage license, or arrange a wedding ceremony. Couples can reconfirm ties of affection by making plans to renew vows.

2. MONDAY. Complex. The demands of those in your immediate environment add stress and pressure to the day. Although as a Sagittarius you generally like to assist other people, this might not be the case now. You need to stand firm and only take on what you can comfortably handle. An overall lack of tolerance could make it upsetting having to cope with other people's shortcomings. Put forth more tact and diplomacy than you have recently been exhibiting. Endeavor to remain calm and avoid conflict. Double-check all important paperwork before signing on the dotted line. An intriguing book recommended to you can provide fascinating information for you to devour.

3. TUESDAY. Changeable. A sense of laziness pervades the atmosphere. You may want to opt out of some of your obligations. Try enlisting assistance to increase your enthusiasm. If hosting a Fourth of July party, get friends to help by bringing food, serving, or doing some cleaning up. Combine work, socializing, and a meal and the work will be done in no time at all, ready to greet your guests. It isn't in your nature to turn people down, but be careful today. Someone could try to take advantage of your good nature, wanting you to do tasks that are assigned to them, not you. Use your charm and politely explain that you have a large workload and are unable to take on any more commitments.

4. WEDNESDAY. Busy. This is an excellent day to prepare and recommend new ideas to your family members for deliberation and feedback. Together you can decide whether these can work and are suitable for all household members. A desire to spruce up your home might occupy you if you are not going to work or attending a special holiday celebration. Cleaning the house from attic to basement could be rewarding. Adding new plants, accessories, or furniture will produce interesting changes in your environment. An art and crafts exhibition may open your eyes to new materials that can be used to produce creative and colorful work.

5. THURSDAY. Active. Be prepared for an unexpected but pleasant change within the family fold or around home base. A compulsion to clean could again be evident, so strike while the iron is hot. Your domestic or work environment will soon be fresh and spotless. Time spent with your family could be subdued due to worry over a problem concerning property or delays to house maintenance or building renovation. Visitors are apt to drop in, and before you know it an impromptu party could develop. This will change your mood from somber and serious to happiness as congenial companionship and a fun time are shared.

6. FRIDAY. Manageable. An invitation to a social function that you would really love to attend might have to be turned down due to another obligation that you cannot back out of at this late date. As a result you will miss out on opportunities to meet important contacts who might encourage your future goals. Think creatively. There can be a way to fulfill your duties and also be present for at least part of the important event. If you need a break from your daily routine, relax by pulling out an uncompleted project, perhaps sewing or quilting started a long time ago. Now you can apply the finishing touches. Don't repeat any gossip you happen to hear tonight.

7. SATURDAY. Eventful. If preparing to travel a long distance, begin your journey early this morning in order to take advantage of the prevailing supportive influences. If you feel that you are stuck in a rut, start an artistic project. Having an outlet for your creative urges could give your spirits a considerable lift and could possibly boost your income. A friend may express interest in buying or marketing your work. An older child may be a concern if you haven't kept the lines of communication open. Time spent indulging a passion for art, film, or music can be very relaxing and therapeutic. A sensual atmosphere brings an exciting element to your romantic relationship tonight.

8. SUNDAY. Lively. Romance is still in the air, making this a perfect time to ask that special someone out on a date if you are currently single. With goddess Venus and passionate Pluto harmonizing together, couples can devote extra time to keeping love alive and lively. Plan a candlelit dinner for two this evening. An involvement with a physical sport would be beneficial, releasing energy, reducing stress, and providing assistance in the health and fitness department. Time is a precious commodity, with never enough to go around. Let other people take responsibility for their own obligations. It is up to you to set guidelines, delegate chores, and give yourself the gift of extra personal time.

9. MONDAY. Auspicious. This is an excellent day to roll up your sleeves and complete the boring but necessary tasks on your current to-do list. Mercury is moving forward in your solar sector of corporate finances and the Moon is in the money-oriented sign of Taurus. As a result, celestial influences are providing the courage for you to ask the boss for a pay increase or a new contract. You will only have to do jobs once to achieve an excellent result. To be more useful around the house and office, utilize your multitasking skills to advantage. This will put you in a good position with superiors.

10. TUESDAY. Unsettling. Workplace conditions could be testing your patience, even making you feel unsettled and nervous. Listen closely to what other people ask you to do. Compromise may be necessary if you are working with partners, ensuring that harmony, the most important requisite, remains strong on the job. Anything that is very sweet or fattening should be removed from your diet to protect and maintain your health and vitality. If seeking an alternative approach to healing for an ongoing or chronic health issue, consider a natural method that involves good eating and exercising habits.

11. WEDNESDAY. Diverse. Morning interactions with other people might cause a whole range of emotional responses. A partner could get on your nerves, possibly because you think mountains are being made out of molehills. Allowing emotions to control your actions or make decisions for you can increase tension. Your self-confidence is likely to receive a boost, although extra moodiness is also indicated. Being put in charge of a public event, presenting a speech in front of an audience, or being asked to head up a special project are possible scenarios that will put you on the spot now.

12. THURSDAY. Promising. This morning you will be in the mood to pamper that special someone in your life. Pull out all the stops and spoil the object of your affections, because by lunchtime your mood may have changed and you could be more inclined to make war, not love. It would be a good idea to spend some time talking about how you each feel. In particular, compare your differences. Think about the many positive and negative aspects of your daily lives and what changes could be made to improve your relationship. Shop around for a lending institution that will give you the best interest rate if you are hoping to increase your overdraft limit or take out a loan.

13. FRIDAY. Empowering. Don't worry about the day and date. Trends similar to yesterday prevail now. Don't keep beating your head against a brick wall if something is not working out as you want it to. Now is the time to make necessary adjustments and get rid of excess baggage. Decide if a certain situation, career decision, or person is making you happy or discontented, then take appropriate action. This is a good time to learn, ask questions, and seek answers based on your own innate knowledge. An interest in the occult could prompt a visit to an astrologer, revealing information that might be both enlightening and confronting, perhaps because you don't realize your true potential and worth.

14. SATURDAY. Renewing. A fresh cycle now begins with the Cancer New Moon culminating in your house of shared resources. This will be helpful if you are applying for a loan or a mortgage, making it simpler to obtain an affirmative answer. This is also a favorable period to make an appointment with a financial adviser, stockbroker, or boss. Venus, the planet that attracts money, has traveled into the reputation and professional status sector of your chart. Even Sagittarius not currently in the workforce can experience a positive flow thanks to some good luck. If you have a talent for crafts, you could turn this into an extra source of income to help pay the bills or to buy yourself some extras.

15. SUNDAY. Insightful. Discussing a diverse range of topics can lead to fascinating insight and some interesting ideas formulating in your mind. This is a time to seriously consider widening your horizons by broadening your knowledge and investigating philosophical theories. Taking a course to study one of the intuitive arts, such as numerology, palm reading, or tarot cards, could open you up to a whole new world. Sagittarius parents with young children might opt for a correspondence course which would provide the flexibility needed to return to academic study. If you don't sign up to take a class, you may be asked to teach one.

16. MONDAY. Challenging. Expect to battle through your daily activities and routine chores. Be careful not to take on more responsibilities than you can comfortably handle. You need to learn to let other people do some things for you. Constantly doing everything for them diminishes their power and lowers their self-confidence. If on vacation you could lose your heart and embark on a romantic holiday affair that might even continue when you return home. Keep your blood pressure from rising by avoiding controversial conversation topics relating to religion or politics. Even people you know well are unlikely to agree with many of your opinions or views.

17. TUESDAY. Exciting. Jump at the chance to take on an interesting challenge. When it comes to shared responsibilities on the job, it might be more beneficial for everyone if you agree to take on a larger portion of the workload. Right now you can complete tasks quicker than most of your colleagues. At the same time you can impress those who matter most. Making progress in a new business venture may be as simple as brushing up on existing skills, retraining yourself and staff members, or studying new procedures to increase productivity. Share your evening with a person who offers entertaining and stimulating conversation.

18. WEDNESDAY. Bumpy. There may not be much joy and good times around work today. A superior might want you to take the blame for something you didn't do. Although good fortune usually smiles on the sign of the Archer, don't push your luck today. If you value your job you might just have to take the blame in the short term to avoid long-term harassment. As a Sagittarius you are an idea person, always willing to try anything at least once. Of course, not all of your plans will work out as envisioned, but today's efforts should be successful providing they are based on practical and realistic approaches.

19. THURSDAY. Restricting. The wistful and vague sensation to the day is likely to make concentrating on any one thing extremely difficult, even for the usually attentive Archer. Take care with your words. There is a risk of going too far with criticisms or thoughts. You could be viewed as overly pushy or aggressive. This is not a good time to follow a sudden impulse or to take rash action. Family friends arriving unexpectedly could dominate the evening. Much time and energy spent ensuring their comfort will be irritating if you have to forgo your own more enjoyable plans for amusement.

Be patient, however. Loved ones are bound to be grateful for your efforts.

20. FRIDAY. Fair. If it seems your life is not moving fast enough right now, look over the wish list of goals you are hoping to achieve. Choose one of them and take necessary steps to make that dream come true. The arrival of unexpected guests accompanied by children may require a quick revamp of your home to make it child proof against breakage. This will put less stress on you and on your visitors. Also be careful about leaving a child alone with your pet. Friends or associates might call on you for suggestions on planning and organizing a fund-raising event. Be generous with ideas without falling into the trap of doing most of the work.

21. SATURDAY. Good. Enjoy your day off. The morning should begin well if you don't need to be anywhere special early today. Don't be afraid to cash in on a few favors if this can help you achieve one of your cherished dreams. You can return the good deed when you are in a more favorable position to do so. A group event or social function in your area might put you in contact with exciting new people who eventually become part of your ever-growing friendship circle. If you are without organized plans for this evening, focus on your romantic partner and spend time entertaining each other. The night is made for love.

22. SUNDAY. Fruitful. This is a day of contentment with decisions, sacrifices, and challenges that you have made and faced in the past. Reviewing these will lead to inner growth and self-empowerment. A secret love affair might demand that you meet out of town, perhaps at an exotic resort that can become your secret hideaway. Giving your time to a charity or volunteer organization can be the result of your belief in the goodness and equality of all human beings. Be as generous as possible. Leave well enough alone if an in-law or relative shows signs of becoming difficult. Being conciliatory could inflame the situation instead of defusing it.

23. MONDAY. Dynamic. The greatest pressure today will be what you put on yourself. You might be tempted to cut corners because you cannot be bothered exerting the appropriate amount of effort. Think carefully before doing this because there are possible future implications. The errors that occur now might prove difficult and costly to correct. Overnight the glimmering Sun entered into your ninth sector of regal Leo, creating a more playful atmosphere and enhancing creativity and inspiration. Accept as many social invitations as you can handle. At any gathering you are likely to meet many interesting people and experience lots of amusing diversions.

24. TUESDAY. Tricky. Today's aspects are creating unfavorable trends for most activities throughout the day, with little relief in sight. A confidential issue might cause some tension, keeping the matter under wraps could prove challenging. Accept that inevitably secrets are likely to be revealed. This could lead to a showdown with someone, even though this is not what you wanted or had planned. Once all problems involving a special project have been resolved, move quickly and follow your intuition, which is unlikely to let you down. The stars look brighter this afternoon, bringing out the social side of your nature and a need for companionship.

25. WEDNESDAY. Uncertain. Confusion continues to reign, with your vim and vigor diminishing as Mars, the planet of drive and motivation, continues to argue with befuddled Neptune. Unsettled conditions at home and at work could increase anxiety, causing impatience and irritability with loved ones and coworkers. It is time to do yourself the favor of taking a step back from the situation that is causing stress. Book a relaxing massage or a new hairstyle, or head for the mall and indulge in some retail therapy to ease pent-up pressure. A lunchtime date with someone special could put a smile on your face, but be careful not to overindulge.

26. THURSDAY. Distracting. Restlessness could strike and make you easily bored. Unless you add plenty of variety to your day, you may find it a struggle concentrating on anything for very long, reducing productivity. If traveling to your place of birth or a destination that holds lots of pleasant memories, keep in mind that people and places change. If you don't expect everything to be exactly as you remember it, you will have a more pleasant trip down memory lane. If you do expect perfect memories, minor disappointment is likely. Romance is possible if you are willing to approach someone who interests you but might be too shy to be the first to speak.

27. FRIDAY. Uneasy. If money worries are causing stress, talk over your options with someone you trust who really understands your current situation. Venus, goddess of romance, is in retrograde motion, providing an opportunity for you to review and resolve current issues affecting your love life. If suffering from a lack of affection in your life, examine why this is the case and make any appropriate changes that are needed. Career-minded Sagittarius and business operators should analyze whether value received reflects the time and effort you are applying to your professional interests and whether you are still happy with your line of work.

28. SATURDAY. Enjoyable. Cosmic influences are improving, although financial commitments might put a strain on your own sense of freedom. If you have some spare cash to invest, seek financial advice from a professional consultant. If you are supposed to be putting funds aside for a major purchase, consider trimming your household or social budget for a few weeks to swell your savings. Finding amusement that is stimulating and reduces the strain on your wallet is not that difficult if you put your mind to it. If going out with a group of friends, look forward to a day of fun and laughter.

29. SUNDAY. Sensitive. People around you might appear more cranky and touchy than usual. Raised voices and criticism could upset your plans for enjoyment. Tonight's Full Moon in the quirky sign of Aquarius indicates that some serious tension is likely to manifest in the sky for everyone, not just for Sagittarius, so be on guard. Drivers out on the road this evening should take more care because the impatient attitude of other people could quickly turn into road rage or a nasty scene. This is a good day to put the finishing touches on a novel, screen play, or any written work that has creative undertones.

30. MONDAY. Trying. Keep your thoughts and opinions close to your chest and avoid being dragged into a debate. Computer problems at home will be frustrating and annoying. It's no fun when electronic equipment goes haywire. It would be advisable to call a tech person rather than stress out as you try to resolve the problem yourself. A professional can find and fix the problem in half the time it might take you. Complaining or talking to your mate or partner this evening about business or work problems is likely to cause arguments. Instead, concentrate on lighthearted topics and enjoy a pleasant time together.

31. TUESDAY. Tense. There is a limit to what even you can do now. Pace yourself so that your energy remains constant. Don't shy away from situations that appear negative. Although daunting, it is possible that these could prove rewarding in the long term. The resignation of an associate could put you at the top of the list to take their place. Although there could be some facets of the job that you are not overly thrilled about, this might be the first step up the career ladder. Coworkers may become upset it they think you are ignoring them. Older people are also more likely to take affront and will require careful handling.

AUGUST

1. WEDNESDAY. Cautious. Be on guard throughout the day. Just when you think you have everything under control, a relatively minor matter can blow out of proportion and make the atmosphere tense. Brighten up your life by putting some fresh flowers on your desk or coffee table. Their beauty and smell will be a constant reminder of the wonders of nature. If you decide to experiment in the kitchen this evening, be extra careful when handling sharp instruments or equipment that you do not use a lot. A minor injury is likely if you rush around without watching what you are doing. If you stay up later than usual you may have trouble falling asleep.

2. THURSDAY. Fortunate. Sagittarius confidence is high, but beware that your ego is not also on the rise, even spiraling out of control. A helping hand is available today, especially if you are traveling for business or as part of your vacation. Students should do well with assignments and exams. Your ambitions are focused, making this an excellent period to expand career aspirations, seek new clients to increase business profits, or decide how to further your professional knowledge. Invite friends over for a spur-of-the-moment dinner party, sharing your friendly hospitality, congenial companionship, and good food.

3. FRIDAY. Bright. This is another good day for the luckiest sign, with the possibility of unexpected money widening your smile even more. It might not be enough to allow early retirement but may help you go on an overseas jaunt or attend a conference involving one of your philosophical or New Age interests. If there are issues disrupting your romantic relationship, this is a good time to take affirmative action in order to restore harmonic vibes. Singles can afford to let nature take its course. Your love life should begin to look up thanks to a new romance sparked by a common interest group, neighborhood gathering, or Internet chat.

4. SATURDAY. Favorable. New electronic equipment or computer software could be a source of problems unless you read the instruction manual first. Reduce frustration by proceeding slowly and in the right order. New equipment should then provide envisioned pleasure in no time at all. Your tolerance for the views of other people rises now with the entrance of intellectual Mercury into your Leo ninth home of overseas travel, education, and publishing. If you have been contemplating a return to school on a part-time or full-time basis, begin to put plans in place. Attending a workshop or seminar on a favored topic can stimulate your mind and also be relaxing.

5. SUNDAY. Active. People are likely to be more congenial and cooperative through the morning hours than later in the day. If you have been working longer hours than usual, become involved in more relaxing pursuits. Put aside household chores and fully enjoy the day. If you must keep busy and on the go, a swim, bike ride, or long walk will release excess energy, assist physical fitness, and get you out of the house. Parents with children to entertain can plan a fun-filled outing that will be amusing for all age groups. A new romance could begin to take off now as you realize that you have a great deal in common.

6. MONDAY. Promising. With health and fitness on your mind, it is time to put in more effort. Focus on improving your current diet and exercise program. It might be wise to purchase a gym membership as a motivator. You will be kept interested and upbeat if you have other people around to share the gain and the pain. A writing talent might be recognized by a publisher or editor. Realizing that your name could soon be on a book cover or as a byline is an exciting prospect. An honor bestowed or a graduation ceremony would be the ultimate fulfillment for reaching an educational goal. Set your sights high.

7. TUESDAY. Spirited. A bevy of activity is occurring in the heavens, ensuring that the day will be interesting and certainly not routine. A very productive time in your life begins now. Your confidence will rise as feisty Mars begins transiting your seventh zone of personal and professional relationships until September 28. With Mars also currently dueling with Venus, goddess of love, arguments about love, money, or business interests are likely to erupt more frequently than usual between both personal and professional partners. Aim to avoid domestic disputes by steering your passion toward making love instead of war. Intimate moments are good for the soul.

8. WEDNESDAY. Diverse. Competitive urges are high, ensuring that you will come out a winner in activities and pursuits that you become involved with now. This could come in the form of winning a vacation getaway or other valuable prize in a competition that you enter. You may seriously look at a colleague or neighbor as a potential romantic interest, especially if your attention is being returned. Proceed cautiously, however, because your timing may not be right. Some potential drawbacks have not yet been revealed to you. Steer clear of touchy subjects with your partner or loved one that may bring old resentments back to life.

9. THURSDAY. Opportune. Timing is always important, and today you have the ability to know the right place to be at the right time. With Venus still traveling backward in the sky, you can use this time to revise and edit what you recently wrote before sending it off. A vacation may be long overdue and really needed now if you have been working long and hard. Plan to spend some time in the sun, sightseeing, reading a book, fishing, or just soaking up the rays. As a Sagittarius you need to escape occasionally into nature's paradise. If you can't get away just yet, plan an activity that at least gets you outside and away from your desk.

10. FRIDAY. Manageable. You may become overwhelmed by all you have to do and just not enough hours in the day to accomplish everything. Writing out a to-do list and pacing yourself should help you complete all the urgent jobs that are waiting for action. Try not to take on more than you can handle. As a Sagittarius you hate to let other people down, but this may happen if you do not say no more often. Review your cash on deposit before making a financial promise that you might not possibly be able keep. Instead make realistic arrangements that you are less likely to default on. Take a night off from cooking and head for an inexpensive restaurant that serves your favorite meal.

11. SATURDAY. Lively. A great deal of activity is occurring in your Leo ninth house of gaining knowledge and broadening horizons, where five planets currently reside. This is definitely the time to push your plans for business travel, a vacation, or to further your education by returning to some type of formal study. If you have been dreaming of an overseas trip or of working abroad, now is the time to act. If your dream is currently unattainable due to environmental conditions or your age or lack of finances, look into the pros and cons of becoming an exchange student or working for a humanitarian organization abroad. Tonight is party time. A celebration is sure to be fun, enjoyable, and very memorable.

12. SUNDAY. Ideal. This is another perfect day to make travel plans, to expand your mind, or to explore a new educational path. Relocating could be an ever-present thought as the lure of a distant state or overseas destination continues to call. This evening's New Moon in Leo favors making your decision and beginning new endeavors, especially in regard to a trip, education, or legal affairs. Business travel arranged now should be successful. Creative inspiration can come through researching foreign cultures and examining artifacts and architecture. Books that deal with spiritual subjects can be a worthwhile investment.

13. MONDAY. Mixed. Confusion reigns, so keep your thoughts on a realistic level and avoid going off on a tangent. Defer making any major decision that cannot be changed at a later time. Your thought process is unlikely to be clear. Creative inspiration is enhanced, assisting Sagittarius people employed in public relations and advertising. You might have plans to travel interstate or overseas, but there is a strong possibility that your flight will be canceled or delayed. Make sure you have plenty of cash and activities on hand to keep you and other family members amused. This is a starred day to become engaged or to formalize a romantic relationship.

14. TUESDAY. Fine. The emphasis is squarely on your career. If you have work that needs to be done, catch up now while celestial influences are supporting your aims. If seeking to pursue a different career, employment connected to travel or a job that takes you to unfamiliar destinations could be worth considering. For self-employed Sagittarius and those working on a commission basis, this is an excellent time to ratchet up advertising. Also do some extra networking to let people know that you are available and to highlight your products and services. Meditation or yoga can provide an excellent form of relaxation for the busy Archer.

15. WEDNESDAY. Passionate. Your natural ability to come across in a gracious and openly affectionate manner wins you new friends and admirers today. Sexy Venus in harmony with Pluto is giving your love life an extra zing. If your mate or partner is not the tender type, make romantic arrangements yourself in order to take advantage of the passionate trends. Obtain a baby-sitter for the kids and go out together on the town. Or turn on the music, lower the lights, and experience love and affection at home. Traveling to less fortunate places might spark your compassion and lead to thinking about what positive steps you can take to help.

16. THURSDAY. Favorable. Sagittarius people in a committed relationship need to avoid a tendency to be overly friendly or openly flirtatious. This type of behavior is likely to create issues not easily resolved. Over the next few days the Leo Sun is moving toward a merger with strict Saturn, increasing the pressure that is already being exerted on you. Everything should work out in your favor as realistic and practical plans begin to bear fruit. A sale of an item that you no longer want or need could introduce a new era in your finances, reducing debt and eliminating high monthly payments. Look around home base to see what can be sold at a maximum price.

17. FRIDAY. Positive. With plenty of celestial action taking place, life is unlikely to be boring. Make sure that you have an open mind when it comes to suggestions from your team at work or from a group or organization that you belong to. By examining and experimenting with an assortment of techniques and processes you can discover a better way to handle new and old tasks. It could be very easy to read something more personal into what might be just a friendly social encounter. To save yourself some embarrassment, remain friendly but distant. Take a walk outdoors to clear your mind through gentle activity this evening.

18. SATURDAY. Reflective. A cautious, pessimistic mood prevails even among outgoing Sagittarius. Don't be too proud to accept or give an apology. Forgiving and forgetting your own misdemeanors as well as those of others should be balm for the soul. Look to the future rather than the past. Be more tolerant of the invariable setbacks encountered along the way. A reclusive attitude might still be evident tonight, with you preferring to stay home rather than going out to meet, greet, and mingle. If visitors come calling, it will not take long for you to put a smile on your face and become the gracious host or hostess.

19. SUNDAY. Lively. Celestial Archers are now experiencing the movement of Mercury into Virgo, your solar tenth house of vocation and reputation. For the next three weeks keep careful track of business appointments. Meetings and discussions are likely to increase, with the possibility that some will overlap. A flagging romantic relationship might begin to move in a positive direction if you mull over past mistakes and make some adjustments. Past love could resurface and perhaps be rekindled. Going back is not something to do lightly, but this could be the chance to right some wrongs.

20. MONDAY. Assertive. Conditions make this a day for action. You can get things done, especially behind closed doors. A little daydreaming is in order as you draw comfort by escaping into the fantasy world. You will be able to create magic through your vivid imagination and artistic flair. The process of dismantling or rebuilding will take time but be worth the effort. Avoid gossip. It can otherwise involve you in something you would prefer to stay out of, and it would be wiser if you did. Find a stimulating new hobby or recreational pursuit that combines both mental and physical challenges if you feel that your life is slipping into a rut.

21. TUESDAY. Successful. Focus time and energy on satisfying some of your personal needs and wishes. Although it is great to be giving and generous to others, you might be tempted to leave yourself short of cash, energy, or both. There is a tendency to go overboard in a number of important areas during the next few days while your ruler, Jupiter, is brawling with Mars. Make sure that this does not affect you directly. Arguments with the public, associates, or your partner could erupt very quickly and without warning unless you are forgiving. Planning and preparation for a group outing should be coming together nicely, with plenty of support for your suggestions.

22. WEDNESDAY. Encouraging. With an optimistic Sagittarius Moon spreading good cheer, your self-confidence should be on the rise. Of course, not everything you hear will be pleasant. Some criticism is bound to come your way. Don't let this upset you, as it is probably just sour grapes due to your current level of success. A superior could ask you to learn new technology, or expect you to alter the way your job is performed. Comply with this request since change provides variety, which should work in your favor. Children can receive positive benefits from learning about customs and religions practiced in other countries and cultures.

23. THURSDAY. Buoyant. The life-giving Sun joins Mercury in your Virgo sector of business and professional interests, bringing ambitions to the fore. Review your working life to ensure that you are fulfilled and happy with the direction you are going. Your willingness to take on difficult tasks or to give a little bit extra when dealing with customers could find you being recognized by your peers or by the boss for a special award. Contact with a politician or someone else who has made a name for themselves could be a highlight of the day. Don't forget to ask for an autograph or have your camera ready.

24. FRIDAY. Helpful. Your prime concern centers around your financial flow and whether it is flooding in or has slowed to a trickle. Expenses could be increasing, but the good news is that more money should be coming in very soon. Make boundaries with regard to your time and spending. A new goal requires implementing a savings plan. Your ability to see the big picture will help you make plans and examine your priorities. However, success will only come if you devote time to the minor details as well. Don't rush a decision for the sake of convenience, especially if other people are rushing you. Wait until you have thought things through thoroughly.

25. SATURDAY. Energetic. The sign of Sagittarius is known to be clumsy, so watch your step. Rushing around and impatience will be key factors if any accident or injury occurs. If you are behind the wheel of a motor vehicle, drive within the speed limit, obey the laws, and be more alert than usual. It is never too late to implement a savings plan. Even though you may not be a great saver, preferring to live for the present, you have enough willpower to change your saving and spending habits. Love can lift your spirits, boosting self-confidence and making your heart sing. Just tread warily with a relationship that is in its infancy.

26. SUNDAY. Variable. If seeking fun, excitement, and a possible romantic encounter, a local club or neighborhood center could be the best place to meet new people. Keep a new plan or idea to yourself until you have done enough research to ensure that it is viable and is the best of all possible alternatives. Only then should you bring it up for discussion. Ongoing obligations with respect to an older relative may be burdensome. Finding an alternative solution is likely to become more pressing as the level of care has to be increased. Learn from the experience of others.

27. MONDAY. Calm. As a Sagittarius you need to regularly escape from the same old activities in order to keep your motivation and enthusiasm high. If you plan your day to include some variety, productivity will increase. Associates or colleagues might be more inclined to ask you questions rather than the boss, aware that you have the answers and will not be judgmental when responding to their queries. Lose yourself in music of your choice if chatter around you becomes too noisy during lunch or while commuting. It might be wiser for younger Archers to steer clear of an older relative to avoid a lecture comparing the behavior of kids today to those in the past.

28. TUESDAY. Important. The eclipsed Moon is full and big in your Pisces house of home and family matters. This is an excellent and powerful period to meditate on your life's direction, destiny, and emotional issues. You should come up with some clear ideas of your path to fulfillment. An ongoing activity is coming to a climax and will need to be handled expeditiously within the next two weeks. If working from home you could find that there is not enough of you to go around. Working from nine to five won't begin to ease your workload, and loved ones might not be valuing your effort in terms of financial worth to the family. Set aside some private fun time to avoid mental burnout.

29. WEDNESDAY. Fulfilling. Home and family affairs are in the spotlight. You might want to consider moving. Or your offer to purchase a home may be accepted, or someone may put a deposit on property you have for sale. An urge to fix up your home could lead to purchasing new covers for furniture, colorful plants to brighten a drab corner, or paint to spruce up certain rooms. Make sure you have a full fridge since visitors who drop by may not want to leave because your home is so comfortable and your hospitality so congenial. Spend time helping children with their homework, or go out together for a walk before it gets dark.

30. THURSDAY. Uplifting. You can mix business with pleasure. However, when you are relating with other people watch that you do not reveal too many secrets. If without formal plans this evening, enjoy a relaxing bath full of your favorite aromatherapy essences to soothe and calm your nerves. A work romance is likely to move faster than you envisioned, taking on a life of its own. It is not too late to slow things down a little if this will make you more comfortable. Check all paperwork carefully so that small errors do not creep in and possibly create future problems if not discovered quickly.

31. FRIDAY. Inspiring. Don't stay home tonight. Accept an offer to go out and enjoy yourself. A client or associate may be captivating your notice and imagination. However, try not to expect too much. People might be put off by a pushy approach. As a Sagittarius you love to gamble on all sorts of things. A trip to a casino could be on your agenda, but make sure you only risk money you can afford to lose. If heading overseas soon, stock up on items to make your trip more comfortable. Begin with the purchase of new luggage that is easy to pull and hard to damage. Also shop for clothes suitable for the climate that you will soon be visiting.

SEPTEMBER

1. SATURDAY. Cooperative. Your knack of viewing the big picture will give you insight into a disagreement. Look at who stands to gain. You will then understand where the problem is being created and be able to sidestep explosive reactions and sensitive emotions. Before you head out to a social engagement take care of household chores. This will put you ahead for the rest of the weekend, enabling you to chase your dreams uninhibited. Sagittarius sportspeople will benefit from extra training for a crucial game. If you apply yourself to the tedium of practice, your opponents won't be able to match your performance.

2. SUNDAY. Auspicious. There is an opportunity to further your career or to enter public life, but consider your loved ones when it comes to making a definite decision. If you are feeling pressured by someone in particular, talking to them honestly can resolve the problem. This is an excellent time to finish an artistic project. A handmade item that has been in the closet or the garage for ages might be a masterpiece worth putting on exhibit. Career opportunities should be plentiful. Sagittarius people who are out of a job at the moment should update their resume and send it off to as many prospective employers as possible.

3. MONDAY. Tense. Think before you act. Plan out your schedule as thoroughly as possible. The day could get hectic and cause stupid mistakes that would otherwise be avoided. Tension is all-pervasive.

If you don't keep your mind on matters at hand, you will miss what is most important. Your mate or partner might push your buttons by changing their mind or imposing restrictions on you. Try not to lose your temper or you may say words you regret later. If your partner seems remote and restless, give some space rather than thinking it's all your fault that they are dissatisfied in the relationship. Have faith that they will share their thoughts and feelings with you when the time is right.

4. TUESDAY. Uneasy. Neighbors might lend a hand when it seems your friends have deserted you. This is sure to renew your faith in humanity. You may experience a crisis that leaves you aware of your personal vulnerability. Partnered Sagittarius people experiencing relationship difficulties need to look closely at what is really wanted from a lover. Be aware of your dreams, which may blur the boundary between your inner and outer worlds. If a dream keeps replaying in your mind, it might be personally rewarding to write it down and then meditate on the symbolism that you see.

5. WEDNESDAY. Demanding. Friends and associates expect a lot from you, which will sidetrack you from important personal matters. If you have been tardy with paying bills or keeping financial records, this would be a good time to get it done. Don't put too much faith in information and advice given by friends or relatives. See a professional if specific questions are gnawing away at you. The cost of their advice might save you much more in the long run. If a credit card debt is worrying you, investigate obtaining a personal loan that will enable you to pay off the high-interest debt with lower interest and more manageable payments.

6. THURSDAY. Independent. Your ability to think outside the box gives you some exciting new possibilities for your direction in life while putting your skills to the test. A romantic interest might start to move in an unexpected direction, adding excitement to your life. Someone close may claim to support your ideas, but when crunch time comes you find out otherwise. Do not let this deter you, for the chance to act independently will be best for your self-confidence. A legal matter may have to be dropped in order to protect someone close to you, even though it goes against some of your principles to do so.

7. FRIDAY. Encouraging. If you can't actually travel, let your daydreams take you into new realms and feed your ideas for the future. You may feel that in-laws or other older relatives are working against you, trying to undermine your relationships. However, try to view them as wanting to help. Sagittarius parents of young children might be able to have more time socializing if grandparents are willing to baby-sit. Students could absorb more through study groups rather than spending hours studying alone at home. The chance to discuss concepts and ideas, even to tutor a fellow student who is behind, will lead to better overall comprehension and better grades.

8. SATURDAY. Favorable. No matter what problems you may be experiencing, you are likely to do well today. An attractive stranger might let you know that they are interested in you, but proceed with caution. What seems very intriguing might turn out to be something completely different. You may be seduced by an exotic new place and think about moving there permanently. However, first check out all aspects of this new territory, such as social restrictions and everyday customs that might become tedious over time. Do not turn down any offer to further your skills and education. Opportunities for travel and advancement will also multiply if you are open to new ideas.

9. SUNDAY. Disquieting. Unconscious drives that surface now could lead to some form of compulsive behavior or action. A discussion or debate with other people might highlight your one-sided views on certain issues. Try to listen with an open mind and consider all views so that you get a more informed and balanced understanding of the subject. A sports competition or other performance that attracts a large crowd will be uplifting and inspiring. Just losing yourself in the crowd can be an awesome experience. Your ambition may be ignited when you are offered a position of authority within an organization. However, keep in mind that what may seem to be fantastic opportunity could turn out to be a series of very bad headaches.

10. MONDAY. Expansive. You can make headway in your career by showing emotional sensitivity and empathy toward the people you work with, thereby winning them over. Be assertive, but don't trample over other people in the process. Public relations should come naturally to you. An opportunity to represent your colleagues or to speak at a meeting will work in your favor. A family issue may have to stay on the back burner due to your career and public responsibilities. Just be sure to call home and let loved ones know you are thinking of them. If a female relative tries to dictate terms to you, be firm with your reply without getting emotional. You should then also be able to sort out a much larger issue with her.

11. TUESDAY. Constructive. The emphasis is on your career and professional life. An unexpected opportunity could prove very beneficial. Stiff competition is indicated, but this will have the effect of stirring up your own ambitious nature and making you able to cope with anything. Don't hesitate to speak your mind on an important issue. Just be sensitive to other people's points of view and you will avoid losing a valuable connection. An invitation to a prestigious affair is likely to boost your confidence and be a good way to impress a person you have been admiring by asking them to accompany you. If you have an ailing relative or neighbor, take time out of your busy schedule to visit and to offer some help.

12. WEDNESDAY. Supportive. Take stock of your current goals and compare them to your hopes and wishes for the future. You may find that some of your goals are no longer relevant, stemming from an earlier time. A female friend might take center stage in your life, providing emotional contact on a much deeper level than usual. This may be a major turning point in your life. Travel plans can be upset due to unforeseen circumstances. If your departure time is canceled, you might decide to abandon the whole trip because you have something more important and more interesting to pursue. Excitement prevails close to home base.

13. THURSDAY. Uplifting. Don't shy away from any and all types of communication that comes your way. You may have to act as mediator between a close friend and their partner to help them understand the cause of ongoing problems. A writing assignment or a position as representative might seem daunting, but you will be able to rise to the task. Your sensitivity toward other people is a big help now. Romantic arrangements might stall as one of you experiences cold feet, but do not take this as the final result. Having misgivings is usually part of the process of preparing for a lifetime commitment. Don't deprive yourself of a special treat.

14. FRIDAY. Changeable. When a personal project encounters a few problems, you will be surprised at the help you receive from family members and friends. A promotion offer could involve moving away from your area, leaving relatives and friends behind. This doesn't have to be the end of your relationships, just a part of your climb to reach career goals. Although change can be scary it doesn't have to be bad. Changes are coming anyway, so it is better to pick and choose them for yourself. A neighbor may ask you to drive them to an appointment or to go shopping. Helping despite your busy schedule will mean a lot to them.

15. SATURDAY. Unsettling. Inner restlessness could drive you to exaggerate, making mountains out of molehills. If you sit at home and brood over your troubles you are only giving them more energy. Instead get outside in the fresh air and engage in some physical exercise. Gardening, hiking in the mountains, or swimming would be excellent pursuits to clear your head and relax your body. Someone close to you who is ill or recovering from an accident would appreciate a visit. Even if you do not know what to say, buy a bunch of flowers and go anyway; conversation will take care of itself. If you are going away for the weekend, be sure to lock up your home securely and let a neighbor know when you will return.

16. SUNDAY. Manageable. A second job to bolster your income could be taking up almost all your leisure time, as well as costing you extra money in travel, uniforms, and self-gratification. Think about budgeting better so that you have more time for rest and relaxation. There are many activities that don't cost a lot. One possibility would be growing a vegetable garden, which would not only be fun but would save money on organic fresh food. A romantic alliance with a foreigner may be strained due to different cultural expectations. Without understanding from both parties it might start to seem nearly impossible to continue the relationship.

17. MONDAY. Comforting. Your emotions are likely to go up and down depending on the influences of your environment. If you are prone to any addiction you may be sorely tested now. A relationship can arouse confusion over what you really believe. If your mate or partner keeps saying that you are wrong, look on the other side and consider that they may be wrong. The Moon has moved into your own sign of Sagittarius and will remain there for the next sixty hours, making this the perfect time to put energy into yourself. Give yourself the nurturing that you usually give to other people. Be kind and treat yourself to something that will make you feel special. After all, you are the main person in your life.

18. TUESDAY. Exciting. A home beautification project could turn out to be a lot less expensive and easier than you imagined. Don't believe all the negative stories that people tell you. Go and tackle the job. Once you read do-it-yourself information, you shouldn't have too much trouble and will be glad to cut out the cost of middlemen. An urge to travel and see the world might become more tangible when you hear of work overseas. Quickly sending in your resume might be the best thing you ever did. You may experience an awakening of your psychic faculties and decide to join a circle of like-minded people to learn more about different metaphysical and spiritual teachings.

19. WEDNESDAY. Intense. An argument early in the day might infuriate you, but don't let thoughts of revenge ruin the rest of your day. Thoughts of forgiveness could actually turn the whole event into a positive experience. A strong urge for freedom could put you at odds with someone in a position of authority. No matter how strongly you feel about a matter, use recognized channels to have your say and thus avoid the risk of recriminations. The ability to make great changes in your life is dominant right now, and your ability to charm and influence other people is also at a peak. Use your time wisely and you will be well satisfied.

20. THURSDAY. Useful. How to spend money, not save, may be on your mind. You may be planning to blow your budget on an expensive item, or find you can no longer afford your preferred lifestyle. Sit down with paper and pencil and calculator and work out a budget that will keep you out of debt. Then deciding what to save for could be the hard part. Consider what you really want out of life. Or, more to the point, can money buy what you really want. Once you answer these questions, you can solve other problems more easily. A romantic situation could start to fall apart due to fixation about ideal love. Relish the moment for what it is and you will gain something worthwhile from it.

21. FRIDAY. Revealing. You may no longer be happy with things the way they are, finding fault with your partner or idealizing them so much they can't possibly remain on the pedestal. With all that is going on in your life, it is time to take a long hard look at yourself. By talking to a friend about your problems you can gain an objective view of what you are doing. You may be judging yourself too harshly. There may be someone who is leading you astray because they are jealous of you. Stop getting caught up in petty dramas and look at the big picture for better understanding. Regardless of other problems, you can excel at work and earn a satisfying bonus.

22. SATURDAY. Stimulating. This is a good time for hard mental work. You have more energy than usual and can tackle difficult problems. You will impress people with your ability and confidence. Work as part of a group could be very satisfying. Don't be surprised if you are nominated at a club meeting for a responsible position. You are in everybody's good books at the moment. Political issues could consume your thoughts and actions, whether it be in local government or international affairs. You may decide to walk the streets delivering pamphlets and obtaining signatures on a petition. Friends and neighbors could drop by or call unexpectedly. There is someone who really needs your help to solve a problem.

23. SUNDAY. Serene. Expect a late start on this day for day-dreams and intimacy. The weather may have a lot to do with your activities since you are more in tune with your surroundings than usual. You could be in great demand socially, so if you are trying to hide out with your lover you might need to turn off the phone and go out for the day to escape all callers. The Sun now moves into Libra and shines its warm light onto your solar house of friends and contacts. You may be invited to attend an important function for somebody you admire or possibly for yourself. Be careful not to overindulge in food, drink, or anything else that is hard for you to resist.

24. MONDAY. Happy. With your loved ones and your home the focus of attention, you might cancel an important appointment simply to be there for a loved one who needs your support. If you have taken on extra responsibilities at work in a bid to get ahead, you could now be experiencing the pressure on family life. With a positive approach and open discussion within the family, you can together make the necessary sacrifices without creating any suffering. The important thing is to make it a collective effort. Consider having weekly meetings where even the youngest family members get to speak and be listened to.

25. TUESDAY. Surprising. A situation which looks worrisome can turn out to be anything but, even changing the way you look at life. The lesson to be learned is to have hope and faith in the goodness of the universe. Would-be teachers might receive a teaching offer and suddenly get cold feet. However, stage fright is part and parcel of doing anything for the first time. Throw yourself into the activity you fear and you will learn a lot. Guard against rushing. The chance of accidents is higher than usual. If you feel stressed, stop and take a few deep breaths. If someone near you is stressed, offer to give a massage. Or make a cup of tea and get them to slow down in that way.

26. WEDNESDAY. Creative. Today's Full Moon in Aries shines its light on your solar house of creativity and love. A romantic alliance can add insight to a personal project and turn it into a masterpiece. If you feel your life is lacking inspiration, taking a course in one of the arts might turn the tide. If music or painting doesn't turn you on, acting might. Sagittarius singles are likely to meet a potential new love interest. Your whole life may be turned upside down overnight. Career-minded Sagittarius may start to look for a position that allows more creativity and scope for personal development. Don't continue to put up with a position that pays the bills but doesn't promise anything else.

27. THURSDAY. Reflective. With Mercury, the planet of communication, moving into Scorpio and your solar house of receptivity and secrecy, you will be inclined to keep your thoughts to yourself and simply reflect on important matters. The feeling that you cannot trust other people with your secrets may not be correct. If you don't express yourself, you can't be heard. Keeping a diary can be invaluable in providing insights. Gains that come through reading your own words can be very enlightening. Social injustice could figure prominently in your thoughts, and you might decide to travel overseas to offer aid.

28. FRIDAY. Dynamic. Your employer may use you as a sounding board for ideas. Don't be afraid of saying the wrong thing. State what you honestly think and you might be offered the next position that opens up. You are very receptive to the feelings of other people and could sense that there is someone gossiping about you behind your back. If you get noticeably upset they will win, so ignore the gossip and you won't have as much to worry about. If you are not happy with your weight and find that diets are generally useless, rigorous daily exercise might surprise you with the results.

29. SATURDAY. Problematic. Mars, the planet that rules action and aggression, moves into Cancer and puts the focus on your sector of joint resources. The sign of Cancer is renowned for its possessiveness, and with it now in your area of shared possessions you have a great reason for a fight. What you value and what another person values will never be exactly the same. If you are in a partnership, it is vital that you respect each other and share decision making. At the very least try to be a benevolent dictator. You have a lot on your agenda today and will have to be selective about what you choose to do and what you put off. You can try to please too many people, but should put yourself first and foremost.

30. SUNDAY. Successful. Social activities should be lots of fun. You might go to see a child performing in a show, videoing it as a priceless gift for all those close to you. Differences of opinion can be aired with love and understanding. If you and your mate or partner have experienced a rough patch, spend the day in meaningful communication. A grandparent or other older relative might need some help sorting through their possessions as they start to share the possessions they worked hard for. They will be pleased with what you value and want to keep.

OCTOBER

1. MONDAY. Volatile. Pamper your nervous system as your busy schedule keeps bombarding you with new information, disruptive situations, and hardly any time to relax and have a meal. Practice deep breathing, even for just ten minutes here and there. Also make sure you take some vitamins, eat fresh fruit, and drink plenty of clean water. A desire to be free from the responsibilities and expectations of people who depend on you can upset those you hold dear and put yourself out on a limb. Rash, impulsive behavior can cause some hassles and make a difficult situation even worse. Sagittarius people in the process of looking for new employment by actively applying for work are well starred now.

2. TUESDAY. Rewarding. Your hard work and proven ability won't go unnoticed. Someone behind the scenes is likely to be pulling strings in your favor. A business meeting should be conducted in private to protect your ideas and eliminate interference. If mixing with well-regarded movers and shakers you will find their high energy infectious. Watch, listen, and learn, and soon you could be on your way to the top. Innuendos won't be missed by you. There could even be some intrigue in high places that gives you an edge on your competitors. You might receive some information about your past that is both fascinating and challenging.

3. WEDNESDAY. Intense. Checking the Internet might turn up some very good investment prospects. Apply for an online loan and you will probably be able to get a favorable interest rate. Visiting a sick friend or attending the funeral of an elderly friend may bring you together with people from the past that you had forgotten about. A lack of funds could be holding up your travel plans, but events conspire today to make you feel that the universe has something very interesting in store for you. Take a well-calculated chance and you might be pleasantly surprised. Just don't risk your money or your reputation. Listen to favorite music to calm your soul tonight.

4. THURSDAY. Exhausting. Avoid taking on too much. You are bound to encounter people who have problems that you feel able to remedy, but your own problems could then get out of hand. Be discerning and save yourself from heartbreak. Make plans to go on a date to a quiet, intimate restaurant that offers entertainment. You will both have a laugh and be entertained together, taking off a bit of the pressure of socializing. If already in a relationship you are likely to experience deeper feelings and a desire for a stronger, more lasting commitment.

5. FRIDAY. Prosperous. Whatever you do or wherever you go today, you will have fun if you are open to learning new things. You might find a discussion group very stimulating and inspiring. If you are having a problem in any area, it could be productive to try brainstorming solutions with a friend. Computer or mechanical problems could be the result of a poor technician. Ask around for the name and number of someone who comes highly recommended. Then what seemed like a major repair may only be a minor matter. Your mediation skills are superb and can be used to negotiate an excellent business deal. Schedule a meeting for lunchtime, using the relaxed atmosphere of a comfortable and upmarket restaurant to set the scene.

6. SATURDAY. Spirited. Your imagination can produce a flurry of creative activity resulting in a beautiful work of art. A new romance can have the effect of turning your life around so that you feel you are finally headed in your true direction. You may be getting ready for a wedding or anniversary celebration, planning a trip to some exotic place. Or you may be inspecting real estate for the right house in the right locale. An interest in philosophy and metaphysics might tempt you to join a group in order to broaden your perspective. This is sure to put you in touch with some interesting, intriguing people.

7. SUNDAY. Demanding. Your generosity and kindness could be pushed to the limit, or you might jump to the defense of an elderly person who is being put down. The changing face of society might also cause problems within your family as a young person questions older traditions and beliefs. Try to take the middle ground in order to keep the peace, regardless of your true feelings. You may come up against unyielding and unmoving authority as well. Beware of sudden impulses that influence negative actions and could lead to a fine or other punishment.

8. MONDAY. Harmonious. Venus, the planet of love and harmony, cruises into the sector that rules your business and professional life. This will attract persons and circumstances that facilitate your work. You may get involved in artistic matters such as design layout, office redecorating, even public relations for the purpose of making the company look more attractive. Today's very impulsive influence might cause you to act on a whim, perhaps putting in an offer on a costly item being sold via the Internet without the benefit of personal inspection. You may then lie in bed all night wondering what you are doing. A love affair with a person in authority, such as your boss, teacher, or lawyer, is another possibility.

9. TUESDAY. Significant. Bad news travels fast, but don't believe the worst until and unless you get confirmation. Rumor is just as likely to be a false call. A meeting could hit on one of your pet peeves and set you off in front of everybody. Audacity and daring are admirable attributes in the right context, but you might be viewed as insulting. If your employer asks you to represent the company, make sure you know exactly what to wear and what outcome you are trying to achieve. Then be sure you do the right thing. An artistic friend having an exhibit may ask you to help organize or host the event, which will put you in contact with some interesting people.

10. WEDNESDAY. Manageable. This evening's New Moon in Libra heralds fresh beginnings among friends and colleagues. Although there is a possibility that some associations will end, others will move to another level. This is a good time to take stock of your expectations and the people you mix with. Be honest about the reasons underlying some of your friendships. Free yourself from any that are based on unequal relations or dishonesty. You are in an altruistic frame of mind. The idea of helping out disaster victims, the handicapped, or homeless people might touch your heart and make you volunteer money or time for a local charity organization.

11. THURSDAY. Opportune. Quirky behavior is the order of the day. If it isn't you who is acting up, someone you see every day is bound to be getting into some strange situations. This is a very favorable time to get a handle on subconscious issues that seem to control much of your life. Formal therapy or counseling from a friend who knows you well could be a big help. Do something special to put some passion back between the sheets. Hardworking Sagittarius might finally start to feel that labor has not been in vain. An extra bonus could appear in your pay this week, or a promotion could come your way. You may come into an inheritance or win a prize that will take the worry out of finances and enable you to finish a pet project.

12. FRIDAY. Disruptive. Mercury, the planet of communication, starts to move backward today and will do so for approximately three weeks. During this time you can expect numerous and assorted misunderstandings and delays. Contracts may seem to go into limbo with neither side knowing why. Or your computer might shut down and cause you to lose a few important files. Work behind the scenes suits you right now. If possible, take some work home so you can give it total concentration without any interruptions. A brother or sister may call for some advice. Who better to counsel them than the person they grew up with in the same house and with the same parents.

13. SATURDAY. Sensitive. An urge to withdraw from life's rat race is probably your unconscious telling you that you need to relax and flee from stress for a while. If you find that you are always getting interrupted, it might be worth arranging a private space at home where you can work or simply be alone. If your mate or partner is away on business, you may find that you are so used to their company that you don't know what to do with yourself anymore. If you go out for a drink, you are in danger of losing the day to the bottle. Instead, go for a walk around the neighborhood, preferably with a friend or just taking the dog for a long stroll. If still feeling lonely, make a long-distance call.

14. SUNDAY. Renewing. Enjoy a lazy Sunday. Sleep until lunchtime, or stay in bed with coffee and the newspaper. The Moon moves into your sign of Sagittarius later in the day, putting the focus on what you want and what you feel. Use this opportunity to pamper yourself. Even if your day is already planned, perhaps to take the kids somewhere or go for dinner with friends, let it all happen in your own time. Don't let anyone rush you. If this seems hard to do, resolve to sign up for a class in meditation and find some peace that way. Just ten to twenty minutes a day and you can relax and regain your center.

15. MONDAY. Enjoyable. With the Moon and Jupiter in your own sign of Sagittarius, it is going to be hard not to have a good time today. Feelings of benevolence, kindness, and popularity are running high. If you are not feeling on top of the world, those around you will cheer you. Contact with people in foreign countries is indicated. This might be through actually traveling to another country or just communicating with overseas customers in connection with your business. Impulsive behavior could get you in trouble, especially if you exceed your budget or make important plans without first consulting your mate or partner or boss.

16. TUESDAY. Productive. Purchasing property for future speculation is favored. Although negotiations are apt to be slow and drawn out, the outcome will be successful. People around you could be moody. Gossip and spiteful conversation should be avoided unless you can talk to the person and help them see how negative they are thinking. If you have been involved in a clandestine romance you may both decide to come out in the open and declare your love, no matter the consequences. You could be voted into a highly respected position that boosts your confidence and renews faith in your own abilities.

17. WEDNESDAY. Opportune. A prior investment might start to increase in value, rewarding your perseverance and faith. Your employer may ask you to be the company representative at an important meeting. This will be the chance to show your abilities for an up-and-coming promotion. Being optimistic in an initially negative situation is one of your talents. Don't let an aggressive and competitive business associate wear you down and put doubts in your mind. Realize that such a person probably wants to usurp your position. An older family member will have some very valuable advice to share if you take the time to consult them. Your partner may be able to pull a few strings on your behalf, so don't let pride keep you from making a request.

18. THURSDAY. Risky. Extra responsibility may fall on your shoulders as part of achieving a long-term goal. You are willing and able to do whatever is necessary. Sagittarius businesspeople may have to spend less and invest more hours in the business. The motto that says you have to spend money in order to make money is very true at this time. Any hardships will be short-lived. You have a natural talent in one of the arts and may now decide to develop this talent into a career. This means taking a gamble on your own ability and might necessitate leaving your present job to go back to school. As a Sagittarius you always land on your feet, so the risk is likely to be well worth it.

19. FRIDAY. Problematic. Your biggest problem may be that you are disorganized, have overbooked your schedule, or have lost important paperwork. Stop rushing around in circles and start getting better organized to gain control. It is better to do a few things well than to do a lot in a slipshod manner. A friend may call and ask you to do a favor. With your natural generosity you might find it hard to refuse, and end up feeling totally overloaded and used. Travel is likely to cause another headache. If you must be on the go, give yourself plenty of time to get where you are going. It would be wise to listen to local radio to hear the latest traffic reports.

20. SATURDAY. Helpful. A person you recently met is likely to introduce you to a new group of people that enhance your self-image. At the same time, take extra care with old friends so they don't feel left out of your life.. A nosy neighbor could be eavesdropping on you. Make sure your private conversations are discreet or they could be used to discredit you in the neighborhood. A brother or sister who is down on luck may need a place to stay for a few days. You might enjoy sitting up late into the night sharing childhood memories and offering sympathy, but don't let this become the norm. To get back on the right track requires courage and a leap of faith.

21. SUNDAY. Empowering. Your personal attributes are being fully recognized by your friends and associates. You might be talked into entering a beauty contest or some other competition and do a lot better than you had thought. In fact, you might even win. Sagittarius students who have completed some studies may be able to earn extra money tutoring. This can enhance your own comprehension of the subject at the same time. A need for mental stimulation can put you on the Internet if you are home alone with nothing to do. You can meet some very interesting characters from all over the planet through the airwaves.

22. MONDAY. Disconcerting. Fear and conflicting emotions can paralyze your ability to make an important decision or choice. Sit down with your family and be prepared to hash out concerns and worries that are causing conflict. Even if you can't solve every thing all at once, you will start to get a good idea of options and of which way you should go. A relationship could be causing so many problems and issues that you are considering breaking it off. If the problems are external you should be able to fix them by working together. However, if your friend or lover wants you to be someone you are not, you may have no choice but to part ways.

23. TUESDAY. Exhilarating. Being offered a position in the public eye can both frighten and delight you, but don't let the chance go by. You will love the adrenaline rush that comes with public performance. However, if you remain undecided for too long you won't do it. An attraction for art and beauty might take you out of your comfort zone as you accept a date with a bohemian character or go to a theater or exhibit that is far out for you. Do-it-yourself renovators need to be aware of legal requirements before starting work. A phone call to the proper government agency beforehand can bring you up to date about development, applications, and the fees that go along with them.

24. WEDNESDAY. Confrontational. A seemingly harmless action could trigger an angry response from you. In turn this should give you cause to look at what triggered your anger. You may not be conscious of some aims and ambitions due to viewing yourself as a nice person who tries to accommodate everybody's desires at the expense of your own. Later in the day you can look forward to having fun with friends and to an interesting night of romantic possibility. An argument with your mate or partner over a child's behavior could be hard to resolve, mainly because you are two different people with your own experiences and values. Acceptance and compromise are needed.

25. THURSDAY. Strained. Conversations are apt to be anything but light. In fact, they may end up resembling analysis, which makes this an excellent time for investigative work or just to get to the bottom of a problem. A company meeting can lead to transformational resolutions that change the face of the organization for good.

A get-together with workmates after work might not be very productive or much fun. You would be better off going out with friends. This is also not a good time to invite your boss to your home. All sorts of minor matters could color their opinion of you, such as unsuspectingly serving food they don't like or having the dog act up.

26. FRIDAY. Accomplished. Daily routine gives you the structure you need to apply yourself to a difficult task and get it done. Your employer will look on you favorably and may even single you out for a job that sets you apart from coworkers. If this happens, be prepared for the cold shoulder from a certain person who resents your good fortune, but that shouldn't last long. Health might occupy a lot of your attention, especially if you are suffering from an allergy which is not bad enough for you to stay home but leaves you in discomfort. Read up on different types of treatment, or make an appointment to see a natural therapist who can help you treat the cause as well as the symptoms. Go to bed earlier than usual tonight.

27. SATURDAY. Perplexing. Listening to what people say and then seeing what they do could leave you wondering about reality. This is a good time to reflect on your own lack of consistency rather than concentrating on other people's flaws and engaging in gossip. Someone around you has a hidden agenda. What you say can be twisted for another purpose, so keep your thoughts to yourself and you can't be misquoted. Turn down a social invitation and spend the day getting odd jobs out of the way and your kitchen stocked with good food. Physical exercise will do you good and give you an appetite for a nourishing meal.

28. SUNDAY. Mixed. If you are away from home this weekend you might wake up in a motel or hotel room that leaves a lot to be desired, even though it seemed fine when you booked it. On a long drive the disappearing miles can be a great backdrop for an intimate conversation, airing feelings and hopes without a critical response. Sagittarius on the first leg of a long journey will be full of expectations and dreams about what lies ahead. It would be wise to start a travel diary so that you have something to look back on. Opt for postcards rather than taking pictures yourself.

29. MONDAY. Turbulent. What you see is not what you get in today's scheming climate. A business partnership might be heading for serious trouble and you are the only one who thinks you can salvage it. A tax audit could turn up discrepancies with your accounts that cause you to doubt a certain person's integrity. Loving relationships can also suffer from issues involving lack of trust. Trust is a two-way street, and if you find it hard to trust your mate or partner that fact in itself says a lot about the depth of your love. A partner who gets jealous every time you talk to someone of the opposite sex is reflecting personal attitudes that don't bode well for your continuing relationship.

30. TUESDAY. Reassuring. Problems that looked like black holes yesterday might seem to have closed up overnight. Whether it is a change of heart or a brighter mood, you should definitely be back to your cheery self. As a normally gregarious Sagittarius, you may need to get away by yourself to sort through matters and to finish a project that is important to you personally. Your sense of honor is stronger than usual. You could leap to defend somebody you deem falsely accused. This will put you in the firing line, but you are apt to enjoy the fight. A friend might ask you to invest in a company they plan to start, but put terms and conditions in writing beforehand.

31. WEDNESDAY. Demanding. Business deals, investments, and even credit card payments can go wrong and cause you all sorts of problems and headaches. Beware of fraud if you are tempted to purchase anything over the Internet. A friend might stand you up for a lunch engagement, probably due to having their own problems and simply forgetting, so try not to hold it against them. An internal office memo with confidential information could get in the hands of the wrong person. Play it safe and deliver confidential information in person. A sudden realization that a deadline has arrived could put you in a frenzy, causing you to cancel everything to focus on priority number one.

NOVEMBER

1. THURSDAY. Fruitful. A meeting behind closed doors will be very productive, with innovative new business ideas providing inspiration. Just be careful to keep your thoughts and plans to yourself or they could be stolen by someone hiding in the wings. A property investment that is proposed quite unexpectedly is well worth considering. Inner doubts and resentment will disappear as your confidence builds and praise for your work behind the scenes is forthcoming. With an element of luck at work for you, you can afford to let intuition be your guide, within reason.

2. FRIDAY. Imaginative. Today's tendency is to daydream. If it isn't you, it will be those around you. This might make it hard to get much work done, but creative solutions can come through discussion and information sharing. Legal matters will clear up when the truth is discovered. Expect to gain better understanding as the day progresses. Back pain can be eased with the magic touch of a good masseuse. To find such a person, ask friends for recommendations you can trust. If watching your weight, consider joining a group for a more effective and sociable method of losing excess pounds and keeping them off.

3. SATURDAY. Encouraging. Expect some strong criticism from an older relative. If you listen objectively with an open mind, their words will serve to guide you in making a major decision and any self-doubts will be vanquished. A spiritual retreat would be a great benefit at the moment. You could also gain great inspiration from research and private learning so long as you stay away from anything that is too structured and serious. There is a chance of being let down by someone close to you. Although this person probably has a perfectly good reason for doing so, it won't become clear to you until another day. Meanwhile, try not to show your annoyance.

4. SUNDAY. Eventful. An important event scheduled for today could lead to rising early, full of excitement and expectation. Nervous tension will be another manifestation of this energy, and the people around you might also be jumpy and unpredictable. This situation can be handled positively if you are aware of the underlying tension. You can then avoid reacting in a negative way, which could lead to arguments and more bad vibes. Political views can grow through the experience of personal injustices. You might decide to climb up on a soapbox to speak your mind, but be careful to stay within the legal limits or your freedom could be curbed.

5. MONDAY. Misleading. Make the most of your Sagittarius attributes and you are sure to be positively received in public. An ability to understand what makes other people tick puts you in a strong negotiating position at work and in forging a business deal. However, be careful that you don't box yourself into a corner and promise more than you can or will care to deliver at a later date. A power play between work associates could be to your advantage if you can manage to stay out of it. This evening is a good time for romance. Leave work early and surprise your mate or partner by going out for an intimate dinner at a favorite restaurant.

6. TUESDAY. Motivating. Be quick to say yes to a new offer. A promotion that puts you in charge of coworkers can be a real challenge. The trick involves how you communicate. You need to talk honestly with them while at the same time maintaining control. You may come up against a few problems with your bank, probably involving falling behind in your payments or having to find someone financially able to guarantee a loan for you. Be very careful who you approach about such matters. Sometimes it is better to cope with your situation alone rather than get friends involved. Considering a move to a new neighborhood can raise concerns about the unknown, but try not to project these worries. Take one step at a time and enjoy the adventure.

7. WEDNESDAY. Inspirational. A childhood dream could be on the verge of becoming reality. Sagittarius lovers might finally find that special spiritual connection that has been a lifetime search. Artists can start to tap into an inner genius, and travelers should not have too many hassles. On the other hand, you run the risk of neglecting important family matters and people who depend upon you, so try to maintain a balanced perspective. Involvement in a group project could load you down with extra responsibilities that should be shared collectively. Don't resign yourself to taking on extra work. Ask for a hand and only do your rightful share.

8. THURSDAY. Interesting. A desire for change can inspire home renovations. This might just involve landscaping part of your yard and creating a private place for meditation and reverie. Or you may want to clear away clutter inside the house to make a more relaxing atmosphere. A hunt through local thrift shops could turn up some older objects that you can make new again without spending a large amount of money. Stress and worry should be evaporating. Make life easy on yourself and do only what you know you are good at. This is an excellent time for study and research. Whether you are a student, a journalist, or just interested in furthering your knowledge, you can't go wrong reading an almanac.

9. FRIDAY. Loving. Venus, the planet of love and harmony, moves into Libra today, projecting love in your sector of friends and associates. Friendships with women will become closer and more intimate through a common bond. You will be increasingly popular on the social circuit and receive more invitations than usual. Some of these could be to prestigious events that definitely put you in the social spotlight. The New Moon in Scorpio heralds new beginnings. This may involve a love affair with someone you have known a long time. Inner awareness of who you really are is starting to blossom, and this new relationship complements the process.

10. SATURDAY. Reflective. New ideas may be starting to inspire new plans to achieve your dreams quicker. Spend as much time working alone on these plans as you can. You can get things sorted enough to start implementing some positive changes. With the Moon moving into your own sign of Sagittarius later today, the next two days are perfect for starting personal projects and working on improving yourself. Focus on developing an artistic talent or teaching a skill to other people. You may need to pay off a social debt or disentangle yourself from a stale relationship. With conscious planning this can be achieved with a minimum of fuss and hurt feelings.

11. SUNDAY. Impulsive. Be quick to put new plans into action. You may have to approach certain authorities to gain approval, or you may be able to just start the ball rolling. Make sure you understand exactly what you are tasked to do. Also stay aware of any laws or regulations you must comply with before starting. Only then can you expect to make significant headway. If you are trying to keep your actions from a certain person's attention, you will probably have enormous difficulty. A nosy neighbor or acquaintance will delight in telling tales. This is a good time to focus on your personal habits. If you want to make some changes, start by eliminating habits that you don't like.

12. MONDAY. Optimistic. Your positive approach to life means that you can achieve far more than most people expect. However, you need to be aware of your limitations as well, so that you don't take on too much and end up wasting your energy. Contact with foreigners could be complicated by communication difficulties. Don't take every word that is said at face value. A group or movement may appeal to your ideals and inspire you to volunteer to aid a charity or other good cause. Issues involving the environment and equality may be especially important for you. You could be on the receiving end of another person's generosity, making your faith in humanity stronger than ever before.

13. TUESDAY. Encouraging. Mixing in a new social circle offers the chance of becoming upwardly mobile but can cost a lot more than you want to keep spending. Financial worries may be resolved by working out a practical budget and living within your means, avoiding the excessive use of credit cards and cutting out extravagance. It is a good time to put in for a promotion or apply for a responsible position. You are conscious of your objectives and can do what it takes to achieve them. Movers and shakers behind the scenes can give you a helping hand, so call on them for assistance before you start any important project or negotiations.

14. WEDNESDAY. Changeable. Change is in the air, and with change comes insecurities which can lead to disagreements. Personal values differ from one person to the next, and there are no two people with the same. You will become increasingly aware of the differences that make you and those close to you unique. What starts out as an argument can lead to innovative changes, passionate lovemaking, or something equally pleasant and surprising. You may be told a valuable secret, one that puts you ahead of your competitors. Treat this information with kid gloves and it will work in your favor. However, any form of blackmail is certain to fail.

15. THURSDAY. Vexing. This is a good day to keep to yourself, working on what is most important to you. Ignore morning irritations until the evening, when you can work them out peacefully. If you push for a resolution earlier in the day you may only make matters worse. Giving advice over the phone provides a degree of distance, but when your advice is acted upon you will become involved, whether you like it or not. A parent might voice criticism of your lifestyle, but try not to lose your cool. Offer respect for being your parent and then get on with your own life as you intend to live it.

16. FRIDAY. Useful. An appointment with a specialist can clear up a problem that has been worrying you. Sagittarius students taking final exams will benefit from studying with fellow students. The chance to discuss the topic together can develop total understanding. News of a romance between friends may cause some jealousy and resentment, but you would be better off staying away from a publicly negative reaction. Devote a couple of hours to paperwork and paying bills so that you can see the top of your desk. With your filing cabinet and computer files in good order you will thank yourself for a job well done.

17. SATURDAY. Uplifting. If you want to sleep in and start the day slowly, take the phone off the hook and don't bother to answer a knock on your door. Shopping at local markets will turn up some unique works of art as well as putting you in contact with friends and neighbors you haven't seen in ages. Lunch at a Middle Eastern or Asian restaurant could inspire an interest in new styles of cooking. An attraction to the unusual can lead to an evening of entertainment in an unknown part of town, meeting new people and coming up against new political and ideological viewpoints.

18. SUNDAY. Stressful. Other people's expectations could be putting you under extra pressure that you do not need. Be honest with yourself. Know your limitations and you can't go wrong. You are very receptive to other people's feelings. A family member may be in a worrisome situation, but they may not want or appreciate your help. You have to know where to draw the line. If you live with one or more roommates you may be in the process of interviewing prospective new people. You are bound to be in for a few surprises as you talk. Follow your intuition rather than socially determined influences.

19. MONDAY. Stimulating. If you feel like a change but can't afford to do much, simply make some changes to your present home to brighten it up. A relative might come to stay so that they can study, get a job, or just visit while passing through. Conversation with them is bound to give you food for thought and a different outlook on a few subjects. A disagreement between family members and you might seem pointless, but you know you have to say you are sorry even though it might not be entirely your fault. Whatever course of action you choose to take will not totally resolve the issue. It is apt to come back to haunt you in the future, so don't apologize if you don't mean it.

20. TUESDAY. Energetic. A creative project can both energize and inspire all of your actions. New horizons attract you, bringing out your pioneer spirit. Be careful not to overreact impulsively or rashly and you can't go wrong. With a vacation coming due, you may want to get away from it all by traveling to some far distant corner of the globe and testing your endurance, such as hiking in the Himalayas or sailing one of the seven seas. Your child may be preparing to go away to school in the New Year and you may start to have second thoughts. Sometimes ideals are a little too coldhearted for the warmth of human relationships. It's not too late to change plans.

21. WEDNESDAY. Insightful. If you have lots of videos or pictures from your last journey, ask a few friends over so you can share the memories and sort them out at the same time. You will all have fun reviewing your travels. A new relationship might put you at odds with some of your good friends or family members, probably because you seldom call them now or because they do not like this new person in your life. Someone who can't accept you as you are and insists on imposing rules and regulations on your relationship may not fit in your current life. Live and let live should be your motto.

22. THURSDAY. Fortunate. The Sun moves into your own sign of Sagittarius today, adding its warmth and creativity to everything you do over the next month. You may be asked to speak on behalf of your entire family to welcome a new member. A new project that you have been secretly planning can finally get the green light and is likely to be more successful than you envision. A new diet and exercise program may start to show results, drawing compliments from people everywhere. Plan on shopping for some new designer clothes to add flair and pizzazz to your current wardrobe and fit with your new healthy, trim appearance.

23. FRIDAY. Difficult. Contracts or agreements could fall through. Be sure to read all the fine print before signing anything since there are sure to be some conditions that you are not aware of. A written assignment could be delayed due to a computer printer problem or simply due to your inability to apply yourself to the task. Writer's block is a common ailment, and the only way to fix it is to sit and wait until something comes to mind. As a Sagittarius you are a generous person, but don't let yourself be used by those around you. If you find that work is always left for you to do, begin to ask for assistance. If you are ignored, only do your own work and leave the rest.

24. SATURDAY. Complicated. The Full Moon in Gemini turns up the volume on your relationships. If you have issues that are unresolved, you can expect them to surface now. You may have to endure various forms of disapproval and criticism, but these should not lead to major upsets. Plan an intimate evening with your mate or partner so that you can talk openly and honestly with each other. You can work out problems without any interference from other people. Be a leader, not a follower. Think for yourself. By considering what other people say you might find an angle that they haven't considered, one that will work in your favor.

25. SUNDAY. Romantic. Today's atmosphere favors close ties and intimacy. Once you and your mate or partner have sorted out your differences you will feel secure in each other's love. Single Sagittarius might meet a fascinating stranger and fall head over heels in love. A family member could make you a business proposition that you can't refuse. Just be sure to put all the terms and conditions in writing to protect all parties in the future. You may prefer to spend the day with that special person in your life. Escape into the countryside for a picnic at a stunning landmark, or lovemaking.

26. MONDAY. Cautious. Do your homework before signing anything. Business deals are fraught with all sorts of dangers and pitfalls for the uninitiated and uninformed. You could be caught up in family negotiations which are at the mercy of family power plays. This is not the time to take sides. Stand back and watch, and you will come to a valuable understanding of your family situation and where you fit into the grand scheme of things. You are likely to be very popular now and have strong charisma. Use this time to encourage people to accept your ideas and develop your own talents and abilities.

27. TUESDAY. Successful. Notice what other people are talking about and you will get a very interesting perspective on an important personal issue. A higher-up could give you some advice that you are not willing to follow, but at least acknowledge this information and do not totally disregard it. An elderly relative may be disagreeable, putting you in a position of having to parent this loved one. Although this is an unpleasant position, it is a natural progression of life. A teaching position could be offered. You may doubt your potential, but this is your chance to reach a significant goal. Do not shy away from accepting. You can do it and do it well.

28. WEDNESDAY. Positive. Conversations and discussions are likely to be very informative and will open your mind to some interesting new concepts that you can develop. This is a starred time to consider going back to school to further your skills and expand your chances of making a good living. Inner restlessness can turn your thoughts to new plans and ideas that you would normally think are above and beyond your scope. Keep in mind that you have to stretch yourself to get better. Travel plans may be the result of a job application in another state. The chances of success are starting to look good, so keep up the hard work.

29. THURSDAY. Idealistic. You may need to examine some of your beliefs as you come up against someone who holds a different cultural perspective. Neither is right and neither is wrong, they are just different. This also applies to the ideals that you are striving to live up to, the ones that are behind many of the life choices you are making. Someone or something could upset some of these today, possibly changing forever more the way you look at life. Be careful what you say as there is a likelihood of a message getting conveyed to the wrong person or group. Be especially cautious when sending an e-mail message.

30. FRIDAY. Tricky. Problems can arise through minor misunderstandings if you do not take the trouble to explain your words, deeds, and actions. Someone close to you could be nursing hurt feelings but won't tell you what is wrong. Instead of reacting emotionally and creating a chain reaction, keep assuring them that you care and sooner or later they will open up to you. A public appearance could be on your mind, and distracting you from important negotiations. Try practicing deep breathing. Be sure to dress appropriately for an important dinner engagement. What you wear as well as what fork you use will be duly noted.

DECEMBER

1. SATURDAY. Promising. You could be easily led, so keep alert and on guard when making decisions. An investment opportunity may sound very inviting but also force you to stretch your budget more than is comfortable. If you are a bundle of nerves because of stress, consider your preferred lifestyle before letting momentum get you into something you don't really want to do. Sagittarius singles may be introduced to someone who fires up passion. This person could even change the course of your life. Because your mind is overactive you might find it hard to get to sleep unless you have a nightcap before going to bed.

2. SUNDAY. Upsetting. An overoptimistic attitude can cause your downfall if you don't keep focused on what you are doing. All sorts of interruptions involving helping other people will detract you from your goals. A nosy neighbor could overstep the mark and become the victim of your wrath. Think ahead and don't push yourself to the breaking point. Your family's expectations of you might be straining your relationship as your desire to break free gains momentum. It might be time for you to step out on your own and test your abilities. However, don't let this conflict build to the boiling point. Tell your family what you have planned and then find ways to compromise with them.

3. MONDAY. Deceptive. This is not a good day for making large purchases or investments. Check out all information you are given, then if everything appears to be okay go back tomorrow and check all over again. A social outing may become unpleasant if someone won't leave you alone. Maintain your personal boundaries and be selective with whom you choose to socialize. You have the gift of gab, but avoid gossiping. A friend might need a shoulder to cry on, and you can be a great help by listening and empathizing. Take it easy on the roads. Watch your alcohol consumption and you will escape a fine as well as traffic hazards.

4. TUESDAY. Sensitive. Emotions color all communications and will nurture your creative writing, public speaking, and other artistic pursuits. Misunderstandings that arose yesterday can be smoothed over. Well-researched business deals will be winners. Group activities are highlighted as many interesting and attractive people come into your sphere of influence. Beware of altruistic ideals if dealing with a charity organization. Keep the focus on what is practical and you can have a real impact. A surprise windfall invested in the stock market could give you more than a reasonable return and might give you enough capital to buy property.

5. WEDNESDAY. Revealing. Try to be aware of your own role in the games that other people play. Selfless acts of kindness are valued if they don't come with a price tag. Beware playing the role of martyr, and steer clear of those who do. In this way you can avoid power struggles. An interest in the occult or other spiritual pursuit might inspire you to study independently or to join a group of like-minded people. Work in institutions such as hospitals and prisons is foreseen, or you might volunteer to work with an organization that helps the down-and-out. Time alone would be very beneficial, allowing you to start to plan a vacation that will take you off the beaten track.

6. THURSDAY. Ambitious. If you are surrounded by movers and shakers, stay in the background so that you can listen and take notes on all that is going on. Although you probably don't feel like being in the thick of things right now, you are fairly popular. Study options to further your career should be considered. Even if you are already established in a rewarding career you might benefit from further studies in a specialized field. A wealthy relative or family friend is worth contacting if you need a benefactor to provide start-up capital. You might be surprised at the help that is offered, and all you had to do was ask.

7. FRIDAY. Stressful. Set your alarm if you don't want to be late this morning. A night of restless sleep spent worrying could leave you feeling groggy and sap your initiative. A stress-related ailment can be treated with vitamins. It might be a good idea to see a doctor or an alternative healer if stress is a common problem for you. Your ambitions are strong now but you may be aiming too high too quickly. Take stock of what you can practically expect to achieve, where and when. Proceed steadily. You should have plenty of support for your ideas and emotions. If a legal matter is starting to look serious, seek advice regarding how to handle it.

8. SATURDAY. Invigorating. The Moon moves into your sign of Sagittarius today, joining the Sun, Mercury, Jupiter, and Pluto in the sector of self. All of these heavenly influences put a strong emphasis on appearance, personality, and self-opinion. This makes today favorable for focusing on yourself, perhaps going shopping for new clothes, obtaining a health or beauty makeover, or starting a personal creative project that inspires you. You could come on a little strong if you are not careful, forcing your ideas and opinions on people or getting upset at any little slight that is directed your way. Find the happy medium and your popularity should grow along with your charisma and confidence.

9. SUNDAY. Opportune. The New Moon in your own sign of Sagittarius opens up new vistas for exploring and for having fun and adventures. Plans that will eventually take you overseas could get under way. You might decide to study to become a flight attendant, travel consultant, or English teacher abroad. Don't let your generosity toward yourself turn a shopping spree into an orgy of excess, maxing out your credit cards and filling your wardrobe with clothes that you might never have the chance to wear. Your strong power of attraction plus excess charisma will make you the center of attention at a party, leading to new friends or to finding a lover.

10. MONDAY. Transforming. If considering laser treatment or plastic surgery, check out the doctor's credentials and reputation before proceeding any further. A strong desire to instigate social reform may lead to a major role in a social movement. However, if you are attending public rallies, be aware of the power of some people to sway the masses. Exercise your rational mind before getting swept away by a charismatic speaker. If you are having trouble with your mate or partner you might both reach a point where you decide to get some professional counseling, which could be the best thing you ever did.

11. TUESDAY. Favorable. If you stay behind the scenes and work, you will be surprised what you can achieve. You might even receive an extra bonus for your effort. A senior position may soon open up, and people in high places will pull strings to get you in, providing a huge boost to your self-confidence. Properties in your area have probably gone up in value. If you check with your bank you might be able to get extra credit to either purchase investment property or renovate your present one. In both ways you stand to come out ahead in the long run. If you have talents that can earn you money, this is a good time to think about setting up your own business from home.

12. WEDNESDAY. Powerful. If involved in a legal matter you may need an expensive lawyer to prove your case. Despite the cost, you will be investing in your freedom and in your future. No matter how tight money is for you, you can come up with the required amount if you decide it's the right thing to do. Payments could be getting higher and higher. You would do well to examine your loyalty to your bank or credit card, which probably doesn't go overboard for you. You might be given a tough assignment at work and enjoy the challenge a lot more than you thought you would. By the end of the day you should be feeling very pleased with yourself.

13. THURSDAY. Variable. If employment conditions are causing stress, consider changing your job. Also look into getting training to put you in a better position. If you earn higher pay you will be able to pay off any loan you need to put yourself through the course of study. A romantic affair might be taking over your life and forcing some difficult decisions. Obtain legal advice before doing anything permanent so that you make an informed decision. Your course of action now will affect you for years to come. A new computer program at work can leave you in the dark. Get some extra help and before you know it, you will be the expert training your workmates and earning extra points with the boss.

14. FRIDAY. Confusing. You can sense the thoughts and feelings of other people to such an extent that you may not remember what you were doing. Or you may drop everything and join in with whatever is going on. You might write a list of must do's and then lose the list. Or a pile of important papers may not include the particular one you are looking for, leaving you at a loss regarding where it might be. Running into a former sweetheart while shopping gets your heart pumping. Then you may spend the rest of the day fantasizing about renewing the fascination. You can do some exceptional work now once you get started.

15. SATURDAY. Satisfactory. An inheritance or investment windfall may have to be divided between people who are entitled to varying amounts. Although this situation can be difficult and stressful, an amicable arrangement can be reached. You may feel that your mate or partner is asking you to give up your personal interests for the sake of family considerations, but try not to argue about this. Instead, talk about how you feel and listen to the response. If you can rationally handle such an emotional issue, it could be a turning point in your relationship as you each start to see the other person's side of the argument.

16. SUNDAY. Tantalizing. An investment made today will not only give you years of enjoyment but can appreciate in value over time, either financially or as a family heirloom. Your intuitive understanding of other people as well as your ability to think laterally could make you a guru among your friends. They are apt to ask for your advice regarding their troubles and woes. Itchy feet could take you out and away from home for the day. In fact, you might go so far and enjoy it so much that you decide not to turn around and go back, unless it is to pack up the things you need and lock up the house for safety's sake.

17. MONDAY. Pleasant. When you contemplate the future it is always helpful to reflect on the past as a way to understand what lies ahead. Although a very good friend may be a strong influence in your life, now is the time to break away and make a major decision for yourself. Sagittarius parents who are worrying about a child's future and trying to steer them in the right career direction should speak to older family members who are already well established. They might even offer your child a start in their business. You have a lot of mental energy and are likely to enjoy a lively debate wherever you go. Just be aware that in some circumstances you might have to keep some of your views to yourself.

18. TUESDAY. Surprising. Certain childhood experiences that were traumatic and affected you psychologically could bubble to the surface at the moment. Sit with your thoughts and feelings and you might learn more about yourself in one day than you have in the past few years. This should be a very positive experience. An exciting, intimate evening with your mate or partner could leave you feeling invincible, giving you the confidence to make life-changing decisions that might normally scare you. The future is beckoning. A taste of what could be is spurring you on, so take the plunge and don't look back.

19. WEDNESDAY. Expansive. Your ruling planet Jupiter, the planet of expansion and learning, moves into your sector of money and values today. For the next year it will give you the chance to make money and grow in the sphere of material possessions and resources, or whatever else you value. On the negative side, it can mean wastefulness. You could have the tendency to invest recklessly and unwisely, or borrow more money than you can comfortably pay back. Travel is also indicated. You might finally decide you can afford your dream trip. Or a vacation may come due as you begin the trip you have looked forward to for so long.

20. THURSDAY. Rewarding. You may feel like quitting your job due to constant nagging by a senior staff member. However, if you don't want to be unemployed, confront this person openly and honestly. In this way you can dispel any backbiting and power play that may have been going on. A relationship that seems to be breaking down must not be ignored or it might break down totally. Call a truce and start talking about divisive issues. Get a third party to mediate if necessary. Just trying to do something shows how much you really care. Fixing your problems will have a transformative effect and boost your confidence. On a lighter note, having to repair an automobile or appliance can produce a different sort of headache but also be rewarding.

21. FRIDAY. Coping. Reassignments at work might have everybody vying to make a good impression and secure a better position. If you are the subject of gossip and power games, focus on your work and ignore all that is going on. Imagine you have a hard shell like an armadillo, and words and thoughts that hit it just ricochet back to their origin, leaving you untouched. An artistic pursuit would be a great way to take the stress out of your life. If you take a class in an area of art that interests you, you may find that you have hidden talent in that area and gain some recognition for it. Practicing meditation is also recommended as a coping device.

22. SATURDAY. Pressured. The Sun has moved into Capricorn, joining Mercury and Jupiter in your solar house of money and resources. This may highlight money worries or exaggerate a need to show off the things you value. You are apt to run short of money at this time of year, frustrating your desire to shower those you love with gifts. But there are things that money can't buy and that might provide special happiness, while saving your budget. Offer a service or write a special poem. You may be coming under fire from your mate or partner regarding your spending habits. Sit down together to work out a new and better holiday budget. Be willing to compromise and you can find the halfway point.

23. SUNDAY. Confrontational. Impulsive reactions and hasty decisions can contribute to disharmony at home. A social function could be full of pomp and ceremony, boring you to tears. However, you know you have to keep up appearances and do what is expected. Your mate or partner may be unusually quiet and cause you to become suspicious, but don't jump to conclusions. Show a little trust and ask what is bothering them. It may be that they simply don't want to pile their worries on top of yours. An older relative might need a hand but be too proud to ask. Just turn up and do it and you will make them appreciative and proud.

24. MONDAY. Intuitive. Your intuition is operating at peak performance while your mind questions almost everything. If you trust your impulses you are sure to do what is best. Buying a few last-minute gifts could be a breeze if you go with your first choice and stop procrastinating. With your loved one's feelings first and foremost on your mind, and your desire to please very strong, be yourself and you can't go wrong. Sagittarius businesspeople might have several deals and contracts coming due at the same time. Delegate so that you can be in more than one place at the same time. Just be sure to choose your agents wisely and you will finish the day on a high note.

25. TUESDAY. Merry Christmas! A day full of love and laughter is assured so long as you don't try to overextend yourself or show off in front of others. Focus on a few surprises you have in store for your loved ones. Your sense of timing will impress and amaze them. Luck is on your side at the moment, so your plans should work out far better than you dared to imagine. If you are currently a fair distance from home you might be with your family and friends in spirit only. At least try to make a special phone call to them or send an e-mail. This evening you might be among people who are from another culture and have the experience of looking at life from their perspective.

26. WEDNESDAY. Changeable. Contacting friends and relatives can be so difficult that you give up on your initial objective and go out for some fun and relaxation instead. A public gathering could be very enjoyable and also give you food for thought and conversation while putting you in touch with people who you haven't seen for a while. A simple change such as this can be as good as getting away. Contact with foreigners or travel in another country can open your mind to different ways of perceiving the world. In turn, this will lead to an expansion of your understanding of the world and of global politics in particular. A phone call could jolt your memory, bringing news you thought you would never hear.

27. THURSDAY. Exacting. Organizing a large social function can fall on your shoulders and put you in a position where you have to encourage and push other people to get things done. At times you may feel that you would rather not have to deal with this, but your ambition and enthusiasm will keep you plugging away. The event should turn out to be a great success, earning you respect for your talents and for your way of handling people. Your financial position could be far healthier than you expected and allow you to plan a weekend getaway. Sagittarius people with a partner should be sure to discuss plans together before proceeding. This will help avoid a confrontation.

28. FRIDAY. Spirited. If you apply yourself you can do anything you want to right now. A parent may need your help and will reward you if you are willing to give up some of your personal time. A job opportunity to earn higher wages might come at the price of moving away from your home and loved ones. Think twice before you accept the offer. It can be lonely being on your own, and you might end up spending most of your hard-earned raise trying to amuse yourself when you have finished work for the day. This evening promises good fun. You might get a visit from a dear friend, sitting up for hours sharing news and stories.

29. SATURDAY. Sparkling. An important upcoming event may keep you up half the night going over all the possible scenarios that might take place and planning how to make the right impression. Regardless of how late you get to sleep, you are likely to wake up ready and raring to go. Don't let envy regarding other people's success color your perception of your own standing in life. You don't know how those people feel. They may be just as envious as you but better at hiding their feelings. Trying to get in touch with a loved one could be very frustrating and cause you all sorts of worries, but they will turn up and there is likely to be a simple explanation.

30. SUNDAY. Vibrant. The compassionate and loving side of your nature is strong and out there for everybody to see. A gathering might give you a forum to make your feelings public as you join with like-minded people. With Venus, the planet of love and harmony, moving into your own sign of Sagittarius today, her attributes will combine with yours. You might spend a lot of time and money improving your appearance and grooming, but even if you do nothing you will exude far more charisma than usual. A new love affair may bloom out of a friendship, with the advantage that you both know each other really well.

31. MONDAY. Sociable. A falling out with a friend due to a misunderstanding can be patched up if you are willing to listen to what others have to say. With Mars, the planet of energy and aggression, moving back into Gemini and your solar seventh house of relationships, it is time to work cooperatively. You can achieve far more with partners than you can on your own. Be prepared to compromise and you will avoid needless controversy. Legal conflicts and lawsuits can occur at this time, and again you will need to compromise. Your New Year's Eve resolutions should focus on love and cooperation at home and in the world at large.

SAGITTARIUS
NOVEMBER–DECEMBER 2006

November 2006

1. WEDNESDAY. Surprising. Being eccentric is being original. This is a day to do things differently. Finding new ways to handle chores will increase your productivity. Changes are foreseen in your love life, so be prepared for the unexpected. A situation could occur that takes you completely by surprise. Domestic affairs show signs of improvement. Problems that occur on the home front should work out well if everyone involved is willing to compromise. An attraction to interesting new people increases pleasurable interaction when socializing. A new romantic relationship entered into now promises excitement but may not be enduring.

2. THURSDAY. Unsettled. Dress to impress people you don't know. A secret or confidence that you and other people have been trying to keep is about to burst out into the open. It might be time to reveal the information before you are upstaged. Although lots of contact with other people provides stimulation, close interaction today could lead to an unwelcome flu or virus. Do all that you can to protect yourself since you are now susceptible to minor ailments. The talented Sagittarius could find restoring old artwork or furniture adds style to a home and is pleasant and fulfilling.

3. FRIDAY. Reassuring. This is not the time to resist changes. It will be necessary for you to go with the flow. You will probably not be content sitting around doing nothing. Strive for an environment where you have an opportunity to mix and mingle with a diverse group of people. As an added benefit to this, you could cross paths with someone who can enhance your future development and open new doors for you. Something that has been stalled should begin to move forward, coming to a head demanding action or an immediate decision. Find a stimulating recreational pursuit to occupy your mind if you have some free time late in the day.

4. SATURDAY. Fulfilling. Arrange to share your artistic or creative talents with those who could benefit the most. The young, aged, infirm, or needy may fit that category, and the feedback you receive should be an enriching experience. Begin a diet or a new health and fitness regime if you want to be in better shape for the upcoming festive celebrations. A period of hard work to achieve long-term goals begins now. For the Sagittarius business owner or anyone who is self-employed, examining work techniques and procedures can show where to implement changes to increase efficiency and productivity.

5. SUNDAY. Sensitive. Emotional tension and sensitivity are in the air due to the influence of the Taurus Full Moon affecting your health sector. This could cause some sparks to fly, so be on guard for confrontation, angry words, or physical action. Hurt feelings from a past incident could come back to haunt you. Tension is likely for some time. It may be better to either do a disappearing act or at least keep in mind the motto silence is golden. Pay attention to pets. One of them may need to visit the vet. The health of an uncle or aunt might be the cause of concern among all family members. Stay in touch by phone if you can't visit in person.

6. MONDAY. Inspiring. This is a time for positive action. If a love triangle or entanglement has been causing doubts, getting to the truth of the matter can confirm or deny your fears. It is not a good time to sign an important deal because you may be tempted to compromise too much in order to avoid potential difficulties. Use your artistic talents and you will excel. Focus on an exciting project that both challenges and inspires your creative juices. You may have to tap deep into your inner resources, but you are capable of pulling it all together. There may be some issues surrounding a female friend or relative.

7. TUESDAY. Satisfactory. A generous and tolerant atmosphere prevails. This is a time to be with people and to share your talents to benefit others. Communicating on a social level with those in your immediate environment should be worthwhile as well as pleasant. Just watch that you don't become involved in too much gossip. Reevaluating your relationship with certain people can lead to greater understanding of where you need to make adjustments in your attitude or behavior. Confidential issues may need attention. Going for drinks after hours with your colleagues will be a pleasant way to relax and unwind.

8. WEDNESDAY. Cautious. This is not a very good day to let your mate or partner loose with the checkbook or credit card. Doing so is likely to lead to problems later on when all the bills start arriving. Take extra care with important documentation and legal paperwork to avoid double handling if mistakes occur. Presenting ideas, plans, or points of view to those who hold more authority than you should result in you being taken seriously. Your ability to express thoughts clearly and concisely ensures that other people will take note of your comments. Buying, selling, and negotiating would be better left until later in the month.

9. THURSDAY. Mixed. A desire to evade normal obligations and duties could overcome you. Best results are likely to stem from working on a mental level rather than emotional. Make a to-do list and follow through on it. Don't allow yourself to become the scapegoat for errors made by other people. If you were not involved in the problem, let those who were stand up and take the blame. It would be wiser to refer youngsters to someone with precise experience or knowledge if they seek advice or guidance. Objectivity is not your strong suit right now, and you could accidentally misinform or steer someone in the wrong direction.

10. FRIDAY. Deceptive. Attend to financial paperwork, making sure everything is in good order. Spend time on the phone calling about overdue money. If you are self-employed, be sure to balance the books yourself. Taking this job on personally should bring a more positive reaction from those who currently owe you money. Avoid a get-rich-quick scheme or unwise investment. You are in a self-deceptive period. Delusions of grandeur could spur you on to speculate with funds which you cannot afford to lose. Your home base will be a hive of activity, possibly creating a feeling of disquiet or disorientation. A family purchase or gift will bring enjoyment.

11. SATURDAY. Eventful. Restlessness and agitation are likely to emerge. If you feel harassed, a change of scenery would be both stimulating and educational. Taking a long trip may be tiring but well worth the effort in terms of scenery and sights. If someone outside your inner circle is trying to delve into your affairs or is giving unsolicited advice, this is the time to let them know that prying is not appreciated or welcomed. Sagittarius home owners may need to call a plumber to check for a gas or water leak. Don't try to repair a major problem yourself because this might end up costing a lot more in the long run.

12. SUNDAY. Imaginative. Finding a creative way to complete chores will make the day easier and less of a hassle. A strong astrological influence in your private sector leads to difficulties expressing emotions to your loved ones. If they feel hurt or neglected by your behavior, try not to overreact. Explain that you are not having

a good day. Those who love you will understand. As an independent Sagittarius you can usually resolve problems. However, it
would be wise to seek help sorting out any travel difficulties. Long-
distance communication may be required, which could be a problem if you cannot speak the language fluently.

13. MONDAY. Stimulating. There may be a strong urge to travel
or participate in something new and exciting. Planning for the future and having to take family concerns into account could occupy
your thoughts. Trying to tie up loose ends and resolve complications could have your head spinning for much of the day. Sagittarius employees may be under extra pressure. You will have to think
on your feet, ad-lib, and sound confident and convincing even if
you do not feel secure. You should be able to manage the task ex-
pertly and without any problems, earning the respect of colleagues.
You will revel in the experience and in the ongoing benefits and opportunities that could be presented.

14. TUESDAY. Variable. Unless you avoid becoming bogged
down by a perfectionist attitude, the day won't bring the rewards
you are hoping for. Although passionate about a particular cause,
do not allow an obsession to interfere with work activities or home
life. Problems could begin to appear insurmountable if you lose
your sense of humor. Loved ones or your partner might demand
that concessions be made so that you will spend more time at home
with family members. Purchasing a new piece of furniture that adds
personal comfort may be a priority. A trip arranged at short notice
either for pleasure or business provides a change of routine and
stimulation.

15. WEDNESDAY. Smooth. There will an exciting atmosphere at
home or on the job. A lot of your energy might be expended performing tasks in a secluded place or in the background. Your energy might be a little low, so give your body time to regenerate by
taking things a little slower and resting every now and then. If you
must work, find a job that you enjoy doing. Sagittarius in charge of
hiring staff could find the people being interviewed compatible
with company aims and a good fit with other employees. Displaying
a compassionate demeanor and showing people that their welfare
is important to you will be emotionally rewarding.

16. THURSDAY. Encouraging. Today may not flow as smoothly as
yesterday, although optimism continues to be high. Trying to orga-

nize a group affair could lead to frustration if you cannot persuade other people to go along with your arrangements or if members are not willing to contribute time or ideas. Do your best under the circumstances. Extra chores plus a new project will add to your already heavy workload. Other people in your environment could act against your advice. Although you might have the last word when a job has to be redone because of errors, the amount of time lost will be annoying and costly.

17. FRIDAY. Hopeful. A number of planetary influences are in play, making anything possible. A special work task could bring kudos and the likelihood of extra income. However, this is not the right time to approach an employer or other authority figure for extra perks or to discuss a salary increase. Be gentle with yourself. Seek relaxing leisure pursuits during your free time. Listening to music, slow dancing, or a long soak in the hot tub should assist relaxation and restore vitality. Even though Mercury moves forward now, it is still not an auspicious time to sign any important document or to arrive at a major decision.

18. SATURDAY. Invigorating. Venus, the planet linked to love and creativity, has now moved into your own sign of Sagittarius. This will increase your participation in social functions within your circle of friends. Deceptive and confusing influences still surround you, so take special care with romantic affairs and business matters. Imagination is strengthened, assisting you to create party decorations or organize an innovative festive theme. If holding a celebration at home, try to tie up loose ends and carry out private responsibilities early in the day. Avoid procrastination since your energy is likely to flag as the day progresses.

19. SUNDAY. Helpful. Catch up on extra sleep by staying in bed an extra hour this morning or taking an afternoon nap. This could help alleviate stress and restore your good humor. It also is a good time to catch up with private affairs, sift through closets, and do some cleaning out on an inner as well as an external level. You may not feel like socializing with a large crowd, but a special outing with loved ones should be enjoyable. A past friendship could begin to develop again, bringing renewed bonds. Using your intuition and sharp mental facilities can be the catalyst for clever ideas and concepts. Practicing visualization techniques will foster self-confidence.

20. MONDAY. Progressive. Uranus, the planet of chaos and excitement, advances forward in Pisces in your home and family sector. If you have been experiencing delays with home renovations or have had problems arranging professional help, progress should occur now. The New Moon in Scorpio, your twelfth house, means that financial gains could come through confidential dealings. This is a time to follow your hunches and intuition regarding money matters. However, do not allow emotions to overcome your better judgment. Long-cherished ambitions or desires may at last come to fruition. You need to make the effort to attend a social function even if you don't feel like it.

21. TUESDAY. Opportune. Today promises to be extra special as your ruler Jupiter happily merges with the Sun, increasing personal optimism. Good deeds done for those who needed your assistance in the past could now be repaid. If you have favors to ask of those in authority, now is the time to act. Approaching your employer for a better paid position or a salary increase could produce a positive outcome. Opportunities exist to mix with people from around the world, which suits your current expansive mood. Gaining more knowledge and insight is an important priority. A formal, elegant occasion should be a wonderful experience.

22. WEDNESDAY. Auspicious. Today is the beginning of a new birthday cycle for all Sagittarius. The Sun now moves into your own sign, bringing your personality and personal interests to the fore. Over the next four weeks you should experience life from a different perspective. This can be a profitable time to travel for business purposes. Trips for pleasure should also be very enjoyable. Physical energy is high, assisting professionals who can expect a boost in revenue. Keeping active or energetic in a stimulating task will appeal. Boredom could quickly descend if chores become too tedious and routine too precise.

23. THURSDAY. Exhilarating. If you are in the market to purchase a piano or other musical instrument, an excellent bargain could be discovered today from a private seller. A major cycle begins as your ruler Jupiter, planet of abundance, moves into your own sign of Sagittarius at midnight tonight. So the Sun, Venus, Jupiter, and Pluto are all impacting your first house of personal affairs and aims. Your charisma and self-confidence are on the rise, so don't hide your expertise and talents from the rest of the world. Exploit your skills without exaggeration or ego tendencies. Relationships are under promising trends, with Sagittarius couples sharing happy rapport. If you are inclined to put on weight easily, care will be needed during the next twelve months.

24. FRIDAY. Optimistic. Your greater sense of optimism improves your outlook on life. A financial meeting that you have been looking forward to should be as successful as you anticipate. A new personal project can be launched now, providing you don't take risks that you later regret. Although vitality should be rapidly increasing, beware of burning the candle at both ends. At times you will still be a little sluggish. The antidote for any burnout is rest, relaxation, and recuperation. Relations with in-laws and with people at a distance are good, with the possibility of a financial gift coming your way.

25. SATURDAY. Promising. Look forward to an interesting day ahead. Resist pressure to act hastily or to go against your better judgment or intuition. Avoid impulsiveness with romantic and financial matters. Excessive spending could greatly reduce the amount of funds available for the forthcoming festive celebrations. Don't neglect your daily routine even if tasks do not seem stimulating. You could get so caught up in pleasurable interests that you forget to act on important matters. Treat loved ones tenderly, especially your significant other. If there are relationship difficulties, bring these out into the open for honest discussion.

26. SUNDAY. Manageable. Staying in touch with loved ones living abroad is easier thanks to the Internet. You are apt to be spending a lot more time contacting people in this way. Profitable gains can be made from buying or selling. It may not be easy to get people interested or organized for a family outing or gathering. If you are not in charge, let someone else worry about getting everyone involved in activities. If embarking on a journey this morning leave home early to avoid a minor mix-up in reservations, seating, or costs. Frustrations with younger family members are likely if you have to share space with them.

27. MONDAY. Stormy. You may be prone to irritability or a temper tantrum this morning. Try to curb an impatient attitude, especially with family members. Also be cautious about rushing around, which could cause an accident. This is a good time to handle legal matters or conduct a confidential investigation. If you have been neglecting those most dear to you due to employment pressures, rectify the situation by taking loved ones out for dinner at a local restaurant as a special treat. This will give everyone including you a break from routine, especially if you are usually the chef in the household. Driving requires extra care and attention.

28. TUESDAY. Disconcerting. Today's strange and confusing circumstances could prove disconcerting, making it difficult to face reality. Property matters are highlighted, but proceed carefully if you are entering into negotiations since misrepresentation of facts or figures is possible. You could crave sweet or rich foods, something you probably experience problems with at times. Remember to keep everything in moderation. Spend time with those who love you the most and you may not need to overindulge as a form of comfort. Offering to baby-sit for relatives or friends so they can enjoy a night out alone would be appreciated.

29. WEDNESDAY. Hectic. The key issues center on your home, family, and personal life. Any changes implemented now are likely to only cause confusion. You may consider that you have plenty of time available to complete daily chores, but you are apt to run out of time and have to rush to complete everything on your to-do list. Try to pace yourself at a steady rate, which should lessen the chance of errors occurring and also help you meet deadlines. An unexpected situation could require a quick change to prearranged alternative plans. If attending meetings or appointments, be sure that you have the correct time and venue since miscommunication is likely.

30. THURSDAY. Enjoyable. Fashion could attract you. If you are going to attend a glamorous social event in the near future, it may be time to shop and make your selections of what to wear. The current planetary influences assist this endeavor, giving you a greater appreciation of what is beautiful and stylish. Discussions regarding the future education of a child should lead to agreement with your partner. Sagittarius singles could meet someone special who over time becomes a very important part of life. Expect more invitations and social occasions to fill your already overflowing calendar. Creativity is to the fore, so explore new ways to implement your great ideas.

December 2006

1. FRIDAY. Interesting. You begin the new month with four planets moving through your first house of personal goals. This places you in the spotlight. Entertainment, social functions, and celebrations combine to make this a fun and interesting time. There may be a slight problem in regard to some domestic duties, although you should be able to sort this out fairly quickly. Try to be patient with children. Their misbehavior may be a way to try to claim more of your time and attention. Give serious consideration to changes or improvements needed to make you happier and more contented. Tantalizing romantic possibilities are likely for the solo Sagittarius.

2. SATURDAY. Problematic. Home owners who are expecting tradespeople to complete last-minute decorating or repairs in anticipation of the upcoming festive season should prepare for a stressful day. Having a variety of people coming and going as well as trying to resolve problems will add variety to your day, although you would prefer a quieter time right now. You may need a change from routine, so at least stop what you are doing for a five-minute break or do something different. A minor accident-prone period prevails, so be patient and avoid careless behavior. Relationships with those you live with could be a little tense unless you compromise.

3. SUNDAY. Trying. This is another day when the gods may not be smiling or as friendly as you would prefer. Unexpected situations are probable, throwing plans and arrangements into disarray. This is not the time to be stubborn or resist change. Go with the flow. If disruptions occur, which is more than likely, embrace these as a chance to make the adjustments that are required. Don't play games with the emotions of your mate or partner, even if you feel your relationship needs revitalizing in some way. Pets enter into conversation. You may be asked to mind a friend's favorite companion while they are away from home.

4. MONDAY. Tense. More hassles are in store. You have a lot to accomplish in a short period of time. Staying cool and calm might be difficult but not totally impossible. Go for a short walk or stroll around the office if everything becomes temporarily overwhelming. This will give you second wind and help put things in better perspective. The Gemini Full Moon is affecting your relationship sector. An examination of business and personal partnerships will reveal whether there is an equal distribution of labor or if you are being taken for granted. Your ability to convey a good first impression is limited, so try to put off situations where you need to present a confident demeanor.

5. TUESDAY. Manageable. Family members or those who have an influence on your future may not be as optimistic or thrilled by your current plans as expected. It is important to consider their objections since these may have merit. A complex monetary arrangement needs to be reviewed before a more serious problem develops. You could decide to contribute more time and effort to assist those who are less fortunate than you. Just make sure that this is not taking time away from your loved ones and that your own needs will not be neglected. You can expect to win a prize or raffle, so enter as many competitions as possible.

6. WEDNESDAY. Dynamic. Mars, the planet of motivation, moves into your sign of Sagittarius and your first house. Over the next few weeks exert a lot of hard work into furthering your own aims and interests. Put forth a more assertive and dominate personality. This will be best suited for self-employment or for working by yourself wherever possible. Your competitive drive and energy are high, making this a time when stressful physical work can be carried out. Just be careful and utilize appropriate safety precautions and rules. In your hurry to start or complete jobs, not taking due care could result in mishaps and accidents.

7. THURSDAY. Diverse. People may disagree with your more traditional approach and methods. If these are working effectively, it would be counterproductive to make sweeping changes. Expect a welcome boost to your income either through your own or the effort of others. Your judgment is sound, ensuring that financial decisions will be based on a realistic and logical approach. Investments can be safely made on items that are beautiful to look at and offer the potential to grow in value. Just be sure to deal with accredited companies or dealers. Deep emotions could rise to the surface, bringing greater intensity to your romantic relationship.

8. FRIDAY. Optimistic. You may get tied up with a number of problems, obligations, or personal issues. However, your cool demeanor and approach will ensure that difficulties can be resolved promptly and to everyone's satisfaction. Talkative Mercury moves into your first house of personality, enhancing your communication skills. People will delight in your congenial company and happy frame of mind. As a Sagittarius you are known for your honest, straightforward approach, but it can sometimes become known as foot-in-mouth syndrome. Over the next few weeks this direct manner of speaking is enhanced. Avoid possible upsets by thinking first before you speak.

9. SATURDAY. Busy. There is restlessness in the air today. New-found knowledge and interesting leisure pursuits could keep you busy and on the go. Explore out-of-the-way places in order to obtain a wider perspective. Spiritual and mystical events appeal. Visiting an astrologer or clairvoyant might give you interesting facts and guidance that can assist self-empowerment. This is also a good time to attend or speak at a conference or workshop where a high level of concentration is required. If you haven't already started holiday shopping or writing out greeting cards, now is the perfect time to do so. A social function should be a fun event, giving you pleasure just to know that you were invited.

10. SUNDAY. Successful. You should be in a more assertive and demonstrative mood, appreciating warm affection from friends and loved ones. A long-overdue guest could finally arrive, much to the joy of your family. Make sure you are prepared to entertain. Stock the pantry, clean the house, and prepare guest sleeping arrangements to avoid the possibility of embarrassment. Social life should be in full swing, with a good chance of meeting someone in the public eye who could provide future benefits. Planning the catering and entertainment for a party is favored. Your creativity and ability to put ingenious ideas to work are enhanced.

11. MONDAY. Accomplished. Your reputation could be enhanced in some way. You could receive a bonus or promotion. Or you might receive rave reviews about your expertise from new clients, either in person or in the media. Venus, goddess of love and values, moves into Capricorn and your sector of shared finances. This planetary placement brings a more practical and conservative approach to your compulsion to go on a spending splurge at this time of year. Any careless approach to financial obligations is also lessened. Obtaining money on credit is likely to be easier, but remain vigilant since spending more than the budget allows can cause problems.

12. TUESDAY. Challenging. Attend to problems as soon as they arise. If action is not implemented quickly, difficulties will increase making it harder to find a solution. The misuse of personal assertiveness could lead to attempting to dominate or manipulate other people. Trying to control people or situations can cause a power struggle which proves more upsetting than the situation warranted. People may not be so quick to forgive or to let you off the hook. Use energy in a more constructive manner by making improvements at home or at work. Take care if trying to resolve an emotional tangle with a loved one.

13. WEDNESDAY. Changeable. You are apt to be in a party mood, and there should be plenty of opportunities to fulfill your wishes. Be discerning in choosing which social events or venues to attend since not all will offer the entertainment and conversational stimulation you crave. Currently single Sagittarius looking for an ideal partner may need to reexamine expectations. Be more realistic to avoid future disappointment when people are unable to live up to your standards. Ask a close friend for advice if you have a dilemma to solve. Watch your tone of voice since irritability and impatience could make you whiny at times throughout the day.

14. THURSDAY. Motivating. Sagittarius popularity is at a high. You are likely to star in any social event you attend. A casual chat with someone important to your long-term career could lead to an interesting new offer. Shopping for holiday gifts could produce a number of bargains that excite you and also leave you with a surplus of cash. Joining a local association or club may appeal. Look for an interest group that caters to some of the activities that you appreciate. However, before committing yourself and paying a membership fee, attend a few meetings and get to know the people to see if you relate easily to the topic and to other members.

15. FRIDAY. Spirited. You won't be inclined to pursue normal everyday matters. By putting routine tasks and activities on a more efficient footing, it should be easier to accomplish what needs to be done. Sagittarius intuition is heightened, helping to lessen any challenges that erupt at home. An interest in material and speculative matters can bring you into contact with practical and organized people who are willing to provide assistance. Be careful when handling machinery and electrical equipment, especially if known to have a malfunction or other fault. An involvement with younger people through teaching or imparting specialized skills can be fulfilling but very hectic.

16. SATURDAY. Uplifting. Approaching a superior or other authoritative figure with a confident attitude could result in favors being granted. Concentrate on specific tasks that you have been continually putting off. If you are planning a special birthday celebration for yourself or for a loved one, everything should proceed smoothly. You have the ability to know exactly what each guest requires. Be generous in planning the menu. People who are lucky enough to be part of your inner circle should find your presence both uplifting and infectious. This can buoy up other people who are not as enthusiastic as you are.

17. SUNDAY. Festive. Using your creative talents and expertise can save money. Instead or purchasing ready-made festive decorations or gifts, try making these yourself. You should be very pleasantly surprised by your efforts. This is also an ideal time to prepare and organize for the upcoming holiday period. If you are hosting a holiday celebration, gather family members together to sort out who will take over various tasks to make the day a success. Romance is heightened, providing the impetus for a display of love and affection to that special person in your life.

18. MONDAY. Starred. This is an excellent time to pursue training needed to move up the career ladder. You may be promoted due to your excellent work ethics and effort. If you are at home, cleaning neglected areas could reveal an item that you assumed was lost forever. If you are on the job, lost files or paperwork may be discovered that helps to reduce the workload. Intense personal situations and issues are likely to emerge, requiring a thorough examination of the entire situation. You may need to rethink a current stand, especially if this has led to criticism from someone you trust and respect.

19. TUESDAY. Active. Your home life may be extremely busy, with tasks and activities that require attention prior to the festivities getting into full swing. There might even be so much to do that feelings of not being able to cope crop up. Although difficult, try your best to stay calm. Act on what you can and ignore the rest. Write a list and tick jobs off as you go, which will give you a sense of accomplishment once the list is completed. A romantic interest who is hard to resist might appear on the social scene. Have fun flirting, but be prepared for the relationship to fizzle out after a short duration. You'll find love very close to home.

20. WEDNESDAY. Refreshing. A special project that calls on your creative talent and aptitude will bring out the best you have to offer. The Sagittarius New Moon illuminates your personal interests and desires. A sociable, happy frame of mind prevails, ensuring you are ready for fun activities and experiences. Professional, financial, or a personal opening could pave the way for you to turn in a new direction. You have more than one option, making this an exciting and productive period. If planning on spending the Christmas holidays away from home, be sure that all essential arrangements and details are taken care of before the last minute.

21. THURSDAY. Satisfactory. You need to apply organization and discipline if you want to make good progress. Finding new ways to handle old problems or situations will assist the process. Rushing around at a frantic pace could lead to more haste but less speed. There is an increased chance of an accident occurring around the home, so take care. Don't bottle up your emotions or express feelings in a destructive manner. Use this energy in a constructive way by working around the house and organizing domestic concerns. Today the Sun enters conservative Capricorn, bringing your solar second house of income into prominence until January 21 of the new year.

22. FRIDAY. Pleasant. Something you have always wanted could begin to move closer to reality. Your financial instincts and money-making abilities are to the fore, possibly providing extra income to be enjoyed throughout the festive season. If you haven't already completed Christmas purchases, finishing this task now will free up the remaining days to spend visiting relatives or organizing a party. A gathering of coworkers and business associates for a festive celebration should be a happy time, with stimulating conversation to keep you occupied as well as entertained. An early surprise gift could be forthcoming this evening.

23. SATURDAY. Exciting. You have plenty of enthusiasm to act on whatever occupies today's agenda. If you are planning a party or other gathering that could become loud, it would be a sensible idea to either invite your neighbors or advise them beforehand of your intentions. Sending over some party food or drink will ensure that complaints are not made about noise. If planning to travel by public transportation over the holiday break, confirm departure and arrival times to ensure nothing has changed since you purchased your ticket. Although you might be extremely busy throughout the day, try to make time to consume a proper meal. Eating on the run could cause minor digestive problems.

24. SUNDAY. Sparkling. Any tasks that need attention to detail can be accomplished without too many problems. Writing, editing, and publishing pursuits are favored if you have an interest in such activities. Sagittarius students could use this time to complete homework assignments. Finishing off all of the odds and ends needed for tomorrow's festivities could take up a considerable amount of your day. However, everything should be under control by this evening, leaving time to enjoy the company of friends and family or to attend a special celebration. Try to have an early night so you have plenty of energy to face tomorrow's busy schedule.

25. MONDAY. Merry Christmas! Today brings out the best in the gregarious and jovial Sagittarius. Sharing good times with family members may be preferred rather than visiting friends or neighbors. If you are hosting the traditional festive fare, guests will appreciate your culinary skills and attention to detail. Try to avoid becoming involved in an intense discussion with an elderly family member who has very different views and opinions from yours. Avoid talking about politics with anyone. Although you have energy to spare, you may be happily exhausted by the end of the day. Sagittarius singles could become romantically inclined toward a guest who has traveled some distance.

26. TUESDAY. Variable. Use humor to diffuse any tense moments as the day begins, especially if everyone is feeling slightly the worse for wear today. You might be entertaining or be getting ready to enjoy someone's hospitality. An issue you feel passionate about might reemerge, leading to possible discord with a family member. Handling this in a positive manner should resolve any lasting difficulties and reduce the tension. If you thought the holiday rush was over, you may need to revise these thoughts as invitations roll in for New Year's celebrations. It would be smart to go to bed early.

27. WEDNESDAY. Favorable. If you are still enjoying a holiday break, enjoy spending time with your favorite people, especially a child. Mercury moves into the practical sign of Capricorn and your second house of income. As a result, communications involving property or commercial interests are likely to be a priority if you are back at work. You could embark on an ambitious venture that leads to personal financial gains. However, there is a need to guard against thinking too big or being overly optimistic. If you have done the research and checked all of the details, a successful outcome is most likely. An unexpected romantic encounter shows potential for Sagittarius singles.

28. THURSDAY. Unpredictable. Unexpected guests might add extra strain to your already depleted finances. Try not to get upset or embarrassed. Explain that the festive season has left you short of funds and that everyone will need to contribute toward the cost of food. People will understand. Spending time with your true love should bring harmonious vibes providing any possessive tendencies are kept under wraps. Parents could enroll children in a new activity that is fun for all the family to participate in or to be a spectator. Singles may attract the attention of a new romantic interest who has a ready-made family.

29. FRIDAY. Fair. If you have been burning the candle at both ends, today brings an opportunity for relaxation. Try to observe a more moderate approach for the sake of your health and well-being, particularly if you have been overindulging with alcohol and rich foods. Problems may arise for the career-minded if work responsibilities are intruding on home and domestic life. Your mate, a partner, or another family member may be critical of the hours you spend away. This could spark dissension in the household. If looking for a particular article to purchase, you should be in luck finding it at an affordable after-Christmas sale price.

30. SATURDAY. Useful. Relationship issues could be a cause of concern for you. If you feel that interest is diminishing, work harder to bring zest back and to make life more interesting. If the problem goes deeper, perhaps it is time for an open discussion or counseling to try to resolve differences. Starting any project now may be a waste of time. If hosting friends for a New Year's celebration, ask for assistance if the planning and preparations are too much to handle on your own. There is a possibility that a minor ailment could slow you down, so take care to avoid getting chilled or overheated.

31. SUNDAY. Good. You are apt to start the day on a low as a few frustrations cause problems. As the hours progress, excitement builds to a high wave of optimism and enthusiasm. If you are celebrating at home, try to get an early start with food preparations. Shop during the morning hours to avoid crowds. Add extra delight to the night by including a secret fun activity for guests to enjoy. Helping someone who is going through a rough period will give you emotional satisfaction. If you are drinking, don't drive anywhere this evening. Hire a taxi, designate a driver, or choose a local venue within walking distance if you are not celebrating at home.

WHAT DOES YOUR FUTURE HOLD?

DISCOVER IT IN *ASTROANALYSIS*—

**COMPLETELY REVISED THROUGH THE YEAR 2015,
THESE GUIDES INCLUDE COLOR-CODED CHARTS FOR
TOTAL ASTROLOGICAL EVALUATION,
PLANET TABLES AND CUSP CHARTS,
AND STREAMLINED INFORMATION.**

ARIES	0-425-17558-8
TAURUS	0-425-17559-6
GEMINI	0-425-17560-X
CANCER	0-425-17561-8
LEO	0-425-17562-6
VIRGO	0-425-17563-4
LIBRA	0-425-17564-2
SCORPIO	0-425-17565-0
SAGITTARIUS	0-425-17566-9
CAPRICORN	0-425-17567-7
AQUARIUS	0-425-17568-5
PISCES	0-425-17569-3

Available wherever books are sold or at penguin.com

B093

Star of Animal Planet's "Pet Psychic"

SONYA FITZPATRICK THE PET PSYCHIC

She can talk to the animals.
Read their minds.
Diagnose their problems.
Heal their illnesses.
Find them when they're lost.
And offer comfort from
beyond the grave.
This is her story—and the remarkable
success stories of her "clients."

*Includes Sonya's 7 simple steps to
communicating with pets
Plus—practical information on care and
feeding, emergency preparedness, illness, moving,
and introducing new pets into the household.*

0-425-19414-0

Available wherever books are sold or at
penguin.com

B096

Cell Phone Psychics